How to borrow a million dollars

Other books by Mark Stevens

The Big Eight

Model

How to Run Your Own Business Successfully

Small Business Mistakes and How to Avoid Them

Leverage Finance

Like No Other Store in the World:
   The Inside Story of Bloomingdale's

How to borrow

a

MILLION
DOLLARS

MARK STEVENS

MACMILLAN PUBLISHING CO., INC.

NEW YORK

Macmillan Publishing Co., Inc.
866 Third Avenue, New York, N.Y. 10022
Collier Macmillan Canada, Inc.

Library of Congress Cataloging in Publication Data
Stevens, Mark, 1947–
    How to borrow a million dollars.
    Includes index.
    1. Credit—Handbooks, manuals, etc.   2. Loans—
Handbooks, manuals, etc.   3. Small business—Finance
—Handbooks, manuals, etc.   I. Title.
HG3751.S69   1982   658.1'5224   82-17143
ISBN 0-02-614480-8

10 9 8 7 6 5 4 3 2 1

Printed in the United States of America

Excerpts from Chapters 4 and 5 of this book appeared
previously in Venture magazine; excerpts from
Chapter 6 appeared previously in INC magazine.

Contents

How to borrow a million dollars

1

Mastering the art and the science

A fifty-six–foot sailing yacht moving gracefully through the blue-green waters off St. Croix . . .

A waterfront condominium, shaded by palm trees, nestled on a perfect crescent beach on Tortola, British Virgin Islands . . .

A silver Mercedes 380 SL, powdered with snow, parked beside a contemporary ski chalet in Aspen . . .

A cruise on the *QE II*—caviar, champagne, and a picture window to the sea . . .

A thriving beachwear boutique, crammed with multinational millionaires, just blocks from the famed casino at Monte Carlo . . .

Rolex, Dom Perignon, Van Cleef & Arpels, Harrod's, Savile Row, Rolls-Royce, Neiman-Marcus Christmas Catalogue . . .

All it takes is money.

The best things in life are free; the close seconds are anything but. Life's glittering prizes sport fabulous price tags. Most people only dream of them; others go out and buy.

Quite often, the difference between the haves and the have-nots boils down not to the legendary "silver spoon" but to a knack, a flair, and a skill for borrowing money.

Although the man on the street moans about the difficulty of borrowing a buck, most people have never tried for anything more than a car or student loan. At this end of the market, the competition for dollars is keen. Those who think big, however—who bring big ideas to the major money sources—find that there are fewer outstretched hands at the zenith and more of a chance of convincing lenders to open their purses. The old saw that bankers are tightwads is nonsense. Money lenders are in business to lend money. That's the only way they profit.

Billions of dollars are up for grabs. Not only banks but insurance companies, venture capitalists, private investors, finance companies, factors, government agencies, sheiks, princes, captains of industry, film stars, oil companies: all are cash-rich and actively seeking investment outlets. Today more than ever before, money must work for a living. It cannot sit in a Chase Manhattan vault collecting dust. Show that you can make money work, and the coffers will swing open. You, as an individual or a small-business owner, can borrow $50,000, $500,000, $1 million, or more, enough to launch a business of your own, expand an ongoing venture, make opportune investments, parlay personal assets, drive a Mercedes-Benz, create a graceful and luxurious lifestyle. It's not easy and it's not guaranteed, but it can be done.

The secret is recognizing that simply filling out forms is not enough. Beyond the hard and fast rules of collateral, contracts, and covenants, there is the human factor to consider. Persuasive arguments can sway lenders despite the risks involved, and can do more than anything to achieve the go-ahead on loans.

"It is my experience that if you know how to approach cash sources—if you know the art as well as the science of borrowing—you can have lenders and investors competing to give you money," says Joseph Mancuso, president of the Center for Entrepreneurial Management, a nonprofit organization geared to help individuals and small companies raise money. "Given the same individual seeking a loan from the same banker, one approach will yield a loan and another will come up dry.

"The owner of a small medical electronics firm recently got turned down for a modest loan. We suggested that he repackage the request and return to the same bank for another try. The second time he walked away with a sizable sum. Success in borrowing depends, to a great extent, on how you pinpoint your sources and how you sell yourself to them."

The fact is that not that many of the rich were born that way, and many of those who made big money used borrowing as their first step toward wealth. All they started with was a good idea and a system for raising money.

Anyone can learn to borrow substantial sums of money —$1 million or more. The following are major loan and equity sources available to individuals, small businesses, and, in some cases, to both.

Secured and unsecured bank loans
Venture capital
Certified development corporations
Informal capital
Limited partnerships
Contract loans
Handicapped assistance loans
Student loans
Physical disaster loans
Economic opportunity loans
Farmers Home Administration loans
Surety bond guarantee program loans
Assignment of leases
Chattel mortgages
Commercial factors

Trade credit
Silent partners

Of course, not every cash source will come across for every applicant. Savvy borrowers are not discouraged by this. Those skilled at the art and science of borrowing know that the best way to attract substantial sums is to make the rounds at between five and ten different types of loan and equity sources, taking the maximum available from each and combining them to reach the highest possible total. If the goal is to obtain $1 million, holding out for that sum from a single source is bullheaded and a near-guarantee of winding up with nothing.

Although lenders are about as varied as snowflakes in their lending requirements and their attitudes toward borrowers, some basic rules are applicable across the board.

Make the prospective lender share your enthusiasm. Assemble press clippings, market research reports, and technical studies that project a bright future for your company, product, patent, or idea. Lenders respond favorably to good growth prospects.

Demonstrate that you will be able to repay the loan on schedule. Amass as much evidence as possible to win the creditor's confidence. Provide information on major orders or sales agreements with existing or potential customers.

Toot your own horn. Establish your track record in managing profitable ventures or in other successful endeavors. Prepare special resumes listing educational and business credentials. A solid background can reassure the most skeptical banker.

Turn the tables on lenders by making them compete for your business. Inform each cash source that you are shopping around for the best terms. Don't beg for money. If you prove that you or your business will turn the cash into more cash, lenders will bid for your account.

Avoid so-called loan brokers who promise to win financing with banks or the Small Business Administration. There is no need to pay fees to middlemen, and outsiders cannot guarantee that an application will be approved.

Work with an accountant throughout the borrowing process. Many CPAs are skilled at selecting the best cash sources and preparing needed financial statements, cash-flow projections, and audits. Ask bankers or finance companies for the names of accountants they work with regularly. These professionals may have an inside track.

It is also a good idea for borrowers to have some familiarity with financial statements. A surface view of a business may reveal facts about merchandise, employees, and trucks, but that company's financial statements will provide a look into the world that lies beneath the surface. And it is that world that owners need to penetrate, since it is in the fiscal foundation that the company's assets and liabilities, its strengths and weaknesses, lie. Financial statements are like X-rays, bringing the vital parts into focus.

Two major financial statements—income statements and balance sheets—are useful to virtually every business venture. Confused by these seemingly arcane documents, however, many entrepreneurs simply leave them to accountants to figure out. That's a mistake. Although professionals should prepare the statements, borrowers should incorporate them into the management process.

"By regularly compiling and analyzing financial statement information, management can detect the chief causes of small-business failure," says a vice-president of the Bank of America. "They can spot sluggish sales, high operating expenses, credit and inventory mismanagement, and excessive fixed assets. By comparing statements from different periods, owners can more easily spot trends and make necessary budget revisions before small problems become larger ones."

Put simply, the income statement reports business revenue, expenses, and the resulting profit or loss over a specific period of time. It is prepared on a monthly and year-to-date basis, thus keeping entrepreneurs abreast of current status as well as long-term developments. Net income, a key measurement in the income statement, represents total revenues minus total expenses, including taxes. This is the so-called bottom line.

The balance sheet lists a company's total assets, liabilities, and net worth. It is based on the fundamental accounting equation: assets = liabilities + equity. Current liabilities covers all debts payable within one year or one cycle of operations, including short-term notes, accounts payable, accrued interest payments, and other obligations.

Much of the data contained in financial statements provides the grist for making sound financing decisions, and can help to wrest capital from lenders and investors.

"Virtually all lenders of capital, such as banks, finance companies, and venture capitalists, require these reports with each loan request, regardless of previous successful loan history," adds the Bank of America vice president. "Also, as a condition of granting a loan, a creditor may request periodic financial statements in order to monitor the business's success."

Act now to develop a working knowledge of financial statements. It's an investment in time that can pay off later in dollars.

2

Plotting your hit list

Down to brass tacks. Now that we know there's money out there and that it can be borrowed, the goal is to prepare further for the borrowing process. The first step in the search for money takes place not in a bank or finance company but in the borrower's home or office. Before a single interview is held, the borrower must groom himself or herself for the market much the way a shrewd attorney prepares to face a jury. Keeping in mind that borrowing is both an art and a science helps to ensure success at this stage of the process.

The vast majority of loan applicants seeking substantial sums fails miserably. Most come up empty-handed because they charge headlong into the lending market, giving little or no thought to the complex challenge they are about to tackle. Others fail because they face the challenge deferentially, the way they have been meeting similar challenges since they were children. Unfortunately, this is inappropriate and self-defeating when it comes to seeking money. Humility, courtesy, and timidity hinder rather than help the borrowing process. The rule is: Facing lenders with hat in hand, pleading for financial support, is the best way to get kicked out the door like an itinerant beggar.

Savvy borrowers—like our shrewd attorney—know the importance of putting on a show: of impressing, dazzling, and mesmerizing lenders; of making lenders so enthusiastic about the project that they are afraid to ignore or reject it, afraid they will lose money by doing so. And although outright lying and deception are not ethical in building this enthusiasm (and may even be illegal), there's no reason to be a Boy Scout either. Successful borrowers know how to create an image of success that is based on hype and illusion but that in no way is fraudulent. That's the art of borrowing.

Take the offensive. Use the following steps to prepare for lenders:

Invest $100 in printing up a box of one hundred calling cards. Sure, you can get a hundred cards for a little as $5, but don't. And don't use the cards you use for your routine business calls. Go to a local printer and ask for something exceptional —the Gucci of business cards. Have them printed on silk paper or parchment with real gold lettering. Make sure they are elegant, attractive, and, most of all, memorable. Creative calling cards distinguish you from other applicants and can create that aura of success (well before you have it) that tempts lenders to jump on the bankwagon to fund your idea or project.

Printing your own letterhead is also a good idea. Writing a letter on blank bond tells the financial company that you have no affiliation, no business base, no previous success. Personalized business stationery, on the other hand, presents an image of prestige and finesse. It inspires confidence —and when it comes to raising money, that's vital. Here again, be extravagant. Spend for fine stationery that commands as much attention as the words printed on it.

Keep in mind that the adage about "money going to money" is absolutely true. Look as though you have wealth, and you'll be inundated with offers from financial movers and shakers. Look as though you have none, and you'll be treated like a gnat. In our society, respect from others is often based strictly on how much money you earn. Bobby Fischer, the great chess master, once intimated that one motive for his playing Boris Spassky in their record purse match in Reykjavik, Iceland, was his knowledge that the game of chess and its most accomplished players would never be respected by the public unless it became a high-stakes contest.

Fischer was absolutely right: as soon as the terms of the match were publicized, the eyes of the world turned to Iceland. Chess became an international fad with millions of people learning the game, taking lessons, and gobbling up chess sets in record numbers. What's more, Fischer became a matinee idol, keeping the gossip columnists as busy as Robert Redford does when he's in town. For the first time in Fischer's life, offers for endorsements came pouring in. The image of Fischer-the-millionaire—not Fischer-the-chess-master—turned on the money men and made them want to fill his pockets with more.

The lesson here is not to become a world-class chess celebrity but to use the image of having money to attract money.

While it is not true that clothes make the man or woman, they can unmake them. The financial community is sober and low-keyed, with a penchant for fashion understatement. Dark, conservative clothing is favored by bankers and Wall Streeters. Prospective borrowers approaching this inner circle in trendy, glittery garb immediately cast themselves as outsiders. Worse yet, they are seen as flaky fashion plates not to be taken seriously and certainly not to be trusted with substantial sums of money.

The rule is: Spend as much as you can afford on a superbly tailored suit—perhaps twice as much as you have ever spent on an article of apparel—and make sure it is gray flannel, dark wool, or subtle pinstripes. A fine garment will add to your image of success, to the impression that you know how to make money.

Avoid flashy gimmicks, but don't be afraid of a well-planned flourish. A bowler hat and black lacquered cane make any man on the street look like he's working on his second million. Women might opt for an alligator attaché case. In general, stay away from Gucci, Louis Vuitton, and other name-dropper items. Opt for the subtler signs.

Prepare a "Mark Stevens borrower's profile." This personal inventory of your most significant skills, traits, and experience can be thought of as a resume used exclusively for borrowing money.

The rule is: Accent the positive and avoid the negative. For example, tradition has it that a resume must include a person's educational experience. This is not so with a Mark Stevens borrower's profile. If your education leaves much to be desired—if you dropped out of college or never got past grade school—simply omit education from the resume. Include only those factors that will inspire confidence in your ability to turn borrowed money into more money and to repay the loan with interest. Stress successes in business, together with civic, military, and educational endeavors.

Another point: Personnel experts often cite a silly rule that resumes must be limited to a single page. Again, this does not apply to the Stevens borrower's profile. Applicants with a long list of credentials should flaunt every achievement regardless of how many pages the resume turns out to be. Remember that when it comes to borrowing money, there is no place for humility.

For each component on the Mark Stevens borrower's profile, give the dates of the activity, duties, responsibilities, and your bottom-line contributions, preferably in terms of dollars. For example, tell how your stint as a division sales manager for a dairy company brought a 26 percent increase in sales or $781,000. This is the kind of quantitative data that makes lenders take notice. List the names and titles of references who can attest to your capabilities, but limit this to prestigious individuals. Endorsements from neighbors, relatives, and co-workers have no clout, unless those persons are famous; those of bankers, company presidents, and politicians are as good as gold.

Draw up a "hit list of target lenders," zeroing in on those with a solid track record of making loans to other than the *Fortune* 500. Much like business executives in all fields, some bankers have a taste for high-risk deals and gain a certain satisfaction out of making them work; others want no part of anything that isn't blue chip. Who stands where can be determined by making a dozen or so calls to trade associations, CPAs, stockbrokers, and business associates. This narrowing down of the targets greatly increases the odds of obtaining a loan. All too many prospective borrowers approach the market helter-skelter and become discouraged before they make contact with a single lender likely to be interested in their pitch.

Plan a "door-in-the-face" search schedule, plotting out, on a calendar, exactly how many lenders you will visit on each day of the period set aside for borrowing money, and make appointments with them well in advance. This is important because as the rejections start rolling in, as the doors start slamming in your face, the frustration may prompt you to give up well before the entire hit list is checked off. But with an appointment schedule tacked to the bulletin board— with all the dates set and confirmed—inertia will carry you through the bleakest periods. And it is just this kind of persistence that can net the big loans of $1 million or more.

3

Unleashing the "baron strategy"

Never underestimate the power of personal style to attract and influence others.

In the early 1970s, for example, many of New York's premier restaurants were said to host a very impressive-looking gentleman—a large, bearded fellow in the manner of Orson Welles. This gent, who called himself Baron Maximillian von Altdorf, knew that haute cuisine restaurants genuflect to patrons who present themselves as haughty, demanding, and aloof. He also knew that they live by formality and that they expect their guests to do the same.

Baron von Altdorf was pleased to oblige. Typically, he would select a restaurant exactly two weeks before he planned to dine there, would have his English "secretary" phone for reservations in the name of Baron Maximillian von Altdorf, and would have her demand "the finest table in the house. Anything less will insult the baron."

On the appointed date, the big man would arrive precisely twelve minutes late. Dressed in a black silk suit and black ascot, he would ask for the captain and greet him simply with the words "Baron von Altdorf." Without fail he would reject the first choice of tables regardless of its size or location, would wave off the second, and would settle on the third. Upon being seated, he would immediately raise a finger, signaling the sommelier. Thus would begin a lavish feast of fish and fowl; wine, champagnes, and cordials—interspersed with tastes of sherbet to freshen the palate; with a fine cigar providing the finale. Throughout the grand repast, the baron would never smile nor in any way acknowledge the attentive service of the assembled captains and waiters. When his cigar was smoked down to the tip and the last drop of sherry was licked from his glass, he would signal the maître d' to approach.

"I haven't a dime," he would pronounce with an arrogant air.

"What!" The captain would seethe.

"Baron Maximillian von Altdorf never carries cash. You'll have to send a bill to my secretary. A pad, if you will. I will note the address."

Greatly relieved, the captain would obsequiously comply.

"Of course, Baron, as you wish."

The truth is, the "baron" was a waiter himself in the dining room of one of Manhattan's most elegant hotels. His secretary was a chambermaid. His billing address was as fraudulent as the character he played. Why he did what he did is for the psychologists to consider, but how he did it may be of great interest to prospective borrowers. The baron had learned the trade secrets of a closed community—the restaurant business—and understood how restaurateurs view the world, how they size up patrons and assign them various levels of status. Armed with this knowledge, he simply created a character capable of turning the system's own prejudices against itself. And he succeeded: Baron Maximillian von Altdorf was the beneficiary of many a meal before his notoriety spread throughout the restaurant business and eventually caught up with him.

Certainly, no one is recommending illegal behavior. But it is important to recognize that an appropriate sense of style can be a powerful tool in convincing others to trust us. It can also open doors to the most exclusive circles. To do so, personal image must be meticulously designed and skillfully implemented. As we have seen, the "baron's" success in manipulating the system was due not only to the character he created but also to his portrayal of that character. Prospective borrowers must do the same. Once you have established your image (as outlined in chapter 2) and drawn up a hit list, it is time to venture out into the loan market. Do this with as much flair as you can muster, and don't be afraid to borrow a few pointers from the "baron."

Invite the prospective lender out to lunch at a gilt-edged restaurant. Set the time and the date, and make certain to pick up the tab. This accomplishes two things: it furthers your image of success (that look of working on your second million), and perhaps more important, shifts the meeting place from the banker's office, where he has the edge, to neutral ground.

Prearrange for someone (spouse, child, partner, co-worker) to call you at the restaurant during the course of the luncheon. When you are paged, have the maître d' bring a telephone to your table. Tell the caller that you are too busy to speak at the moment and that you will have to return the call. This too has dual benefits: you appear to be successful, decisive, and accustomed to giving orders; and, in addition, you have balanced the demands on your time and have proven yourself to be a courteous luncheon host.

Have a secretary or a reasonable facsimile of one make all of your appointments with prospective borrowers.

Turn the tables on lenders. State clearly that *you are interviewing* a number of bankers, venture capitalists, and the like, and that you will be deciding within three weeks which source you or your firm wants to work with. In many cases, the scent of competition makes otherwise uninterested parties pursue you. Keep in mind that it is a way of life for money managers to dream of big deals—of the hot loans and investments that pay off handsomely.

Never ask the borrower for anything. Simply tell him what you are planning to do and how much money you need. Close the meeting by presenting your business card and asking the banker *to call you* if he is interested.

4

Real-estate limited partnerships

Now that you are ready to enter the money marketplace from a position of strength—or, at least, with the appearance of strength—here's where to turn for the best cash sources.

Effective methods for raising capital extend well beyond loans. Wise borrowers, be they individuals or businesses, do not limit themselves. They explore every avenue in the search for funds. This includes working with investors who seek equity participation in return for their capital, in other words, people who want a partial ownership stake in your company or commercial project. Many wise entrepreneurs have offered this in exchange for enormous sums of money.

Take the case of Dennis Brown, an attorney and one-time Internal Revenue Service agent, with a passion for promising businesses and a compelling urge to start a company of his own. Like millions before him, he had a promising idea but no money to bring it to market. That was before he turned to limited partnerships. Today, he's one of the leading entrepreneurs in his industry. But to go back to the beginning . . .

"When I was a practicing attorney I was always fascinated by growth businesses, and I noticed something that really intrigued me," Brown recalls. "Some hot new ventures in the lodgings field were making a big splash with the opening of so-called no-frills motels—those offering plain accommodations at low prices. I thought the prospects were great, and I decided to jump in with both feet and become an entrepreneur."

After two decades of movement away from the original concept of motels as simple roadside lodgings—and the building of ever-more palatial facilities challenging major resorts in size and amenities—forces in the lodgings industry recognized once again that "less can be more." A growing segment of the traveling public clamored for clean, efficient rooms equipped with color televisions, telephones, and comfortable beds for less than the cost of a day's pay. This sleep-and-run crowd was more than willing to forgo fancy lobbies with crystal chandeliers, pretentious restaurants, and swimming pools for low prices. Thus was born the no-frills movement.

"As soon as my first no-frills Super 8 Motel [named to stress the $8 per night room charge, which has since climbed to about $20] opened in Aberdeen, South Dakota, we knew we had a winner," Brown says. "It experienced an eighty percent-plus capacity rate from the outset, and we had to expand the facility three times to meet demand. Our major customers were, and still are, traveling sales representatives who either pay their own expenses or are on very limited expense accounts. They don't want to pay for pools, lobbies, or other such features they have no time to use. They want good rooms at reasonable prices, and that's what we give them."

With his firstborn packed to the rafters and his brand of no-frills lodgings a proven performer, Brown thought immediately of building a family of Super 8s across the nation. The problem was that although he had target locations in mind, he found that financing, not market research, determined where he could open additional units. As a privately held company with little assets, the firm could attract fi-

nancing from only a handful of savings and loan associations. Wherever Brown could interest an S & L in lending
money, that's where he built another Super 8. Using this
approach, the firm grew modestly, adding several more
units.

"Then a number of factors converged to make this form
of financing unacceptable," Brown says. "We were getting
some good publicity in the trade press, and we wanted to
capitalize on that by launching a major expansion program.
I had always dreamed of opening units at the major airports,
but once we were big enough to do that, we were shut out of
these markets. The limited amount of S & L funds started
drying up. Suddenly, no one wanted to lend money for
single-purpose real-estate projects. Our backs were against
the wall. We had to come up with an innovative financing
strategy."

What Brown came up with was limited partnerships.
The basic concept is relatively simple: a partnership is
formed with a general partner, who administers the investment, and a group of limited partners, who put up the money
and take depreciation and other expenses as personal tax
deductions. Their risk is generally limited to the amount of
money they've invested in the deal.

The concept works best for transactions with significant tax breaks that can be passed on to partners as individuals. Most commonly, businesses involved in oil and gas
drilling, leasing, real estate, and research and development
turn to the limited partnership approach.

"The big tax breaks, such as the ability to deduct substantial depreciation on commercial properties, make these
deals attractive to many investors," says Gerald Frieder, a
tax partner with the national accounting firm of Touche
Ross. "They might not invest in the ventures without the
tax breaks available to them as limited partners. Although
the IRS has cracked down on many multiple write-off deals
[where investors deduct from taxes several times the

amount they have at risk in the investment] we are still seeing more limited partnerships than ever before."

Limited partnerships can be offered as either public or private deals. The former must be registered with the Securities and Exchange Commission as well as with the states in which the investments will be sold. Private offerings can eliminate registration with Uncle Sam but must still provide disclosure statements outlining all details of the partnership, including material risks to the investors.

"Generally speaking, partnerships with more than thirty-five investors must be registered with the SEC," says John Alspach, an attorney with Petty, Andres, Tufts & Jackson, the San Francisco law firm that handles Super 8 Motels. (Super 8 is now headquartered in San Mateo, California.) "That's the general rule that distinguishes a private from a public offering. Either way the limited partnership has a distinct advantage over the corporate form in that it tends to be more flexible. For example, partners can get shares of the business in consideration for personal services as well as for cash investments. Also, partners can be assigned different rights and obligations. This is harder to do with corporate shareholders."

Although no two limited partnerships are identical, the procedure for taking a public offering from drawing board to marketplace usually involves the following steps:

The entrepreneur—in many cases, the general partner—outlines his or her business objectives, spelling out what he or she wants to accomplish.

A CPA firm works up the numbers, including the specific tax breaks, the amount of money needed to finance the project, the cash flow, and income projections.

A lawyer familiar with securities laws organizes the partnership, including the rights and obligations of the general and limited partners; drafts the partnership agreement; and has it recorded with the SEC and state governments where necessary.

The government officials may demand changes in the deal, and these are made after consultations with the attorneys and the CPA.

Once the offering is cleared, it is sold by the broker-dealers handling the offering.

"As a thumbnail estimate, you can figure expenses will amount to about fifteen percent of the amount of money raised," Alspach notes. "It breaks down like this for a typical five-million-dollar offering: five to ten thousand for filing fees; twenty-five to thirty thousand for the attorneys; five to ten thousand for the CPAs; thirty thousand for printing the prospectus; and eight to ten percent commissions for the broker-dealers on the amount of money they raise."

Super 8's first limited partnership offering was preceded by eight months of negotiations with the attorneys and broker-dealers who would market the investment to the public. The deal had to be structured so that it conformed to the securities laws, would be acceptable to investors from the standpoint of cash flow and tax benefits, and would still be profitable to Super 8. When the terms were finally hammered out, the deal called for investors to receive 90 percent of the cash flow of the motel operations, all of their capital returned if and when the units were sold, and 85 percent of the long-term capital gains from the sale. (Super 8 looks to sell its units to franchisees after seven or eight years of operation.)

The offering proved a sellout, raising $5 million in five months. More than nine hundred investors put up a minimum of $2,000 each (units sold for $1,000) and became limited partners in the deal. The money was used to build three new motels with a total of 332 rooms. Like most of Super 8's deals, the partnerships were treated as franchises that acquire the land, build the motels, and manage them. Brown serves as the general partner in most of the partnerships.

"It's an expensive form of financing, to be sure, but it has worked well for us," Brown notes. "We get a fee of six percent of the money we raise for our partnerships and that becomes quite substantial when you have a lot of deals going. More important, however, we are able to build new units based on market considerations rather than the whims of the S & Ls. We have a presence in a number of major airports now, and these units do extremely well. It wouldn't have been possible without the limited partnership strategy."

In just a few years, Super 8 had six public and two private offerings under its belt. It had raised $20 million, generated an additional $500,000 per week through new partnerships, and had 116 properties in 22 states. That kind of success is hard to argue with.

Brown puts it this way: "With limited partnerships, I'd say our growth prospects are unlimited."

5

R & D limited partnerships

Limited partnerships do more than fund real-estate projects. They are versatile financing devices that come in many shapes and sizes. One species of the genus—the research and development (or R & D) limited partnership—can help investors turn their brainstorms into hard cash. Look what it did for Jim Dunn, an engineer who spent years with Exxon Enterprises, the oil company's high-technology arm. When Dunn came up with a new promising product idea, he left Exxon and searched for some way to finance his product's commercial development. Because most banks and other conservative lenders were not interested in high-risk start-up ventures with no substantial collateral, Dunn needed an alternative. He turned to R & D limited partnerships.

An increasingly popular device, R & D limited partnerships are helping inventors and others with high-risk technology ventures raise millions of dollars that are not available from traditional financing sources. "R & D limited partnerships are successful at generating the funds entrepreneurs need to develop new products and services because they make it attractive for investors to risk money on these projects," says Grover T. Wickersham, a securities partner with the San Jose and Beverly Hills, California, law firm of Freshman, Mulvaney, Marantz, Comsky, Forst, Kahan &

Deutsch. "The expenses incurred by the R & D limited partnership can be deducted on the limited partners' personal tax returns. What's more, the full write-off can be taken as soon as the money is given over to those doing the R & D work."

In a typical R & D partnership, an inventor's corporation that is seeking to produce a high-technology product contracts with a limited partnership to finance the product's development. The corporation gives its interest in the product—such as a patent or license—to the partnership.

The partnership raises money for the research and development, and pays this to the corporation. If the corporation succeeds in developing the new product, it is technically the property of the partnership. Through the option agreement found in most contracts, the corporation is entitled to buy back the rights to the product with a lump-sum payment or, more often, through a royalty agreement assuring the partnership of a percentage of the product's sales.

"The R & D limited partnership enables high-tech ventures to raise money at a lower price tag than is often possible through other types of financing," Wickersham adds. "Sell stock and you give away too much equity. Borrow money and—providing you can get it—you must struggle with debt service. The limited partnership can detour both of these problems.

"Investors are responding to R & D limited partnership offerings for more than just the tax deductions. Another major appeal is that the limited partners' earnings on the rights to the developed product may be treated as long-term capital gains regardless of how long the partners held those rights. It can be less than a year and still qualify for long-term capital gains treatment."

Jim Dunn works with the MicrOffice® Limited Partnership, which traces its roots to a profile of entrepreneur Jerry

Minsky that appeared in the August 1981 issue of *Venture* magazine. "I had just bought control of a company called Alanthus Corporation that was principally involved in tax-sheltered computer leasing deals," explains Minsky. "I wanted to diversify the company's activities to include venture capital, oil and gas limited partnerships, real-estate syndications, and R & D tax shelters. I renamed the company Technology Finance Group. In the *Venture* interview, I talked about the new directions in which I wanted to take it.

"Well, Jim Dunn, president of a start-up called MicrOffice Systems Technology, came to see me as a result of the article. He was interested in developing a sophisticated portable computer terminal, now called the Porta-Writer®, and wanted my assistance in raising money to develop the product. We've been working together ever since."

The Dunn/Minsky meeting started a collaboration that led to the formation of the MicrOffice Limited Partnership, with Minsky as general partner. "We decided to go the R & D limited partnership route because the venture capitalists, my first choice as a financing source, wouldn't even answer my calls at the time," Dunn explains. "When I was able to get through to them, they kept telling me that I needed more and more of everything before they'd consider funding my project. First they wanted a business plan. When I handed that over, they said I needed a management team. That done, they then asked for independent analyses of the product. I saw that it would never end—that they'd run me to death.

"What's more, at this stage the venture capitalists wanted sixty percent equity in the firm, and that was more than I was willing to give up. Jerry Minsky asked me to consider the limited partnership approach when we first met in the early fall, and by November the partnership was formed."

The legal and accounting work involved in preparing the partnership for a private offering was performed mostly by Minsky's in-house staff at Technology Finance Group. The terms of the deal called for selling thirty units at $50,000 each to raise a total of $1.5 million. Investors were to pay for the units in three installments: $25,000 in 1981, $15,000 in 1982, and $10,000 in 1983. In turn, they could claim the full $50,000 as a deduction on their 1981 tax returns. (The signing of a recourse note obligating them to pay the entire $50,000 made it possible to take the full deduction in the first year.) In addition, the limited partners are entitled to 5 percent of the PortaWriter's gross sales once it goes to market.

"When the royalties equal one hundred fifty percent of the partners' cash investment, their percentage of gross sales declines to two percent," Minsky explains. "But, at this point, they may opt to exchange their royalty rights for a hundred thousand dollars' worth of MicrOffice Systems common stock. We expect the limited partners to reach this point quite quickly. The PortaWriter should go to market in the first quarter of 1983, and we are projecting a five-to-one cash return to our investors by 1988."

The investors' faith in this rosy projection is based both on Dunn's reputation as a prominent inventor/engineer with Exxon Enterprises and on the market potential of the PortaWriter. Dunn seems to have found both a void in the computer marketplace and a way to fill it. His product takes the best of minicomputers and programmable calculators, adds some new capabilities, and blends all features into a hybrid device that is convenient and easy to use.

"Our product is a portable computer work station that takes no training to operate, that weighs about five pounds, and that fits into the unused portion of an attaché case [it is 7" x 11"]," Dunn explains. "It has applications for sales representatives, writers, engineers—literally millions of white-collar executives and professionals who need information processing but don't want to learn to be programmers. Insurance salesmen, for example, will be able to take the PortaWriter to a client's home, slip in a cartridge containing data on specific types of coverage, and compute costs and coverage figures right on the spot. The unit doesn't have to be plugged into a central computer or, for that matter, even into a wall socket. It is battery-operated, so you can use it on an airplane. Perhaps best of all, it can be hooked up to standard electronic typewriters that serve as printers when hard copy is required. The PortaWriter has a projected sales price of fifteen hundred dollars."

Sanford Garrett, vice-president and office automation analyst for Paine Webber, is enthusiastic about the Porta-Writer. "I've been impressed by its performance; and, equally important, I think it's a product that is right for its time. The office automation market is exploding—its size and scope are virtually unlimited—and the PortaWriter has found a void in the market. As millions of executives develop their own data base through the use of personal computers, they'll want access to that information when they're at home or on the road. The PortaWriter will help them do that. I also think that Dunn has put together a good core management team for a start-up venture. I'm optimistic about the prospects."

Money raised through R & D limited partnerships is rarely enough to bring a product all the way to market. It is intended to finance research and development only, stopping short of the manufacturing process. For this reason, venture capitalists or other financing sources may be needed at the later stages of the project, by which time the entrepreneur may have the clout to extract better terms.

That's what happened to Dunn. When the venture capitalists saw everything fall into place—when they recognized that Dunn had the management, the product, and the development money—they rang his phone off the hook.

Many wanted to take the deal on and were willing to accept 35 percent of the equity rather than the 60 percent they originally demanded.

R & D limited partnerships range from small private deals in MicrOffice's class to giant public offerings, including the behemoth of the species, Trilogy Computer Development. This $55 million offering, for which Merrill Lynch served as investment banker and agent, proved to be an extraordinary success and in the process greatly expanded the market for R & D limited partnerships.

"We arranged a public offering of five-thousand-dollar units with a minimum investment of ten thousand dollars," says Brent Nicklas, a Merrill Lynch vice-president involved in the transaction. "It sold out in two days in August 1981. The success of the offering proved that we could open the market for R & D partnerships beyond the super-high–net-worth individuals to the medium-size investors playing with ten thousand dollars. They too are interested in investing in high-tech companies if they can get some tax benefits."

Certainly, Trilogy owes much of its success to the reputation of the man behind the company, Gene Amdahl. The former IBM computer whiz who went on to form Amdahl Corporation has a broad following of true believers who think he can do it again. Trilogy's R & D money will go toward doing what Gene Amdahl does best: developing a high-speed mainframe IBM compatible computer that is more powerful and sophisticated than anything on the market. But, as the more recent MicrOffice deal proves, the action in R & D partnerships will not be limited to funding the projects of high-tech superstars.

"We are seeing a proliferation of R & D limited partnerships, and I think this trend will only accelerate in the future," says Seymour F. Bernstein, a partner with Deloitte, Haskins & Sells, CPAs. "The Congress has provided tax incentives to encourage these activities, and it seems as if that strategy has worked. A wide variety of products in a great number of industries is likely to grow out of this."

Have a prototype product, a patent, or just an idea you think can attract funds from an R & D partnership? If so, contact an investment banker (see chapter 15) and have the possibilities explored.

6

Asset-based loans

Sometimes it is possible to have everything and nothing at the same time. That's the case when a company or individual boasts a portfolio of assets but almost no cash flow. All the wealth is bound up in homes, property, artworks, and machinery. The owner is not about to sell these assets to buy a new Mercedes.

But he can use them as a lever to pry cash from a little-known loan source, the asset-based lender. Often referred to as "lenders of last resort," they provide cash to applicants who are judged poor credit risks by more conservative sources.

Asset-based lenders make secured loans. The amount of credit extended is determined by the value of the borrower's assets. Accounts receivable, inventory, machinery, buildings, real estate—and, in some cases, trademarks and patents—may be used as collateral. Because the loans are not based on the balance-sheet criteria used by unsecured lenders (generally a debt-to-worth ratio of three-to-one or better), they offer small, growing firms and individuals the opportunity to borrow up to several times their net worth.

"In many cases, unsecured borrowing doesn't work for small borrowers," says Monroe R. Lazere, president of Lazere Financial Corporation, an asset-based lender. "That's why they come to firms like ours. Thousands need money badly but cannot qualify for unsecured bank loans on the strength of their balance sheets alone. And even those who meet the banks' criteria may be severely limited in the amount of money they can borrow. If a business is undercapitalized, the available credit may be too little to be of real help. Or the business may be too new to interest an unsecured lender. But because we look at prospective borrowers differently, we can offer major loans to the same applicants the banks turn away."

Joe Kassel, president of Kassel Corporation, importers and manufacturers, has found this to be true. "In talks with the banks, we quickly learned that our borrowing needs greatly exceeded the amount they were willing to lend us. So we turned to asset-based lending. We've been using it for six years now and find it to be an excellent business tool. Our balance runs up to a million dollars at a time. Secured borrowing has helped us to keep growing at a steady pace."

Typically, asset-based loans are advanced against a borrower's receivables. The procedure is simple: a contract is drawn providing for a loan of up to 80 percent of the outstanding accounts. As receipts are collected by the borrower, the checks are forwarded directly to the finance company. This satisfies part of the loan and makes new credit available. Interest is charged on a per diem basis and is limited to the amount of the open balance, not the full credit limit. Asset-based financing differs from factoring (see chapter 19) in that the lender does not own the receivables. Because customers do not have to pay a third party, the company avoids the stigma so often associated with factoring. Accounts do not have to know that receivables are being used to secure a loan.

Interest rates for asset-based loans are generally higher than for unsecured loans. They are pegged to float at between three and five points above the prime rate but not exceeding state usury limits. Terms for fixed-rate loans range from five to seven years; loans based on receivables are revolving lines of credit and are evaluated annually. Borrowers can reduce effective interest charges by drawing on credit for short-term needs and repaying the balances as quickly as possible. Since payments are made with the regular flow of collections, this can be accomplished without causing economic hardship.

Asset-based loans may be used to take advantage of supplier discounts, pay trade debts, made advantageous purchases, enhance credit standings, modernize and expand facilities, pay taxes, meet payroll and overhead, and launch advertising campaigns. Individuals and small companies can also use asset-based financing to expand their business interests rapidly through mergers and acquisitions.

One approach is to play the takeover game. Contrary to popular opinion, this is not limited to multinational giants. You can join in, too, personally gobbling up companies in any number of fields. And you can do it with little or no money of your own. The financial sleight of hand is accomplished through a little-known technique called leveraged buyouts. It works like this: when a company or a group of employees or investors seeks to acquire a business, it raises money for the acquisition by pledging the assets of the target firm. The national network of asset-based lenders makes loans on this basis.

"The value of the acquired firm's assets determines just how much money we will lend for any given buyout," says J. Alan Kerr, senior vice-president of Walter E. Heller, Inc., a major finance company. "If that value equals or exceeds the selling price, it is possible for the new owners to make the purchase without dipping into their own pockets. That's a case of maximum leverage. More typically, however, the acquirers have to invest some of their own money. Some lenders will demand this just to make certain that all parties are sharing the risk. They want management to have as much at stake in the venture as they do."

Lenders will commit funds for acquisition financing up to these maximum percentages of the acquired firm's assets:

80 percent of the receivables

70 percent of the appraised value of real estate

45 percent of inventory

75 percent of the appraised value of machinery and equipment

Fixed-asset appraisals are based on liquidation value, which is the price they would bring at auction. This tends to be lower than fair-market value.

Leveraged buyouts range from $250,000 upward. Those loans made on accounts receivable are revolving lines; plant and equipment loans generally extend from five to seven years. Interest rates are quoted at between 2 and 4 percent above prime, with the larger and less risky deals qualifying for the better terms.

Companies interested in conducting a leveraged buyout should start by calling a lender active in the field. (See the address of the National Commercial Finance Conference at the end of this chapter.) These firms will dispatch a team of experts to look into a prospective acquisition's operations and financial statements. "We study the company's books, its management, and its products," Kerr explains. "We also research general market conditions, including consumer attitudes and competitive factors. Based on our findings, we do a series of projections on the company's future. Most important is the 'worst case' projection. This assumes that everything that could possibly go wrong in the next few years will go wrong. If the projection shows that the company could still meet its obligations under these difficult conditions, we'll probably make the loan. If not, we'll decline."

As Monroe Lazere puts it, "Let's say that Company A wants to purchase Company B and that the latter has one million dollars in assets. By pledging those assets to us, Company A can obtain the cash to buy Company B. The loan is then repaid with the earnings of the acquired company."

Entrepreneur Douglas Stevens did just that. For years he watched from the sidelines as a small company, Caspari Greeting Cards, thrived in the marketplace. Familiar with the industry, Stevens gave high marks to the company and its product line. As a result, when he learned that Caspari was up for sale, he jumped at the chance to buy the firm. "But I couldn't get enough money from the banks," he sighs, sounding like a man who knows how it feels to butt his head against a brick wall. "They focused almost exclusively on the debt-to-worth criterion, and I fell short there. Fortunately, the asset-based lenders like Lazere are more interested in the quality of the assets and the cash flow. We pledged the receivables of Caspari to get the loan. The seller took back notes over a period of several years, and we used the loan funds to bridge these payments.

"The deal has worked out wonderfully. I own the firm I wanted in spite of the banks' lack of cooperation. What's more, there is also a side benefit in working with the asset-based lenders. The discipline of the relationship forces you to get good documentation of your assets and to keep close tabs on receivables."

Once the private preserve of finance companies such as Lazere Financial Corporation and Walter E. Heller & Company, asset-based lending is now attracting a growing number of major banks. "Until recently, banks viewed themselves primarily as collectors of deposits who had to make very safe investments with those deposits," says Steven Diamond, president of Chase Commerical Corporation, a subsidiary of Chase Manhattan Bank. "They left the riskier segment of the market to the finance companies and their asset-based deals. But this changed in the late seventies because banks started to see themselves not as collectors of deposits but as financial intermediaries that had to find all sorts of ways to make money lending money. The asset-based market was an attractive growth area because inflation forced many that had previously qualified for traditional unsecured loans to go the asset-based route."

For the most part, the banks have spun off their asset-based activities into separate divisions run, as in Chase's case, by former finance-company executives. The problem here is that prospective borrowers seeking bank loans may be rejected for traditional unsecured or partially secured financing without being informed of the asset-based option. Diamond admits that, in many cases, "you have to know to ask for it."

It is said that the borrowing spectrum ranges from the pure unsecured loan to the pawn shop. Lenders of all kinds dot the curve at different points. This is true even within the context of asset-based borrowing. While some finance companies will make loans solely on the strength of assets, the banks tend to look at cash flow as well. They are more conservative in their approach. As a general rule, those individuals or businesses seeking asset-based loans must meet the following criteria:

Management's ability to demonstrate good moral character. A track record of honest and responsible relationships with financial institutions is a big plus.

If receivables are used as collateral, they must be based on unconditional sales.

For fixed-asset loans, real estate, boats, cars, inventory, equipment, and other items are valued by the lender's appraisers from a liquidation, or "undertaker's," point of view. Loans will be made for up to 80 percent of this value.

The following asset-based lenders belong to the National Commercial Finance Conference, One Penn Plaza, New York, New York 10001. Shop among them for asset-based loans.

Abrams & Company, Inc.
400 Madison Avenue
New York, New York 10017
(Burton Abrams, President)
    (212) 355–4646

Accord Business Credit, Inc.
1440 St. Catherine Street West,
    Room 310
Montreal, Quebec, Canada H3G
    1R8
(Gerald S. Levinson, Vice-
    President)
    (514) 866–2711

Aetna Financial Services Limited
4150 St. Catherine Street West
Montreal, Quebec, Canada H3Z
    1X8
(Denis G. Higgins, President)
    (514) 935–8585

Alabanc Financial Corporation
P.O. Box 2545
Birmingham, Alabama 35202
(Thomas J. Tucker, President)
    (205) 326–5788

Albany Bank & Trust Company,
    N.A.
3424 West Lawrence Avenue
Chicago, Illinois 60625
(Joseph J. Briganti, President)
    (312) 267–0614

Allegheny International Credit
    Corporation
One Allegheny Square, Suite 880
P.O. Box 6958
Pittsburgh, Pennsylvania 15212
(Charles C. Maupin, President)
    (412) 562–4086

Ambassador Factors Corporation
1450 Broadway
New York, New York 10018
(George J. Colon, Senior Vice-
    President)
    (212) 221–3000

American Acceptance
    Corporation
One Montgomery Plaza
Norristown, Pennsylvania
    19401
(John J. Grauer, President)
    (215) 278–2600

American Business Credit
    Corporation
Blue Bell West, Suite 122
650 Skippack Pike
Blue Bell, Pennsylvania 19422
(Knute C. Albrecht, President
    and Chief Executive Officer)
    (215) 278–8901

American Business Finance
1190 First National Building
Detroit, Michigan 48226
(Alfred F. Ryan, Senior Vice-
    President)
    (313) 962–8600

Armco Industrial Credit
    Corporation
225 LBJ Business Park
2995 LBJ Freeway
Dallas, Texas 75234
(David C. Schad, President)
    (214) 247–7044

Associates Business Loans
55 East Monroe Street
Chicago, Illinois 60603
(Russell B. Donahue, Executive
    Vice-President)
    (312) 781–5858

Associates Commercial
    Corporation
400 South Tryon Street
Charlotte, North Carolina 28285
(Norris S. Griffin, Executive
    Vice-President)
    (704) 373–0466

Atlantic Corporation
55 Court Street
Boston, Massachusetts 02108
(Rubin Epstein, President)
    (617) 482–1218

Avco Commercial Corporation
620 Newport Center Drive
Newport Beach, California 92660
(John B. Patterson, Director of
    Commercial Financing)
    (714) 640–5200

BA Commercial Corporation
1105 Hamilton Street
Allentown, Pennsylvania 18101
(Ronald P. Tweedy, President)
    (215) 437–8265

Banco Financial Corporation
780 Northstar Center
Minneapolis, Minnesota 55402
(John H. Olson, President)
    (612) 372–7988

Bank Hapoalim
10 Rockefeller Center
New York, New York 10020
(Harris F. Epstein, Vice-
    President)
    (212) 397–9650

Bank Leumi Trust Company of
    New York
1430 Broadway, 8th Floor
New York, New York 10018
(Howard Ross, Vice-President)
    (212) 832–5152

Bank of Montreal
Current Asset Finance Division,
    19th Floor
First Canadian Place
King Street
Toronto, Ontario, Canada M5X
    1G6
(Allan Taylor, Vice-President)
    (416) 867–5313

Bank of the Orient
233 Sansome Street
San Francisco, California 94104
(Thomas M. Chin, Vice-
    President)
    (415) 781–6565

Bank of Virginia
P.O. Box 25970
11011 West Broad Street Road
Richmond, Virginia 23260
(Harold F. Stierhoff, Senior Vice-
President)
(804) 771–7404

Bankers Trust Company
BT Factoring & Finance Division
1775 Broadway
New York, New York 10019
(Richard L. Solar, Vice-President)
(212) 977–6123

Barclays American/Business
Credit, Inc.
P.O. Box 118
Hartford, Connecticut 06101
(James T. Verfurth, Executive
Vice-President)
(203) 528–4831

Barclays American/Commercial,
Inc.
P.O. Box 31307
201 South Tryon Street
Charlotte, North Carolina 28231
(Edward L. Boyd, President)
(704) 372–8700

Barnett Bank of Jacksonville, N.A.
100 Laura Street
Jacksonville, Florida 32202
(John B. Logan, Vice-President)
(904) 791–7450

Bay Area Financial Corporation
606 Wilshire Boulevard, Suite
604
Santa Monica, California 90401
(Kenneth Pingree, Jr., Vice-
President)
(213) 451–8445

Beneficial Commercial
Corporation
Holiday Park Towers, Suite 219
644 Linn Street
Cincinnati, Ohio 45203
(Ingo K. Kozak, Vice-President)
(513) 241–8822

Boston Financial & Equity
Corporation
P.O. Box 68, Kenmore Station
Boston, Massachusetts 02215
(Adolf F. Monosson, President)
(617) 437–1100

Brancorp Factors
1440 Broadway
New York, New York 10018
(Jack Lindner, President)
(212) 840–2552

The Budd Leasing Corporation
3003 North Central Avenue
#1214
Phoenix, Arizona 85012
(C. L. Gehring, Senior Vice-
President)
(602) 264–4420

Business Loans, Inc.
1100 Glendon Avenue, Suite 759
Los Angeles, California 90024
(Lawrence M. Kohn, President)
(213) 824–5001

CBT Business Credit
Corporation
(An Affiliate of the Connecticut
Bank and Trust Company)
100 Constitution Plaza
Hartford, Connecticut
06115
(Paul Borden, President)
(203) 244–5223

CBT Factors Corporation
1040 Avenue of the Americas
New York, New York 10018
(Herbert A. Schattman,
   President)
      (212) 944–1100

CF International Inc.
One Penn Plaza
New York, New York 10001
(Barry J. Essig, Executive Vice-
   President)
      (212) 239–7100

Central Penn National Bank
Central Penn National Building
5 Penn Center Plaza
Philadelphia, Pennsylvania
   19101
(John H. Van Dusen, Senior Vice-
   President)
      (215) 854–3900

Century Factors, Inc.
444 Fifth Avenue
New York, New York 10018
(Stanley Tananbaum, President)
      (212) 221–4400

Chase Commercial Corporation
560 Sylvan Avenue
Englewood Cliffs, New Jersey
   07632
(Stephen C. Diamond, President)
      (212) 223–7006

The Chase Manhattan Bank,
   N.A.
1411 Broadway
New York, New York 10018
(Frank J. Donahue, Vice-
   President)
      (212) 223–7009

Chemical Bank
Factor and Finance Division
110 East 59th Street
New York, New York
   10011
(Andrew G. Tepper, Vice-
   President)
      (212) 750–7048

C.I.T. Commercial Finance
   Company
650 Madison Avenue
New York, New York
   10022
(Vito "Vic" J. Ascatigno,
   Executive Vice-President)
      (212) 572–6373

Citicorp Industrial Credit, Inc.
450 Mamaroneck Avenue
Harrison, New York
   10528
(Frederick S. Gilbert, Jr.,
   Executive Vice-President)
      (914) 899–7540

Citizens & Southern Financial
   Corporation
P.O. Box 4095
33 North Avenue, NE
Atlanta, Georgia 30302
(Charles S. Mitchell, Senior Vice-
   President)
      (404) 491–4610

Citytrust
961 Main Street
Bridgeport, Connecticut
   06602
(Henry N. Kraver, Vice-
   President)
      (203) 384–5051

Colonial Acceptance
  Corporation
P.O. Box 946
117 North Main Street
Mount Holly, North Carolina
  28120
(Charles G. Johnson, Executive
  Vice-President)
    (704) 872–5853

Colonial Business Finance
  Corporation
101 South Main Street
Waterbury, Connecticut 06720
(Joseph J. Gillooly, Jr., President)
    (203) 574–7215

Commercial Credit Business
  Loans, Inc.
300 St. Paul Street
Baltimore, Maryland 21202
(Frank J. Medeiros, President)
    (301) 332–7963

Commercial Funding, Inc.
230 Park Avenue
New York, New York 10017
(Alan A. Fischer, President)
    (212) 661–4848

Commercial Trading Company,
  Inc.
1440 Broadway
New York, New York 10018
(Gerald J. Grossman, Vice-
  President)
    (212) 244–8600

Commonwealth Financial
  Corporation
3505 Broadway
Oakland, California 94611
(William F. Plein, President)
    (415) 658–4426

Congress Financial Corporation
1133 Avenue of the Americas
New York, New York 10036
(Robert I. Goldman, President)
    (212) 840–2000

Continental Illinois National
  Bank and Trust Company of
  Chicago
231 South LaSalle Street
Chicago, Illinois 60693
(Val F. Pautz, Vice-President)
    (312) 828–9080

Crocker Commercial Services
A Divison of Crocker Bank
595 Market Street
San Francisco, California 94105
(Robert Van Dyke, Senior Vice-
  President)
    (415) 477–8080

Dimmitt & Owens Financial,
  Inc.
3250 W. Big Beaver Road, Suite
  #120
Troy, Michigan 48084
(Clifford G. Dimmitt, President)
    (313) 643–6084

Diversified Discount &
  Acceptance Corporation
Northwestern Federal Building
Minneapolis, Minnesota 55403
(M. B. White, President)
    (612) 339–8958

Equimark Commercial Finance
  Company
Equimark Bank Building
Two Oliver Plaza
Pittsburgh, Pennsylvania 15222
(Gerard B. Knell, President)
    (412) 288–5010

European American Bank and
Trust Company
600 Old Country Road at Glen
Cove Road
Garden City, New York
11530
(Eugene Campbell, Vice-
President)
(212) 437–4652

FBS Business Credit, Inc.
P.O. Box 522
200 Soo Line Building
Minneapolis, Minnesota
55480
(John E. McCauley, President)
(612) 370–4990

Fidelity Commercial Finance
Corporation
15 South Munn Avenue
East Orange, New Jersey 07018
(William J. Cardew, President)
(201) 676–6661

The Finance Company of
America
Munsey Building
Baltimore, Maryland 21202
(Louis Eliasberg, Jr., President)
(301) 752–8450

Financial Guild of America
5730 Uplander Way, Suite 103
Culver City, California 90230
(Bron D. Hafner, President)
(213) 641–9200

First American Commercial
Finance, Inc.
First Amtenn Center
Nashville, Tennessee 37237
(Charles McMahan, President)
(615) 748–2607

First City Financial Corporation
1111 Fannin
Houston, Texas 77002
(Lawrence C. Blanton, President)
(713) 658–6724

First Commercial Company, Inc.
120 North Robinson, Suite 1225
West
Oklahoma City, Oklahoma 73102
(David H. Pendley, Senior
Vice-President)
(405) 272–4693

First Factors Corporation
P.O. Box 2730
101 S. Main Street
High Point, North Carolina
27261
(Earl N. Phillips, Jr., Executive
Vice-President)
(919) 855–8055

The First Jersey National Bank
2 Montgomery Street
Jersey City, New Jersey 07303
(Michael J. Palermo, Vice-
President)
(201) 547–7000

First National Bank in Dallas
P.O. Box 83711
Dallas, Texas 75283
(Stephen Fischer, Senior Vice-
President)
(214) 744–7417

The First National Bank of
Allentown
645 Hamilton Mall
Allentown, Pennsylvania 18101
(William M. Holls, Jr., Vice-
President)
(215) 439–4548

The First National Bank of
  Atlanta
P.O. Box 4148
Atlanta, Georgia 30302
(William T. Deyo, Jr., Group
  Vice-President)
    (404) 588–5469

The First National Bank of
  Chicago
One First National Plaza
Chicago, Illinois
  60670
(Joseph S. Giuffre, Vice-
  President)
    (312) 732–3175

First National Bank of Louisville
101 South Fifth Street
Louisville, Kentucky
  40201
(Charles Reeves, Senior Vice-
  President)
    (502) 581–4200

The First National Bank of
  Maryland
P.O. Box 1596
25 South Charles Street
Baltimore, Maryland
  21201
(William A. Quade, Jr., Senior
  Vice-President)
    (301) 244–3709

First National State Bank of New
  Jersey
550 Broad Street
Newark, New Jersey
  07102
(Robert J. Corcoran, Vice-
  President)
    (201) 565–3705

First Tennessee Bank, N.A.
  Memphis
Commercial Finance Division
P.O. Box 84
165 Madison Avenue
Memphis, Tennessee 38101
(Joseph D. Hardesty, Jr., Vice-
  President)
    (901) 523–4633

First Union Caesar Corporation
First Union Plaza CORP-8
Charlotte, North Carolina 28288
(James B. Wolf, President & CEO)
    (704) 374–6061

First Wisconsin Financial
  Corporation
622 North Cass Street, Suite 200
Milwaukee, Wisconsin 53202
(Frank R. Quinn, President)
    (414) 765–4492

FNB Financial Company
Two Pennsylvania Plaza
New York, New York 10001
(Gabe E. Romeo, Senior Vice-
  President)
    (212) 239–1800

The Foothill Group, Inc.
2 Century Plaza, Suite 600
2049 Century Park East
Los Angeles, California 90067
(John F. Nickoll, President)
    (213) 556–1222

Franklin Commercial Corporation
  P.O. Box 475
South Bound Brook, New Jersey
  08880
(Thomas P. Smyth, Assistant
  Vice-President)
    (201) 745–6044

General Commercial Acceptance
Company
2 Overhill Road
Scarsdale, New York 10583
(William T. Blumberg, Partner)
    (914) 723–0857

General Discount Corporation
60 State Street, Suite 1800
Boston, Massachusetts 02109
(Lawrence R. Seder, President)
    (617) 227–0900

General Electric Credit
Corporation
260 Long Ridge Road
Stamford, Connecticut 06902
(Dennis D. Dammerman, Vice-
    President)
    (203) 357–4540

General Innkeeping Acceptance
Corporation
3760 Lamar Avenue
Memphis, Tennessee 38195
(E. Tucker Dickerson, President)
    (901) 362–4426

Gibraltar Corporation of
America
350 Fifth Avenue
New York, New York 10001
(Herbert C. Hurwitz, Chairman)
    (212) 868–4400

Girard Bank
1 Girard Plaza
Philadelphia, Pennsylvania
19101
(Walter Einhorn, Vice-President)
    (215) 585–2160

Globe Business Credit, Inc.
480 Lytton Avenue

Palo Alto, California 94301
(Robert W. Brophy, President)
    (415) 321–7170

Hamilton Bank
P.O. Box 3959
Lancaster, Pennsylvania 17604
(Robert A. Rupel, Vice-President)
    (717) 569–8731

The Harris Trust & Savings Bank
111 West Monroe Street
Chicago, Illinois 60690
(Neal Elkin, Vice-President)
    (312) 461–6580

Hartford National Bank & Trust
Company
Secured Lending Department
777 Main Street
Hartford, Connecticut 06115
(Arthur R. Beeman III, Vice-
    President)
    (203) 728–2000

Walter E. Heller & Company
200 Park Avenue
New York, New York 10017
(Herbert E. Ruben, Senior Vice-
    President)
    (212) 880–7154

Hempstead Bank
40 Main Street
Hempstead, New York 11550
(George Stofsky, Vice-President)
    (516) 560–2362

Heritage Commercial Finance
Company
Broadway & Cooper Streets
Camden, New Jersey 08101
(Frank Sannella, Jr., President)
    (609) 964–2030

E.F. Hutton Credit Corporation
Greenwich Office Park I
Greenwich, Connecticut
  06830
(Harvey Leibowitz, Vice-
  President)
    (203) 629–3025

Industry Financial Corporation
444 Lafayette Road
St. Paul, Minnesota 55101
(J. Fred McCandless, Senior Vice-
  President)
    (612) 222–7792

Intercontinental Credit
  Corporation
2 Park Avenue
New York, New York 10016
(Barry M. Weinstein, Vice-
  President)
    (212) 481–1800

Investors Lease Corporation
200 Park Avenue, Suite 228E
New York, New York 10017
(David J. Tananbaum, President)
    (212) 697–4590

Irving Factors Corporation
One Penn Plaza
New York, New York
  10001
(Joseph A. Grimaldi, President)
    (212) 239–5030

Irving Trust Company
Commercial Finance
  Department
201 East 42nd Street
New York, New York 10017
(Robert M. Grosse, Vice-
  President)
    (212) 922–7100

William Iselin & Company, Inc.
357 Park Avenue South
New York, New York 10010
(Thomas A. Savage, President)
    (212) 481–9400

ITT Commercial Finance
  Corporation
Community Federal Center,
  Suite 800
12555 Manchester Road
St. Louis, Missouri 63131
(Melvin F. Brown, President)
    (314) 821–7750

JSA Financial Corporation
40 Court Street
Boston, Massachusetts 02108
(David E. Torrey, President)
    (617) 726–7100

Jung Factors, Inc.
P.O. Box 2524
Houston, Texas 77001
(Gordon L. Clemmons,
  Chairman of the Board)
    (713) 522–9861

KB Business Credit, Inc.
450 Park Avenue
New York, New York 10022
(John D. McCormick, President)
    (212) 832–7200

KBK Financial, Inc.
P.O. Box 61463
Houston, Texas 77208
(Doyle Kelley, President)
    (713) 224–4791

Kellock Factors Limited
10 St. Mary at Hill
London, EC3 R8E
(J.N. Oppenheim, Director)
    London 01–44–623–9021

Lakeshore Commercial Finance
Corporation
610 North Water Street
Milwaukee, Wisconsin 63202
(Lawrence R. Appel, President)
(414) 273–6533

Lazere Financial Corporation
(Affiliated with Connecticut
Bank & Trust Company)
60 East 42nd Street
New York, New York 10017
(Monroe R. Lazere, President)
(212) 573–9700

Lincoln First Commercial
Corporation
1325 Franklin Avenue
Garden City, New York 11530
(Robert E. Stark, Senior Vice-
President)
(212) 949–1774

Manalis Finance Company
17141 Ventura Boulevard
Encino, California 91316
(Lowell B. Delbick, Partner)
(213) 872–0193

Manufacturers Hanover
Commercial Corporation
1211 Avenue of the Americas
New York, New York 10036
(Francis X. Basile, Executive
Vice-President)
(212) 575–7300

Marine Midland Bank–New
York
One Marine Midland Center
Buffalo, New York 14240
(Richard W. Parker, Senior Vice-
President)
(716) 843–2424

Marine National Exchange Bank
of Milwaukee
(Commercial Finance Division)
P.O. Box 2033
111 East Wisconsin Avenue
Milwaukee, Wisconsin
53201
(Phillip C. Strobel, Vice-
President)
(414) 765–3000

Maryland National Corporation
120 East Redwood Street
Baltimore, Maryland
21202
(Alfred I. Puchner, Chairman of
the Board
(301) 244–6740

John J. McDermott Company,
Inc.
900 Route 9
Woodbridge, New Jersey
07095
(John J. McDermott, Chairman of
the Board)
(201) 750–0350

M.B.C.H., Inc.
4590 Harrison Boulevard
Ogden, Utah 84403
(Randy J. Bushell, Senior Vice-
President)
(801) 394–3431

Meinhard-Commercial
Corporation
9 East 59th Street
New York, New York 10022
(Carroll G. [Peter] Moore, Vice-
President and General
Counsel)
(212) 572–6346

Mercantile Safe Deposit & Trust
Company
P.O. Box 1477
Two Hopkins Plaza
Baltimore, Maryland 21203
(Donald J. Trufant, Vice-
President)
(301) 237–5781

Mercantile Texas Credit
Corporation
2100 Mercantile Commerce
Building
1712 Commerce Street
Dallas, Texas 75201
(Ray G. Torgerson, President)
(214) 698–5719

Merchants Bank & Trust
Company
59 Wall Street
Norwalk, Connecticut 06852
(Leonard R. Volpe, Vice-
President)
(203) 852–5507

Metro Factors, Inc.
Royal Central Tower, Suite #216
11300 North Central Expressway
Dallas, Texas 75234
(Henry G. Wichmann, President)
(214) 363–4557

Midlantic Commercial
Company
A Division of Midlantic Banks,
Inc.
1455 Broad Street
Bloomfield, New Jersey 07003
(A. Robert Lange, President)
(212) 964–4478
(201) 266–8385

Midlantic National Bank
2 Broad Street
Bloomfield, New Jersey
07003
(Robert A. Klein, Senior Vice-
President)
(201) 266–6110

Milberg Factors, Inc.
99 Park Avenue
New York, New York
10016
(Leonard L. Milberg, President)
(212) 697–4200

Miller Martin & Company
2677 First International Building
1201 Elm
Dallas, Texas 75270
(Richard Miller, President)
(214) 748–8373

The Mint Factors
215 Park Avenue South
New York, New York
10003
(Charlotte Mintz, Partner)
(212) 254–2377

Mirabel Factors Corporation, Inc.
50 Cremazie West, Suite 811
Montreal, Quebec, Canada H2P
1A6
(Danny Aronoff, President)
(514) 382–2000

National Acceptance Company
of America
105 West Adams Street
Chicago, Illinois 60603
(Frank R. Bergen, Vice-President)
(312) 621–7500

National Bank of North America
Commercial Finance
  Department
592 Fifth Avenue
New York, New York
  10036
(Austin Ludlow, Vice-President)
    (212) 730–6000

NCNB Financial Services, Inc.
P.O. Box 30533
1 NCNB Tower
Charlotte, North Carolina
  28230
(Dan J. Crowley, President)
    (704) 374–5087

Nelson Capital Corporation
591 Stewart Avenue
Garden City, New York 11530
(Irwin B. Nelson, President)
    (516) 222–2555

New England Merchants
  National Bank
28 State Street
Boston, Massachusetts 02106
(Leo R. Breitman, Senior Vice-
  President)
    (617) 742–4000

Northwest Acceptance
  Corporation
Orbanco Building, 21st Floor
1001 S.W. Fifth Avenue
Portland, Oregon 97204
(Frank J. O'Connor, President)
    (503) 222–7920

Northwestern Bank
Business Finance Division
P.O. Box 1347
315 9th Street
North Wilkesboro, North
  Carolina 28659
(F. Gareth Beshears, Vice-
  President)
    (919) 667–2111

Old Stone Bank
150 South Main Street
Providence, Rhode Island
  02901
(James V. Rosati, Vice-President)
    (401) 278–2000

The Philadelphia National Bank
Broad and Chestnut Streets
Philadelphia, Pennsylvania
  19101
(Robert R. Chase, Jr., Vice-
  President)
    (215) 629–3100

Pitney Bowes Credit Corporation
72 Heights Road
Darien, Connecticut
  06820
(Henry B. Vess, Vice-President of
  Marketing and Field
  Operations)
    (203) 655–7761

Pittsburgh National Bank
P.O. Box 340700–P
Pittsburgh, Pennsylvania
  15265
(Ronald L. Lambert, Vice-
  President)
    (412) 355–4922

PNB Commercial Finance
Corporation
1900 PNB Building
Philadelphia, Pennsylvania
19107
(Alexander M. Gusdorff, Jr.,
President)
(215) 568–4604

Puritan Finance Corporation
One North LaSalle Street
Chicago, Illinois 60602
(Lawrence A. Sherman,
President)
(312) 372–8833

Republic Acceptance
Corporation
P.O. Box 1329
Minneapolis, Minnesota 55440
(Fred [Bucky] Weil, Jr., President)
(612) 335–3121

Republic Factors Corporation
355 Lexington Avenue
New York, New York 10017
(Robert S. Sandler, Executive
Vice-President)
(212) 573–5500

Rhode Island Hospital Trust
National Bank
One Hospital Trust Plaza
Providence, Rhode Island 02903
(Peter L. Paquin, Vice-President)
(401) 278–8540

Rosenthal & Rosenthal, Inc.
1451 Broadway
New York, New York 10036
(Melvin E. Rubenstein, Executive
Vice-President)
(212) 790–1418

Scotia Factors Limited
1550 de Maisonneuve Blvd., W.,
Suite 300
Montreal, Quebec, Canada H3G
1N2
(H. H. Robertson, President)
(514) 934–1234

Seafirst Commercial Corporation
Irongate Executive Plaza, Suite 102
777 South Yarrow
Lakewood, Colorado 80226
(Charles Overson, President)
(303) 989–6711

Security Pacific Business Credit,
Inc.
850 Third Avenue
New York, New York 10022
(Louis Rubin, President)
(212) 826–3006

Security Pacific Finance
Corporation
Scripps Ranch Business Center
10103 Carroll Canyon Road
San Diego, California 92132
(Barry I. Newman, Chairman of
the Board, President and Chief
Executive Officer)
(714) 578–6150

Shawmut Credit Corporation
One Federal Street
Boston, Massachusetts 02110
(William S. McLaughlin,
President)
(617) 292–3572

The Slavenburg Corporation
One Penn Plaza
New York, New York 10001
(Vincent P. Arminio, President)
(212) 564–8600

Southeast First National Bank of
Miami
100 South Biscayne Boulevard
Miami, Florida 33131
(Robert E. Lerch, Jr., Vice-
President)
(305) 577-3198

Southern National Financial
Corporation
P.O. Box 33849
Charlotte, North Carolina 28233
(Preston L. Fowler III, Executive
Vice-President)
(704) 377-5611

Standard Financial Corporation
540 Madison Avenue
New York, New York 10022
(Louis J. Cappelli, Executive
Vice-President)
(212) 826-8050

State Financial Corporation
1100 Glendon Avenue, Suite 753
Los Angeles, California 90024
(Irving S. Reiss, President)
(213) 208-2200

State National Bank of
Connecticut
One Atlantic Street
Stamford, Connecticut 06901
(Joseph Iannuccilli, First Vice-
President)
(203) 356-0499

James Talcott Factors
1633 Broadway
New York, New York 10019
(William R. Gruttemeyer,
President)
(212) 484-0333

Textile Banking Company, Inc.
51 Madison Avenue
New York, New York 10010
(Joseph E. Mariani, President)
(212) 481-3000

Todd Leasing Corporation
350 Fifth Avenue, Suite 628
New York, New York
10001
(Robert L. Krause, President)
(212) 947-0505

Trefoil Capital Corporation
One Penn Plaza
New York, New York
10001
(Gerald Blum, President)
(212) 736-3515

Trust Company Bank
P.O. Box 4955
Atlanta, Georgia 30302
(J. Thomas Humphries, Senior
Vice-President)
(404) 588-7711

The Trust Company of New
Jersey
35 Journal Square
Jersey City, New Jersey
07306
(Robert J. Figurski, Vice-
President)
(201) 420-2808

Union Planters National Bank
P.O. Box 387
Memphis, Tennessee
38147
(H. Morgan Brookfield III, Vice-
President)
(901) 523-6848

U.S. Bancorp Financial
One Wilshire Building, Suite
  2500
Los Angeles, California 90017
(P. Anthony Yasiello, Executive
  Vice-President)
  (213) 622–3820

United Bank of Denver
Commercial Finance Division
1700 Broadway
Denver, Colorado 80217
(Alan D. Linton, Vice-President)
  (303) 861–8811

U.S. Capital Corporation
525 Northern Boulevard
Great Neck, New York 11021
(Martin Albert, President)
  (516) 466–8550

United Credit Corporation
10 East 40th Street
New York, New York 10016
(Leonard R. Landis, President)
  (212) 689–9480

United Virginia Bank
Box 26665
Richmond, Virginia 23232
(John K. Sheranek, Vice-
  President)
  (804) 782–5458

USI Capital & Leasing
  Corporation
733 Third Avenue
New York, New York 10017
(Alphonse F. Fantuzzo, Vice-
  President of Operations)
  (212) 682–8500

Wachovia Bank & Trust
  Company, N.A.
Post Office Box 3099
Winston-Salem, North Carolina
  27102
(Richard J. Dorgan, Senior Vice-
  President)
  (919) 748–6201

Washington Acceptance
  Corporation
1180 South Beverly Drive
Los Angeles, California 90035
(I. William Zweben, President)
  (213) 553–8595

Webster Factors, Inc.
11 Middle Neck Road
Great Neck, New York 11021
(Alter Milberg, President)
  (516) 466–0200

Wells Fargo Business Credit
12700 Park Central Drive,
  Suite 505
Dallas, Texas 75251
(Thomas D. Drennan, President)
  (214) 386–5997

Westinghouse Credit
  Corporation
650 Smithfield Street
Pittsburgh, Pennsylvania 15222
(Sylvan N. Mack, Manager,
  Commercial Finance)
  (412) 255–4140

Winfield Capital Corporation
237 Mamaroneck Avenue
White Plains, New York 10605
(Stanley Pechman, President)
  (914) 949–2600

Worcester County National Bank
446 Main Street
Worcester, Massachusetts 01608
(Judson J. Mohl, Vice-President)
    (617) 853–7342

Zenith Financial Corporation
The Towers
111 Great Neck Road
Great Neck, New York 11021
(Paul Singer, President)
    (516) 487–0302

7

Hidden-asset and growth-capital loans

An interesting variation on the asset-based loan is the so-called hidden-asset loan. With this, all you have to do is wave a magic wand, and old machines, vans, trucks, and computers will turn into the latest models—and it happens without your investing a dollar in cash down payments.

With inflation pushing the prices of new products through the roof, used-asset values have been rising in tandem. Many assets written off as old and outdated may actually be worth thousands of dollars. Even those assets no longer serving your needs can be applied to the acquisition of new generations of the same assets at advantageous terms.

Leading finance companies involved in hidden-asset loans accept existing equipment as collateral for 100 percent financing of new purchases. This approach differs from standard asset-based loans in that it calls for using one piece of equipment to gain another.

"We will accept the chattel on the used assets as the equivalent of a down payment," says Gerald S. Kessler, vice-president of C.I.T., a financial services company. "This enables the borrower to conserve its cash or to use the money for other purposes. What's more, the borrower retains use of the old assets. It does not have to trade them in but simply takes advantage of the inflated value to secure the financing."

51

Adds Ken Lewis of Kenlee Precision Corporation, a metalworking concern, "In order to keep up with opportunities that were constantly opening up for us, it was absolutely essential that we acquire the latest equipment. But, as with any growing business, we couldn't pay for it wholly through internally generated funds. The solution, which has worked extremely well, was to get finance-company loans secured by our existing equipment. We weren't obligated to use our short-term bank lines, which are essential for day-to-day needs."

The first step in securing hidden-asset loans is to obtain a "resale appraisal" of the existing units, which puts a dollar figure on the wholesale value of the business equipment. Lenders use this estimate to compute the size of the loan they will make based on the secured assets.

"We need a fairly accurate gauge of what we can sell the asset for should the loan go into default," Kessler explains. "That way, we are certain of covering our risk exposure. Certain types of assets that are exceptionally rare or subject to rapid obsolescence may not qualify for this type of financing simply because we cannot be assured of selling them on the open market should we have to."

Financing terms generally range from three to fifteen years, depending on the Internal Revenue Service's guidelines for the equipment's useful life. Those assets likely to remain productive for many years, such as boats and certain heavy machinery, can qualify for the longest terms. Interest rates vary according to prevailing economic conditions, the type of assets involved, the value of the collateral, and the borrower's credit rating. "Virtually any type of income-producing—business assets can qualify for this financing technique.

Loans start at roughly $10,000 and climb to well above $1 million. Even the maximum sums can be secured at 100 percent financing. To qualify, prospective borrowers must have a good track record with creditors and a demonstrated ability to repay the loan from cash flow.

Contact business attorneys or CPAs for the names of reputable finance companies extending hidden-asset loans.

Similar to hidden-asset loans but more liberal in approval terms and the amounts of money available to many borrowers are "growth-capital loans." "Although these loans are based, in part, on the borrower's assets, growth-capital lenders do not set strict ratios correlating asset values to the size of the loan. What's more, they look at the prospective borrower's total picture, including the debt-to-worth ratio, credit rating, and the borrower's experience in the field.

"Sometimes, loan applicants will not meet any of the standard tests for approval that banks rely on so heavily, but we'll make the loan anyway," says a vice-president of Commercial Credit Services Corporation. "Our primary objective, after all, is to make money available to emerging ventures that don't necessarily have a long track record of successful operations. That's why we will work with startups that have made a capital investment of their own and that are thoroughly experienced in their industry."

Growth-capital loans are also flexible because they can be applied to a wide range of needs, including debt consolidation, working capital, inventory, new facilities, acquisition of other companies, and equipment purchases. Terms range from three to ten years, rates float between three and six points above the prime (lower rates are for larger loans), and borrowers can repay, often without penalty, after the first three years. Growth-capital loans are rarely made below $25,000.

Some asset-based lenders make growth-capital loans. Contact any of the firms listed in chapter 6, or ask your accountant to recommend outfits that extend this type of loan.

8

Sale leasebacks

Sale leasebacks are another variation on the asset-loan theme. Like the alchemy of old, this modern-day sorcery turns common assets into instant treasure. And it does so, time and again, without abracadabra, lucky stars, or secret formulas. The "magic" is nothing more than a savvy financing strategy. Ideally suited for today's prohibitive financing market, sale leasebacks enable borrowers to obtain lump-sum cash payments or to finance new projects at highly attractive interest rates, often well below the prime.

"Put simply, we can turn brick and mortar into cash," says Jay M. Messer, chairman of the American Property Fund, a real-estate investment organization specializing in sale-leaseback transactions. "So much equity lies dormant in stores, warehouses, plants, offices, and other structures. We help the owners turn this into productive capital while still retaining control of their facilities."

In a typical sale-leaseback deal, an individual or small company sells a property to the lessor for the full current market value. Simultaneously, the seller/tenant leases back the facility for a primary term, at a fixed rental, for a period of twenty to twenty-five years with between three and four ten-year extension options. In this way, the seller retains control of the property for fifty years or more—virtually its entire useful life. A provision can also be built into the agreement granting the seller the right to repurchase the property at the end of the lease at its then current market value.

"Sale leasebacks can also be used to finance new projects," Messer adds. "We will commit ourselves to purchasing an attractive property more than a year before it is built, and we guarantee the owners one hundred percent of all costs, including land, architectural fees, real-estate commissions, and the like. The client can put up its own funds or secure a gap loan until the project is complete, and we make the purchase. By using the sale-leaseback method, clients can save from two to three percentage points compared to traditional financing."

To prevent financial hardship during the early years of the lease, the new tenant may have the rental gradually "stepped up," with smaller payments due at the outset. This has dual benefits: initial expenses can be slowly absorbed into the budget, and the larger sums can be paid with deflated dollars.

Sale leasebacks are also attractive because, unlike the conventional debt market, there are few, if any, restrictive covenants. The seller can use the cash proceeds of the transaction for any number of purposes and can, if desired, seek additional financing from other sources. By carefully structuring the sale leaseback as an "operating lease," the deal may qualify for off balance-sheet accounting, thus improving earnings reports and credit standing.

Owners of assets often fail to consider sale leasebacks for emotional reasons. Suffering from the so-called family-jewels syndrome, they hold on to property for the sake of tradition or the pride of ownership. But this is often a mistake. The capital they can generate from this can be used to take advantage of promising business opportunities or once-in-a-lifetime investments. Remember, as we have stated, money goes to money.

Of course, sale leasebacks are not always the best alternative. There are a number of drawbacks that must be considered. First, loss of ownership is more than psychological. The firm does relinquish the legal rights and tax advantages that go along with the title to the property. Second, the tenant has no claims on the structure's residual value. In some cases, rapidly appreciating property may be better held by the current owner until the market value levels off. The prospect of substantial capital gains may outweigh the immediate windfall gained from the sale leaseback.

Leasing companies, banks, and other financial institutions can structure or arrange sale leasebacks. Check with an accountant or business consultant to explore the merits of a deal and to select a reputable outfit to handle it.

9

Small business employee ownership loans

Imagine a financing strategy that offers something for everyone. That's the case with an obscure loan plan that gives entrepreneurs instant cash and their employees a piece of the corporate pie. It turns workers into business owners, and for many that's a dream come true.

It is all part of the Small Business Employee Ownership Act. Designed to encourage employee management and ownership of small businesses, the law helps groups of individuals buy into the companies they work for. Now more people than ever can have an entrepreneurial stake in the economy.

The vehicle for this is a loan-guarantee program administered by the Small Business Administration (SBA). It works like this: trusts established by at least 51 percent of a firm's employees can qualify for financing to buy the stock of their employers. Participating banks and finance companies provide the funds based on SBA guarantees. Employees can borrow up to $500,000 at interest rates of up to 2.5 percent above the prime for loans of less than seven years and 2.75 percent for loans of longer term. Most important, the loans are nonrecourse; in other words, lenders cannot require participating employees to provide personal loan guarantees.

The loans can help employees purchase control of small firms. Because the financing standards of the SBA are more liberal than those of commercial banks, employee trusts rejected by banks can turn to the government for guarantees that make the purchase possible. The loan program can also aid the current owners of small businesses, who can sell out for a windfall by creating a buyer through the employee trust. This approach may be easier than selling a company on the open market since some small outfits don't attract buyers that easily.

Employee ownership loans can also help revive failing businesses. Rather than shutting down a troubled venture, the owner may sell to an employee trust. Staff and managers may be able to revitalize the firm with fresh ideas and new leadership.

The Small Business Employee Ownership Act allows for substantial flexibility. Business owners selling stock to employee trusts need not divest themselves of all interest in the firms: they may sell all or part of their stock. Employees must, however, hold enough votes in the company to block its dissolution or merger with another firm. If, on the other hand, the trust purchases a majority interest in the company, the seller cannot remain in control. Should outside management be required to aid in the transition, employee-owners must be trained to take over the reins by the time the loan is repaid.

To obtain an employee ownership loan, the firm's staff should set up an Employee Stock Ownership Plan (ESOP). Put simply, this is a trust that holds stock of the employer and can borrow money to purchase such stock. The National Center for Employee Ownership, based in Arlington, Virginia, offers its members information on starting ESOPs, and recommends the names of attorneys and bankers experienced in the field.

Employee trusts rejected by at least two private lenders may qualify for SBA-guaranteed loans. The SBA will review the loans according to established criteria, basing the decision primarily on the company's ability to repay the debt. Lenders may also require that the firm's assets be pledged as collateral.

ESOPs can be valuable financing tools even without government funding. "Companies often find that borrowing through an ESOP is a desirable alternative to a public or other private offering of stock—if the corporate employer has first committed itself to funding an employee benefit plan," says Peter Baumler, a partner with Arthur Andersen, the national accounting firm. "The funded ESOP becomes the immediate source for corporate financing as well as providing ultimate retirement benefits for employees."

It works like this:

Acting with an attorney and an accountant, the employer corporation creates an ESOP.

The ESOP goes to a lender for a loan to buy stock in the employer corporation. These shares of stock are set aside in the plan for the employees.

The employer corporation guarantees the loan.

The ESOP uses the loan to buy the corporation's stock and pledges it as collateral on the loan.

The employer corporation uses the money obtained for the stock to buy capital equipment, for working capital, or for other business uses.

Every year the corporation makes a cash contribution to the ESOP, which in turn uses this money to retire the loan. Because the corporation's payment is made to a qualified benefit plan, it is tax deductible (within certain limits set by the Internal Revenue Service).

"ESOPS are not widely recognized as financing instruments," adds Israel Press, a tax manager with Touche Ross & Co., CPAs, "but they do represent a sound, legitimate way for some companies to borrow at a lower effective cost."

Small businesses may also use ESOPs to acquire other companies. Baumler illustrates how this can work in a hypothetical case in which Smithco Corp. wants to buy ABC Manufacturing, Inc., for $5 million.

Smithco's ESOP borrows $5 million from a bank and purchases Smithco stock. Smithco guarantees the loan.

Smithco acquires the ABC stock with the $5 million received from the ESOP.

Smithco annually contributes to the ESOP enough cash to service the ESOP debt, including principal and interest.

The major caveat with regard to ESOP use is that the plans cannot be viewed solely as financing devices. They are, first and foremost, employee benefits with strict regulations governing their use.

For example, ESOPs can acquire only voting stock and must allow participants to vote the shares on matters of major interest to the company. Also, if there is no outside market for the shares, the corporation may be required to buy them back at a later date. This obligation must be carefully considered before the company commits itself to any form of ESOP financing.

Wise business owners will compare the relative merits and drawbacks of ESOP financing as well as alternative strategies before choosing a course of action.

"My employees set up an ownership plan five years ago, and I've been selling more of my stock to it every year," says Ed Sanders, president of Allied Plywood Corporation. "It's a terrific concept. If the corporation had redeemed my shares, the proceeds would have been considered ordinary income. But by selling stock to the trust, the payments to me are treated as capital gains. That makes for a big tax savings.

"What's more, the plan has a tremendous impact on employee productivity. Although this has been a difficult period for our industry, Allied Plywood has been doing quite well. I credit employee ownership for a measure of that success."

10

Certified development companies

You may find business financing right around the corner. An obscure network of lenders makes capital available at the local level. The objective is to spur hometown private enterprise—and you may be the beneficiary.

The network is composed of so-called certified development companies. The CDC program, enacted in 1980 as an amendment to the Small Business Investment Act, encourages private lenders to meet the long-term credit needs of small businesses through Small Business Administration-supported loans.

A certified development company may operate on a local, regional, or statewide basis. It may be organized as a private nonprofit corporation or as a for-profit stock corporation. These key requirements must be met:

The company must have a minimum of twenty-five members or stockholders, and a defined area of operation.

Membership in the company must include representation from all four of the following groups: local government, private lending institutions, community organizations, or business organizations.

The development company must have a professional staff with the capacity to package, process, close, and service its loans, and to provide professional accounting and legal services to small businesses.

No member, shareholder or group of shareholders, or members of the development company owning a direct financial interest in the project may have an individual or combined voting control in the development company of more than 10 percent of the total outstanding stock or membership.

The CDC also must contain wording in its incorporation papers indicating that its chief purpose is to "promote and assist the growth and development of business concerns including small businesses," and "any monetary profit or other benefits which flow to shareholders (members) shall be incidental to the corporation and shareholders."

Certified development companies are authorized to sell debentures pertaining to an identifiable small concern with the SBA's 100 percent guarantee. The proceeds from the sale of each debenture are used for plant acquisition, construction, conversion, or expansion for each identifiable small-business concern. The amount of each debenture guaranteed by SBA may not exceed one-half the cost of each project. The remaining one-half is to be provided from nonfederal sources: typically, 50 percent from a private lender, 40 percent from the SBA guaranteed debenture, and 10 percent from the local CDC.

A typical CDC financing of $100,000 is put together with the following private, SBA, and local CDC components.

Source	Percentage	Amount	Security
Bank	50 percent	$50,000	First mortgage
SBA-guaranteed debenture	40 percent	$40,000	Second mortgage
Certified development company	10 percent	$10,000	Third mortgage

The certified development company can provide assistance to small businesses under two basic plans. With the re-lend plan, the small business buys the property being financed; and the certified development company is a conduit through which SBA-guaranteed debentures and the nonfederal financing flow to the small-business concern. The business has title to the property; and under the first mortgage formula, the bank is entitled to make a direct loan to the business in exchange for a first mortgage. Proceeds from the SBA–guaranteed debenture are sent to the certified development company (or a bank acting as its agent), which re-lends to the small business in exchange for a second mortgage. This is then assigned to the SBA.

Another option is the lease plan. Under it, the development company owns the property and leases it to the small business. The arrangement can be a lease, lease-purchase, or lease with an option to purchase. The development company uses the proceeds from the sale of the debenture along with the funds borrowed from the nonfederal sources to purchase property, or it constructs-renovates the property for the identifiable small business.

The proceeds of debentures are used to assist small businesses in financing plant construction, conversion, or expansion, including the acquisition of land, existing buildings, and leasehold improvements. Plant construction includes the acquisition and installation of machinery and equipment. Each loan made from the debenture proceeds must be SBA-approved.

The SBA-guaranteed debenture may not exceed $500,000, and debentures may not comprise more than 50 percent of the project's total cost. Interest on the debentures is set by the secretary of the treasury, taking into consideration the current average market yield on outstanding marketable U.S. obligations with comparable maturities. Current rates may be obtained from local SBA offices.

The maturity on debentures does not exceed twenty-five years, with the exact terms depending on the economic life of the asset being financed. The contract between the certified development company and the borrower in each project sets forth terms acceptable to the small business and the SBA, not to exceed the sum of the following:

Repayment with interest on the debenture and the first mortgage nonfederal financing in the project

Taxes and insurance on the plant

Servicing costs of the debenture, which normally may not exceed one-half of 1 percent per annum on the outstanding balance of the debenture

A processing fee to cover administrative costs of the loan, which may not exceed 1.5 percent of the amount of the debenture

All debentures guaranteed under this program must be secured to the extent the SBA determines as reasonable to ensure repayment. Usually, collateral on development-company projects includes a mortgage on the land and the building being financed; liens on machinery, equipment, and fixtures; lease assignments; and personal guarantees where appropriate.

The best approach is to contact the CDC nearest you for all the details. See if these obscure programs can't inject a healthy dose of capital into your business projects.

A listing of CDCs nationwide follows.

REGION I

Androscoggin Valley Regional
    Planning Commission
70 Court Street
Auburn, Maine 04210
(Jon S. Oxman, President)
    (207) 783–9186
Area of operations:
    Androscoggin, Franklin, and
    Oxford counties

Bay Colony Development
    Corporation
87 Cresent Road
Needham, Massachusetts 02194
(George R. Berbeco, President)
    (617) 449–1694
Area of operations: Throughout
    Massachusetts, except Dukes
    and Nantucket counties

Boston Local Development
    Corporation
18 Tremont Street, Suite 300
Boston, Massachusetts 02108
(Frank Bronstein, President)
    (617) 725–3342
Area of operations: City of
    Boston

Boston Neighborhood Business
    Corporation
182 Tremont Street
Boston, Massachusetts 02111
(John F. Kelly, President)
    (617) 451–3496
Area of operations: City of
    Boston

Brattleboro Development Credit
    Corporation
P.O. Box 1177
5 Grove Street
Brattleboro, Vermont 05301

(Henry E. Merrill, President)
    (802) 257–7731
Area of operations: Windham
    County

Bristol County Chamber Local
    Development Corporation
P.O. Box 250
653 Metacom Avenue
Warren, Rhode Island 02885
(William H. Adair, Jr., Chairman)
    (401) 245–0751
Area of operations: Bristol
    County

Brockton Regional Economic
    Development Corporation
One Centre Street
Brockton, Massachusetts 02401
(Richard Straczynski, President)
    (617) 586–0500
Area of operations: Designated
    area of the Brockton Regional
    Chamber of Commerce

Central Vermont Economic
    Development Corporation
43 State Street
Montpelier, Vermont 05602
(Alan Noyes, President)
    (802) 476–4168
Area of operations: Washington
    County plus a part of northern
    Orange County

Cynosure, Inc.
P.O. Box 786
135 Church Street
Burlington, Vermont 05402
(Dudley H. Davis, President)
    (802) 862–5726
Area of operations: Greater
    Burlington Area

Eastern Maine Development
   District
10 Franklin Street
Bangor, Maine 04401
(Raynor Crossman, President)
   (207) 942–6389
Area of operations: Six counties
   in Eastern Maine

Greater Attleboro Development
   Corporation
42 Union Street
Attleboro, Massachusetts 02703
(Daniel T. Blake, President)
   (617) 226–4119
Area of operations: City of
   Attleboro

Greater Hartford Business
   Development Center, Inc.
c/o HEDCo
15 Lewis Street
Hartford, Connecticut 06103
(James H. Monroe, President)
   (203) 566–6970
Area of operations: County of
   Hartford

Lewiston Development
   Corporation
40 Pine Street
Lewiston, Maine 04240
(Dominique J. Tardit, President)
   (207) 784–0161
Area of operations: City of
   Lewiston

Lynn Capital Investment
   Corporation
598 Essex Street
Lynn, Massachusetts 01901
(T. Russell Webber, President)
   (617) 592–2361
Area of operations: City of Lynn

New Haven Community
   Investment Corporation Local
   Development Company
157 Church Street
New Haven, Connecticut
   05610
(Joseph Disesa, President)
   (203) 787–6023
Area of operations: City of New
   Haven

Newport County Local
   Development Company, Inc.
c/o Newport County Chamber of
   Commerce, Inc.
10 America's Cup Avenue
Newport, Rhode Island
   02840
(Raymond C. Mills, President)
   (401) 273–8050
Area of operations: Newport
   County

North Shore Business Finance
   Corporation
57 Pickering Wharf
Salem, Massachusetts 01970
(John D. Rooney, President)
   (617) 745–7100
Area of operations: North Shore
   Area

Northern Maine Regional
   Planning Commission
P.O. Box 779
Main Street
Caribou, Maine 04736
(James A. Barresi, President)
   (207) 498–8736
Area of operations: Aroostock,
   Pescatguis (six townships), and
   Washington (one community)
   counties

Ocean State Business
Development Authority
42 Park Place
Pawtucket, Rhode Island 02860
(Henry A. Violet, President)
    (401) 722–5800
Area of operations: Providence,
Kent, Washington, and
Newport counties

Pawtucket Local Community &
Industrial Development
Corporation
200 Main Street
Pawtucket, Rhode Island 02860
(Chester C. Benjamin, President)
    (401) 724–5200
Area of operations: Plymouth
and Norfolk counties

Plymouth Industrial
Development Corporation
130 Court Street
Plymouth, Massachusetts 02361
(Edward W. Santos, President)
    (617) 746–3370
Area of operations: Plymouth
County, Kingston, and
Plympton

Providence Industrial
Development Corporation
10 Dorrence Street
Providence, Rhode Island 02903
(James R. Winsker, President)
    (401) 273–8050
Area of operations: City of
Providence

Providence Local Development
Corporation
77 Washington Street
Providence, Rhode Island 02903

(Lombard Basbarro, President)
    (401) 274–5200
Area of operations: City of
Providence

Riverside Development
Corporation
42 North East Street
Holyoke, Massachusetts
01040
(Donald Breen, President)
    (413) 533–7102
Area of operations: City of
Holyoke

Somerville Local Development
Corporation
93 Highland Avenue—City Hall
Somerville, Massachusetts 02143
(Dr. Frank Scimone, President)
    (617) 625–6600
Area of operations: City of
Somerville

South Shore Economic
Development Corporation
36 Miller Stile Road
Quincy, Massachusetts 02169
(Wilham E. Kelly, President)
    (617) 479–1111
Area of operations: Plymouth
and Norfolk counties

Springfield Small Business
Assistance, Inc.
600 Baystate West Plaza
1500 Main Street
Springfield, Massachusetts 01115
(Herbert P. Almgren, President)
    (413) 734–5671
Area of operations: Hampden,
Hampshire, and Franklin
counties

Target Area Development
Corporation
86 N. Main Street
St. Albans, Vermont 05478
(Steven Bourgeois, President)
(802) 524–2194
Area of operations: Franklin
County

Winooski Community
Development Corporation
27 West Allen Street
Winooski, Vermont 05404
(John F. Rinaldi, President)
(802) 655–0773
Area of operations: City of
Winooski and town of
Colchester

Worcester Business
Development Corporation
350 Mechanics Tower
Worcester, Massachusetts 01608
(John Adam, Jr., President)
(617) 753–2924
Area of oeprations: Worcester
County and contiguous areas

REGION II

Albany Local Development
Corporation
155 Washington Avenue
Albany, New York 12210
(Jacob Herzog, President)
(518) 465–7581
Area of operations: City of
Albany

Camden Local Development
Company
101 North Seventh Street,
Suite 201
Camden, New Jersey 08102

(Benjamin A. Smallwood,
President)
(609) 963–8230
Area of operations: City of
Camden

Corning Crossroads, Inc.
42 East Market Street
Corning, New York
14830
(Thomas W. Peet, President)
(607) 936–8443
Area of operations: Steuben
County

Empire State Certified
Development Corporation
(State)
41 State Street
Albany, New York 12207
(Marshall R. Lustig, President)
(518) 463–2268
Area of operations: State of New
York

Erie Niagara Industrial
Development Corporation
107 Delaware Avenue
Buffalo, New York 14202
(Clifford B. Marsh, President)
(716) 877–4320
Area of operations: Erie and
Niagara counties

Hudson Development
Corporation
32 Warren Street
Hudson, New York
12534
(Edmond F. Schorno, President)
(518) 828–3373
Area of operations: City of
Hudson

Local Development Corporation
for the City of Buffalo
920 City Hall
Buffalo, New York 14202
(James Griffin, President)
   (716) 856–4200
Area of operations: City of
   Buffalo

Long Island Development
   Corporation
1501 Franklin Avenue, Suite 209
Mineola, New York 11501
(Steven D. Gurian, President)
   (516) 535–5454
Area of operations: Nassau and
   Suffolk counties and environs

Monroe County Industrial
   Development Corporation
55 St. Paul Street
Rochester, New York 14604
(R. Bruce Carson, President)
   (716) 454–2220
Area of operations: Monroe
   County

Niagara Falls Local Development
   Corporation
745 Main Street
Niagara Falls, New York 14302
(Michael C. O'Laughlin,
   President)
   (716) 278–8018
Area of operations: City of
   Niagara Falls

Onondaga Industrial
   Development Second
   Corporation
1500 MONY Plaza
Syracuse, New York 13202
(Parke W. Wicks, President)
   (315) 422–1343

Area of operations: County of
   Onondaga

Port Jervis Development
   Corporation
24 Front Street
Port Jervis, New York
   12771
(Irving E. Homer, President)
   (919) 856–4444 or
   (919) 856–6310
Area of operations: City of Port
   Jervis

Promote Gloversville
   Development Corporation
Frontage Road
Gloversville, New York
   12078
(Louis Nicolella, President)
   (518) 773–7521
Area of operations: City of
   Gloversville

Syracuse Economic
   Development Corporation
217 Montgomery Street
Syracuse, New York
   13202
(David S. Michel, President)
   (315) 473–5501
Area of operations: City of
   Syracuse

Utica Industrial Development
   Corporation
209 Elizabeth Street
Utica, New York 13501
(Henry F. Miller, Jr., President)
   (315) 724–3151
Area of operation: Oneida and
   Herkimer counties; City of
   Utica

REGION III

Allentown Economic
Development Corporation
P.O. Box 1410
462 Walnut Street
Allentown, Pennsylvania 18105
(Aman M. Barber, Jr., President)
(215) 435–8890
Area of operations: City of
Allentown

BEDCO Development
Corporation
Charles Center South, Suite 2400
36 South Charles Street
Baltimore, Maryland 21201
(Bernard L. Berkowitz, President)
(301) 837–9305
Area of operations: City of
Baltimore

Business and Job Development
Corporation
1411 Park Building
Pittsburgh, Pennsylvania 15222
(Paul D. Nelson, President)
(412) 391–1240
Area of operations: Allegheny
County

Chester Business Development
Service, Inc.
513 Welsh Street
Chester, Pennsylvania 19013
(John Meli, President)
(215) 447–7845
Area of operations: City of
Chester

Delaware County Economic
Development Center, Inc.
602 E. Baltimore Pike
Media, Pennsylvania 19063

(John W. Boyer, Jr. President)
(215) 565–7575
Area of operations: Delaware
County

Erie City Local Development
Company
City Hall, Suite 500
Erie, Pennsylvania
16501
(Michael Veshecco, President)
(814) 455–0961
Area of operations: City of Erie

Northwestern Pennsylvania
Development Company
700 Peach Street, Suite 202
Erie, Pennsylvania
16501
(Thomas F. Manucci, President)
(814) 452–4158
Area of Operations:
Northwestern Pennsylvania

PIDC Local Development
Corporation
1800 One East Penn Square
Philadelphia, Pennsylvania
19107
(Richard J. McConnell, President)
(215) 568–8370
Area of operations: City of
Philadelphia

Philadelphia Industrial Loan
Fund, Inc.
One East Penn Square Building
Philadelphia, Pennsylvania
19107
(James Martin, President)
(215) 568–2630
Area of operations: City and
county of Philadelphia

Urban Local Development
   Corporation (ULDC)
100 South Broad Street, Suite
   2032
Philadelphia, Pennsylvania
   19110
(Joseph J. James, President)
   (215) 561–6600
Area of operations: Philadelphia
   County

Washington, D.C., Local
   Development Corporation
1350 E Street, N.W., Room
   201
Washington, D.C. 20004
(Lawrence P. Schumake III,
   President)
   (202) 727–6600
Area of operations: Washington,
   D.C.

Wilmington Local Development
   Corporation
Two East Seventh Street, Suite
   304
Wilmington, Delaware
   19801
(Elliott Golinkoff, President)
   (302) 571–9087
Area of operations: City of
   Wilmington

REGION IV

Appalachian Wilderness
   Investment Corporation
P.O. Box 537
Highway 411 N.
Chatsworth, Georgia
   30705
(Jimmy L. Davis, President)
   (404) 695–3633

Area of operations: 90 percent of
   Murray County; remaining 10
   percent adjacent Whitfield,
   Gilmer, Fannin, and Gordon
   Counties

Areawide Development
   Corporation
P.O. Box 19806
5616 Kingston Pike
Knoxville, Tennessee
   37919
(Paul D. Goddard, Jr., President)
   (615) 584–2484
Area of operations: Eastern
   Tennessee

Atlanta Local Development
   Company
1350 North OMNI International
Atlanta, Georgia 30303
(Joseph G. Martin, Jr., President)
   (404) 658–7066
Area of operations: City of
   Atlanta

Barren River Area Development
   District
P.O. Box 2120
Bowling Green, Kentucky 42101
(Henry Broaderson, Chairman)
   (502) 781–2381
Area of operations: City of
   Birmingham

Birmingham City Wide Local
   Development Company
710 North 20th Street
Birmingham, Alabama 35203
(William Green, President)
   (205) 254–2832
Area of operations: City of
   Birmingham

CSRA Local Development
Corporation
P.O. Box 2800
2123 Wrightsboro Road
Augusta, Georgia 30904
(Charles Kitchens, President)
(404) 828–2356
Area of operations: Thirteen-
county area in East Central
Georgia

Charleston Citywide Local
Development Corporation
166 Meeting Street
Charleston, South Carolina
29401
(Arthur J. Clement, Jr., President)
(803) 577–6970
Area of operations: City of
Charleston

Columbus Local Development
Corporation
P.O. Box 1340
Columbus, Georgia
31933
(John Edwards, President)
(404) 324–7711
Area of operations: City of
Columbus

Commonwealth Small Business
Development Corporation
2400 Capital Plaza Tower
Frankfort, Kentucky
40601
(Roger L. Peterman, President)
(502) 564–4320
Area of operations: Statewide
except Robertson and Carlisle
counties

Fayetteville Progress, Inc.
2504 Raeford Road, Suite B
Fayetteville, North Carolina
28305
(M.J. Weeks, Chairman)
(919) 323–1313
Area of operations: Southeastern
North Carolina

First Alabama Development
Corporation
2017 Morris Avenue
Birmingham, Alabama
35203
(Russell Jackson Drake,
President)
(205) 323–8331
Area of operations: Statewide
except Sumter, Choctaw, and
Washington counties

Jacksonville Local Development
Company, Inc.
Florida Theater Building, Suite
603
128 E. Forsyth Street
Jacksonville, Florida
32202
(Albert McCowen, Jr., President)
(904) 359–5237
Area of operations: City of
Jacksonville

Local Development Corporation
of Dade County
1001 N.W. 54th Street, Suite L
Miami, Florida 33127
(Alga Hope, Jr., President)
(305) 751–6872
Area of operations: Dade
County

Louisville Economic
Development Corporation
Natural History Museum, 4th
Floor
727 West Main Street
Louisville, Kentucky 40202
(Gerald Toner, President)
(502) 587–3051
Area of operations: City of
Louisville

Miami Citywide Development, Inc.
100 N. Biscayne Boulevard, 9th
Floor
Miami, Florida 33132
(W.R. Ellis, President)
(305) 358–1025
Area of operations: City of
Miami

Sanford-Seminole Development
Corporation
Greater Sanford Chamber of
Commerce Building
400 East First Street
Sanford, Florida 32771
(Clifford McKibbin, Jr.,
President)
(305) 322–8160
Area of operations: Basically
Seminole County

Suwannee Industrial
Development Corporation
205 Houston Avenue, S.E.
Live Oak, Florida 32060
(O.P. Hatch, President)
(904) 362–3103
Area of operations: Suwannee
County

United Local Development
Corporation

c/o Bank of Mississippi
P.O. Box 789
One Mississippi Plaza
Tupelo, Mississippi
38801
(Palmer Foster, President)
(601) 842–7140
Area of operations: Alcorn, Lee,
Prentiss, Itawamba, Desoto,
Monroe, Pontotoc, Union,
Chichasaw, and Calhoun
counties

Wilmington Industrial
Development, Inc.
P.O. Box 1698
508 Market Street
Wilmington, North Carolina
28402
(Ralph L. Godwin, President)
(919) 763–8414
Area of operations: City of
Wilmington and New Hanover
County

REGION V
Akron Small Business
Development Corporation
166 South High Street
Akron, Ohio 44308
(Willis Else, President)
(216) 375–2133
Area of operations: City of Akron

Beverly Area Local Development
Company
9730 South Western Avenue
Chicago, Illinois 60642
(Patrick Nash, President)
(312) 233–3100
Area of operations: Beverly Hills,
Morgran Park

Bucktown Local Development
   Corporation
1942 N. Leavitt Street
Chicago, Illinois 60647
(Peter G. Poulos, President)
   (312) 489–1971
Area of operations: Bucktown
   Community of Chicago

Cincinnati Local Development
   Company
415 West Court Street
Cincinnati, Ohio 45203
(Fred Lazarus III, President)
   (513) 579–7477
Area of operations: City of
   Cincinnati

City-Wide Small Business
   Development Corporation
Miami Valley Tower, Suite
   2080
40 West 4th Street
Dayton, Ohio 45402
(Michael F. Adler, President)
   (513) 226–0457
Area of operations: City of
   Dayton and environs

Cleveland Area Development
   Finance Corporation
690 Union Commerce Building
Cleveland, Ohio 44115
(Thomas W. Adler, President)
   (216) 241–1166
Area of operations: Cuyahoga
   County

Community Development
   Corporation of Fort Wayne
City–County Building, 8th
   Floor
Fort Wayne, Indiana 46802

(Michael D. Mustard, President)
   (219) 423–7995
Area of operations: City of Fort
   Wayne

Detroit Shoreway Community
   Development Organization
6516 Detroit Avenue
Cleveland, Ohio 44102
(Reverend Father Marino
   Frascati, President)
   (216) 961–4242
Area of operations: City of
   Cleveland

Downtown Improvement
   Corporation
4525 Indianapolis Boulevard
East Chicago, Indiana
   46312
(Matthew Junigan, President)
   (219) 392–8258
Area of operations: East
   Chicago

Dupage, Kane, Will
   503 Development Company
628 Ogden Avenue
Naperville, Illinois
   60540
(James A. Schmidt, President)
   (312) 369–9392
Area of operations: Dupage,
   Kane, and Will counties

Elkhart Local Development
   Corporation
514 South Main
Elkhart, Indiana 46516
(John B. Holdeman, President)
   (219) 293–1531
Area of operations: Elkhart
   County

Forward Development
Corporation
1101 Beach Street
Flint, Michigan 48502
(Michael H. Finn, President)
(212) 257–3010
Area of operations: Genesee
County

Gary City-Wide Development
Corporation
504 Broadway, Room 629
Gary, Indiana 46402
(Leonard Pryweller, President)
(219) 883–9691
Area of operations: City of Gary

Grand Rapids Local
Development Corporation
17 Fountain Street, N.W.
Grand Rapids, Michigan
49503
(Tom Malleis, President)
(616) 459–7221
Area of operations: City of Grand
Rapids

Greater Gratiot Development,
Inc.
215 East Center Street
Ithaca, Michigan 48847
(Scott B. Munger, President)
(517) 875–2919
Area of operations: Gratiot
County

Greater Kenosha Development
Corporation
611–56th Street, Room 202
Kenosha, Wisconsin 53140
(Roger Caron, President)
(414) 656–6064
Area of operations: City of
Kenosha

Greater North-Pulaski Local
Development Corporation
4054 West North Avenue
Chicago, Illinois
60639
(John M. Sevick, President)
(312) 384–7074
Area of operations: (S) Chicago
Avenue, (N) Belmont Avenue,
(E) Western Avenue, (W)
Cicero Avenue

Greater Southwest Local
Development Corporation
6249 Southwestern Avenue
Chicago, Illinois
60656
(Thomas Daniel O'Reilly,
President)
(312) 436–1000
Area of operations: City of
Chicago

Jackson Local Development
Company
City Hall, 8th Floor
161 West Michigan
Jackson, Michigan
49201
(Daniel Nuttle, President)
(517) 788–4187
Area of operations: Jackson,
Michigan City Limits

Kalamazoo Small Business
Development Corporation
241 West South Street
Kalamazoo, Michigan
49007
(David T. Harrison, Chairperson)
(616) 385–8050
Area of operations: City of
Kalamazoo

Lawndale Local Development
3210 West Arthington Street
Chicago, Illinois 60624
(Reuben Butler, President)
    (312) 265–8500
Area of operations: Bound by (S)
    22nd Street, (N) Harrison
    Avenue, (E) Western Avenue,
    (W) City Limits

Lawrence Avenue Development
    Corporation
3446 W. Lawrence Avenue
Chicago, Illinois 60625
(Richard Reifler, President)
    (312) 463–5420
Area of operations: Albany Park
    Area of Chicago

Madison Development
    Corporation
23 North Pinckney Street
Madison, Wisconsin 53703
(Rodney E. Stevenson, President)
    (608) 256–2799
Area of operations: City of
    Madison

Mahoning Valley Economic
    Development Corporation
3200 Belmont Avenue
Youngstown, Ohio 44505
(J. Phillip Richley, President)
    (216) 759–3668
Area of operations: Mahoning
    and Trumbull counties

Metropolitan Growth &
    Development Corporation
One Parkland Boulevard, Suite
    715 West
Dearborn, Michigan 48126
(Gary L. Bingamen, President)
    (313) 336–3306

Area of operations: Wayne
    County

Metropolitan Small Business
    Assistance Corporation
c/o Department of Metropolitan
    Development
Old Courthouse Center, Room 301
    Evansville, Indiana 47708
(Clyde Howlett, President)
    (812) 426–5534
Area of operations: City of
    Evansville and environs

Milwaukee Economic
    Development Corporation
734 North 9th Street
Milwaukee, Wisconsin 53233
(Patrick G. Walsh, Vice-
    President)
    (414) 278–2685
Area of operations: City of
    Milwaukee

Oshkosh Commercial
    Development Corporation
P.O. Box 230
120 Jackson Street
Oshkosh, Wisconsin 54902
(Fintan Flanagan, President)
    (414) 235–3000
Area of operations: Winnebago
    County

Scioto Economic Development
    Corporation, Inc.
P.O. Drawer 1606
Scioto County Courthouse,
    Room 1
Portsmouth, Ohio 45662
(Robert J. Stapleton, President)
    (614) 354–7779
Area of operations: Scioto,
    Adams, Pike, Jackson, and
    Lawrence counties

South Central Illinois Regional
Planning and Development
Commission
Marion County Public Service
Building
Salem, Illinois 62881
(Glenn R. Bunyard, Chairman)
(618) 548–4234
Area of operations: Effingham,
Fayette, and Marion counties;
also cities of Centralia and
Wamac

South Shore Area Development
Corporation
7054 S. Jeffrey Boulevard
Chicago, Illinois 60649
(Rosa C. Moore, President)
(312) 288–1000
Area of operations: South Shore
Side (Cook County)

Toledo Economic Planning
Council
425 Jefferson Avenue, Room
1009
Toledo, Ohio 43604
(George W. Haigh, President)
(419) 255–6077
Area of operations: City of
Toledo

REGION VI

New Orleans Citywide
Development Corporation
301 Camp Street, Suite 216
New Orleans, Louisiana 70130
(Brooke H. Duncan, President)
(504) 524–6172
Area of operations: City of New
Orleans

San Antonio Local Development
Corporation
P.O. Box 9365

San Antonio, Texas 78204
(James Saunders, President)
(512) 299–8080
Area of operations: City of San
Antonio

Texas Capital Development
Company, Inc.
511 North Bell Boulevard
Cedar Park, Texas 78613
(J.A. Garrett, President)
(512) 258–8312
Area of operations: Statewide
except Texas Panhandle

Tulsa Economic Development
Corporation
411 South Denver
Tulsa, Oklahoma 74103
(W.R. Hagstrom, President)
(918) 585–8332
Area of operations: City of
Tulsa

REGION VII

Avenue Area Incorporated
503 Security National Bank
Building
One Security Plaza
Kansas City, Kansas 66101
(Jonathan Phelps, President)
(913) 371–0065
Area of operations: Downtown
Area of Kansas City

Central Avenue Betterment
Association
1000 Central Avenue
Kansas City, Kansas 66104
(Fred Meier, President)
(913) 371–4511
Area of operations: Central
Avenue Community of Kansas
City

Certified Development
Corporation of Southwest
Missouri
812 S. Glenstone
Springfield, Missouri 65804
(R.L. Bennett, President)
(417) 864–7540
Area of operations: Southwest
Missouri

Crossroad Economic
Development Corporation of
St. Charles County, Inc.
P.O. Box 1454
207 N. 5th Street
St. Charles, Missouri 63301
(Norbert Wapelhorst, President)
(314) 956–4377
Area of operations: St. Charles

Downtown Fort Dodge
Development Corporation
Municipal Building—Planning
Development
Fort Dodge, Iowa 50501
(Earl C. Underbrink, President)
(515) 573–8321
Area of operations: Original
Downtown Fort Dodge
Business District

Fort Madison Commercial
Development Corporation
P.O. Box 277
933 Avenue H
Fort Madison, Iowa 52627
(Richard Rump, President)
(319) 372–5471
Area of operations: Fort Madison
and environs

Highland Park Local
Development Corporation
102 E. Grand Avenue

Des Moines, Iowa
50307
(David G. Dodson, Agent)
(515) 283–4161
Area of operations: Highland
Park Business District

Iowa Business Growth Company
901 Insurance Exchange Building
Des Moines, Iowa 50903
(Don J. Albertsen, President)
(515) 282–2164
Area of operations: State of Iowa

Kansas City Corporation for
Industrial Development
(KCCID)
1102 Grand Avenue, Suite 310
Kansas City, Missouri
65106
(Edward G. Bruske, President)
(816) 474–3560
Area of operations: Kansas City

McPherson County Small
Business Development
Association
101 S. Main
McPherson, Kansas 67460
(Don Reed, President)
(316) 241–0431
Area of operations: McPherson
County

Mid America Development
Corporation
4414 N. 31st Avenue
Omaha, Nebraska 68111
(William H. Dodd, President)
(402) 453–3300
Area of operations: Omaha:
Council Bluffs Standard
Metropolitan Statistical
Area

North Platte Development
  Corporation
P.O. Box 968
512 North Bailey
North Platte, Nebraska 69101
(Gil E. Wilkinson, President)
  (308) 532–4966
Area of operations: Lincoln
  County

Northeast Economic
  Development Corporation
919 Troup
Kansas City, Kansas 66104
(Gerald W. Hall, President)
  (913) 321–7200
Area of operations: Northeast
  area of Kansas City

Ottumwa Area Development
  Corporation
P.O. Box 308
106 North Court Mall
Ottumwa, Iowa 52501
(William E. Jones, President)
  (515) 682–0828
Area of operations: Corporate
  limits of Ottumwa

Ozark Gateway Development,
  Inc.
2008 Sergeant, 5th Floor
Joplin, Missouri 64801
(W.H. Kelly, President)
  (417) 781–3222
Area of operations: Barton,
  Jasper, Newton, and McDonald
  counties

Rosedale Local Development
  Corporation
3500 Rainbow Boulevard
Kansas City, Kansas 66103

(George Armstrong, President)
  (913) 236–7700
Area of operations: Rosedale
  Community of Kansas City

St. Louis County Local
  Development Company
555 South Brentwood Boulevard
St. Louis, Missouri 63105
(Gayle P. Jackson, President)
  (314) 889–2167
Area of operations: Throughout
  St. Louis County

St. Louis Local Development
  Company
1300 Delmar Boulevard, 3rd
  Floor
St. Louis, Missouri 63105
(Robert J.A. Renard, President)
  (314) 231–3500
Area of operations: City of St.
  Louis

Siouxland Economic
  Development Corporation
430 Insurance Exchange Building
Sioux City, Iowa 51101
(James S. Sherman, Chairman)
  (712) 279–6286
Area of operations: Woodburg,
  Plymouth, Cherokee, Ida, and
  Monona counties

REGION VIII
Butte Local Development
  Corporation
505 West Park
Butte, Montana 59701
(William Sherwood, President)
  (406) 792–1263
Area of operations: Butte Silver
  Bow County

Greater Salt Lake Business
District
DBA Salt Lake Area Central
Business District Corporation
555 East South Temple
Salt Lake City, Utah 84102
(Mayor Ted L. Wilson, President)
(801) 355–3474
Area of operations: Salt Lake
City Valley

Hazen Community
Development, Inc.
Box 468
Hazen, North Dakota
58545
(David Bergated, President)
(701) 748–2708
Area of operations: City of Hazen
and environs

The Historic 25th Street
Development Company
252 25th Street
Ogden, Utah 84401
(Robert J. McDougal, President)
(801) 399–8241
Area of operations: Weber
County

Manitous Springs Development
Corporation
P.O. Box 72
Manitous Springs, Colorado
80829
(Howard Morrison, President)
(303) 472–6385
Area of operations: Manitous
Springs

Metropolitan Denver Local
Development Corporation
38 Broadway

Denver, Colorado 80203
(Jack Machol, Jr., President)
(303) 722–1231
Area of operations: City of
Denver

Old Aurora Development
Company
1465 Boston Street
Aurora, Colorado 80010
(William R. Dominquez,
President)
(303) 364–4360
Area of operations: City of
Aurora

Old Colorado City Development
Company
2504 West Colorado Avenue
Colorado Springs, Colorado
80904
(Gene S. Brent, President)
(303) 471–6962
Area of operations: El Paso
County

Provo Development Company
351 West Center Street
Provo, Utah 84601
(Jerry M. Howell, President)
(801) 374–1025
Area of operations: City of
Provo

Western Slope Economic
Development Company
314 Valley Federal Plaza
Grand Junction, Colorado
81501
(Patrick J. Berry, President)
(303) 245–3430
Area of operations: Western
Slope of Colorado

REGION IX

Arvin Development Corporation
Box 546
200 Campus Drive
Arvin, California 93203
(Jack O. Schulze, President)
(805) 854–5881
Area of operations: Southeastern
part of Kern County

Bay Area Employment
Development Corporation
6460 Hollis Street
Emeryville, California
94608
(Bert Otterson, President)
(707) 778–7823
Area of operations: Within the
Association of Bay Area
Government's Area

Calexico Industrial Development
Corporation
747 Imperial Avenue
Calexico, California 92231
(Bruce Noe, President)
(714) 357–2100
Area of operations: City of
Calexico and contiguous areas

Crown Development
Corporation of Kings County
323 A.N. Douty Street
Hanford, California
93230
(John Hibbard, President)
(209) 582–4326
Area of operations: King County

Economic Development
Corporation of Shasta County
1135 Pine Street, Suite 104
Redding, California 96003

(Richard K. Smart, President)
(916) 241–5361
Area of operations: Shasta
County

Economic Development
Foundation of Sacramento
7844 Madison Avenue, Suite 110
Fair Oaks, California
95628
(Mary Sherman, President)
(916) 966–9303
Area of operations: Sacramento
and nineteen other counties

Greater Bakersfield Local
Development Corporation
1501 Truxton Avenue
Bakersfield, California
93301
(Arthur L. Rockoff, President)
(805) 861–2764
Area of operations: Kern County

La Habra Local Development
Company, Inc.
P.O. Box 377
Civic Center
La Habra, California 90631
(Aubrey G. LeBard III, President)
(213) 694–1011 or (714) 526–
2227
Area of operations: Orange
County

HEDCO Local Development
Corporation
1505 Dillingham Boulevard
Honolulu, Hawaii 96817
(Dexter J. Taniguchi, President)
(808) 847–6502
Area of operations: Oahu, Kauai,
Maui islands, and Hawaii

Long Beach Local Development
Corporation
P.O. Box 7646
Long Beach, California 90807
(James T. Heard, President)
(213) 590–6841
Area of operations: City of Long
Beach

Los Angeles LDC, Inc.
c/o City Economic Development
Office
City Hall, Room 2008
200 North Spring Street
Los Angeles, California
90012
(Bradford S. Crowe, President)
(213) 624–6753
Area of operations: City of Los
Angeles

Los Medanos Fund, A Local
Development Company
P.O. Box 1397
501 Railroad Avenue
Pittsburg, California 94565
(Virginia Spears, President)
(415) 439–1056
Area of operations: City of
Pittsburg

Reseda Local Development
Corporation
6850 Canby Avenue, Suite 107
Reseda, California 91335
(Thomas A. Howard, President)
(213) 996–6035
Area of operations: Central
Business District

San Diego County Local
Development Corporation

4262 Market Street
San Diego, California
92102
(Clarence M. Pendleton, Jr.,
President)
(714) 428–2261
Area of operations: City of San
Diego

San Francisco Industrial
Development Fund
552 McAllister Street
San Francisco, California
94115
(Dean Macris, President)
(415) 558–5626
Area of operations: City and
County of San Francisco

Southern California
Employment Development
Company
3250 Ocean Park Boulevard
Santa Monica, California
90404
(Charles Tatum, President)
(213) 984–1935
Area of operations: Ventura, Los
Angeles, Orange, Riverside,
and Santa Barbara counties

Tucson Local Development
Corporation
c/o Kendall Bert
P.O. Box 27210
Tucson, Arizona
85726
(Ben C. Hill, Jr., President)
(602) 791–4505
Area of operations: Tucson and
adjacent area

Union of Small Cities
   Corporation
2006 N. Fine, Suite 104
Fresno, California 93727
(Raul Martinez, President)
   (209) 896–4420
Area of operations: Fresno,
   Kings, Tulare, Madera,
   Merced, and Stanislaus
   counties

West Contra Costa Local
   Development Company
P.O. Box 1227
Richmond, California 94802
(Gerald Feagley, President)
   (415) 234–4426
Area of operations: Contra Costa
   and Alameda counties

REGION X

C.C.D. Business Development
   Corporation
744 S.E. Rose Street

Roseburg, Oregon 97470
(Shirley Van Loo, President)
   (503) 672–6728
Area of operations: Coos, Curry,
   and Douglas counties

Greater Spokane Business
   Development Association
City Hall, Room 301
Spokane, Washington 99201
(David Jones, President)
   (509) 456–4375
Area of operations: Statewide
   except Pacific County

Seattle King County Community
   Development Association
2111 Smith Tower
Seattle, Washington 98104
(Howard Barkhoff, President)
   (205) 625–4530 or
   (205) 784–9533
Area of operations: Statewide
   except Garfield County

11

Small business administration loans

The Small Business Administration is the big daddy of government loan makers.

Part of the executive branch of the federal government, the SBA is designated to serve as the official guardian of the nation's small-business community. Although it often comes up short in this regard, this bloated and often confused bureaucracy does offer a smorgasbord of loans and loan guarantees that total more than $4 billion a year. The money is available through a network of 110 offices in 100 cities across the U.S. (see the full list of SBA offices at the end of this chapter) and more than 10,000 of the nation's banks.

The SBA makes guaranteed loans through commercial banks and other financial institutions as well as direct loans of its own funds. Interest rates for both vary but are usually below those on the open market. SBA maximum rates on guaranteed loans and lines of credit are based on continuous surveys of the market for fixed-income securities, both federal and private, and on the prevailing rate for loans as determined by SBA field personnel. Rates on SBA direct loans are based on a formula that considers the cost of money to the federal government. These rates are reviewed on a quarterly basis.

Loans made directly by SBA have a maximum of

$150,000; the bank guarantee loan program guarantees up to 90 percent of a loan, or a maximum of $500,000, whichever is less.

Variable interest rates that fluctuate over the course of the loan are also permitted if agreed to by both the borrower and the lender at the time the loan is made. (President Ronald Reagan's 1983 budget calls for eliminating SBA direct loans. Prospective borrowers should check on this development.)

To be eligible for SBA business loans, applicants must not exceed the following annual income levels: *

Service firms: $2–$8 million

Retailers: $2–$7.5 million

Wholesalers: $2.2–$9.5 million

General construction: $9.5 million

Farmers: $1 million

Manufacturers: 250–1,500 employees

By law, the SBA may not make or guarantee a loan if a business can obtain funds on reasonable terms from a bank or other private source. A borrower, therefore, must first seek private financing before applying to the SBA.

In a city with a population over 200,000, applicants must be turned down by two banks before applying for an SBA loan. Applicants also must agree to comply with SBA regulations that prohibit discrimination in employment or services to the public, based on race, religion, national origin, sex, or marital status.

Note: When neither private financing nor a loan guarantee is available, SBA may provide loan funds on an "immediate participation" basis with a bank. The bank

* Ranges are given because maximums vary by industry.

disburses part of the loan, at market interest rates, and the balance of the loan is disbursed directly by SBA, at a lower interest rate. SBA's share of an immediate participation loan may not exceed $150,000.

The SBA accepts the following collateral:

A mortgage on land, a building, or equipment.

Assignment of warehouse receipts for marketable merchandise.

A mortgage on chattels.

Guarantees or personal endorsements, and in some instances, assignment of current receivables.

To apply for a loan, those already in business should:

Prepare a current financial statement (balance sheet) listing all assets and all liabilities of the business as well as an earnings (profit and loss) statement for the current period to the date of the balance sheet.

Prepare a current personal financial statement of the owner, or each partner or stockholder owning 20 percent or more of the corporate stock in the business.

List collateral to be offered as security for the loan, with an estimate of each item's present market value.

State the amount of the loan requested and exact purposes for which it will be used.

Take these documents to your banker. Ask for a direct bank loan or, failing that, ask the bank to make the loan under SBA's Loan Guarantee Plan or Immediate Participation Plan.

If a guaranteed or a participation loan is not available, write or visit the nearest SBA office.

Those seeking to start a business should:

Describe the type of business you plan to establish.

Describe your experience and management capabilities.

Prepare an estimate of how much you or others have to invest in the business and how much you will need to borrow.

Prepare a current financial statement (balance sheet) listing all personal assets and all liabilities.

Prepare a detailed projection of earnings for the first year the business will operate.

List collateral to be offered as security for the loan, indicating your estimate of the present market value of each item.

Follow the final two steps for those already in business.

The table that follows lists those categories covered by the SBA's major business loan programs, and indicates the number of loans granted in a recent year together with the total costs of those loans.

Loan Program	Number	Dollar Amount in Millions
Regular business	28,168	3,604
Physical disaster	69,943	1,202
Economic opportunity	2,434	90.9
Economic injury disaster	1,138	78.5
State development company loans and local development company loans (now certified development company loans)	476	79.2
Handicapped assistance	258	20.6
Small-business energy	183	27.2
Water-pollution control	18	3.0

Physical Disaster Loans are available in areas deemed by the SBA or by the President of the U.S. to have suffered a major physical disaster.

Business facilities damaged during "official disasters," may obtain SBA loans for restoration to predisaster condition. This includes inventory, furniture, fixtures, machinery, equipment, and leasehold improvements.

Maturity ranges up to 30 years, with payments usually required monthly; the first payment is ordinarily due within five months of disbursement. Loans are available for up to $500,000 but cannot exceed the actual tangible loss suffered by the disaster victim. The SBA does not require collateral for disaster loans. A key point is that applicants are not required to pay disaster expenses from personal resources before obtaining disaster loans.

The SBA also makes disaster loans to renters, homeowners, nonprofit institutions, and businesses victimized by officially designated disasters. In 1980, 69,943 national disaster loans were made for a dollar total of $1.2 billion.

Economic Opportunity Loans are available to any resident of the U.S., Puerto Rico, and Guam whose total family income from all sources is not sufficient for the basic needs of that family, or in cases in which, owing to social or economic disadvantage, the applicant has been denied the opportunity to acquire adequate business financing through normal lending channels on reasonable terms. EOLs also help small firms adversely affected by government regulations and small firms engaged in manufacturing, selling, installing, servicing, or developing specific energy measures.

Every applicant must, however, demonstrate the ability to operate a business successfully and must provide reasonable assurance that the loan can be repaid from the earnings of the business. And while character is considered to be more important than collateral for these types of loans, applicants are expected to have some money or other assets invested in the business. This loan program provides for both financial and management assistance. The maximum amount of an EOL loan is $100,000 for up to 15 years.

Loans to Builders are made to those general contractors with annual receipts of less than $9.5 million. Up to $350,000 is available to construct new residential or commercial properties or to rehabilitate existing structures for immediate resale on their own account.

Interest rates vary according to market conditions. For new construction, loans may be used only for labor and materials. The SBA requires evidence that there will be a market for the type of structure being built or rehabilitated and that permanent mortgage money is available in the area where the property is located.

Handicap Assistance Loans provide handicapped men and women seeking more than a handout, more than a job, with a little-known loan program designed to make them self-employed. Funds are available both to established handicapped entrepreneurs and to those dreaming of a business of their own.

The Small Business Administration has allocated more than $20 million for Handicap Assistance Loans in fiscal 1982. The money is designated exclusively for applicants whose mental or physical disabilities place a financial burden on their business activities.

"We make loans under this program to handicapped-owned companies and to non-profit organizations run for the handicapped," says Robert H. Bartlett, chief of programs operations for the SBA's Office of Business Loans. "By handicapped we mean those whose impairment, defect, ailment, disease, or disability is of a permanent nature and limits the selection of employment for which the person would be otherwise qualified.

"Sometimes there is a fine line in determining eligibility. For example, a shirt salesman with one eye cannot qualify for these loans because his disability doesn't limit his career performance. But a double amputee who requires special equipment to compete effectively in business is eligible for handicap assistance."

Direct loans are issued through the SBA at 3 percent interest; SBA-guaranteed loans are made through commercial banks and finance companies at maximum interest rates of 2.25 percent above prime for terms of less than seven years and 2.75 percent for longer maturities. To qualify for either type of loan, handicapped applicants must prove that they cannot obtain assistance from other private or governmental sources.

Handicap Assistance Loans may be used for a wide range of business needs, including working capital, the acquisition of commercial facilities, new machines, promotion, and personnel. Maximum amounts are $100,000 for direct loans and $500,000 for loan guarantees (provided the guarantees do not exceed 90 percent of the loan). Handicapped individuals have used direct and guaranteed loans to start and expand successful businesses.

There are, however, major limitations. First, government financing is not intended to turn every handicapped person into an instant business owner. Applicants must demonstrate more than need. They must have experience in or working knowledge of their field of business and must convince administrators that they will be able to repay the loan on schedule.

Second, there is not enough money in the SBA pipeline to fund adequately all the handicapped entrepreneurs who can satisfy the lending criteria. Even qualified applicants should know that they may come away empty-handed.

"I used a three percent interest, one-hundred-thousand-dollar Handicap Assistance Loan to buy a delicatessen," says a blind business owner. "The deli grew dramatically, with sales rising forty percent in the first two years after I took over from the previous owners. But when I went back to the SBA for an additional fifty thousand dollars to expand the facility, they told me there was a shortage of direct loan funds. I got the extra money, but this time at fifteen percent. It's not as good as the first loan but I'm happy to have it."

Applications for Handicap Assistance Loans may be made at all local SBA offices.

Surety Bond Guarantee Program benefits contractors required to have a bid, performance, or payment bond in order to obtain a contract. The SBA guarantees qualified bonds for contracts up to $1 million, and there is no limit on the number of bonds that can be guaranteed for any one contractor. In consideration of the surety company's paying the SBA 20 percent of the gross bond premium, the SBA guarantees the surety company up to 90 percent of any loss sustained on contracts up to $250,000 and up to 80 percent on contracts up to $1 million. There is a $500 maximum deductible to the surety company regardless of the contract amount.

The bond guarantee program enables contractors in a variety of fields to compete for big jobs they might not ordinarily be able to qualify for. By using this program, most of the financial risk shifts to the SBA, not the contractor. The cost of the SBA guarantee is borne by the contractor and the surety company.

Put simply, the program works as follows:

A contractor cannot qualify for a standard surety bond

The surety company offers to share 20 percent of its premium on the bond in return for an SBA guarantee

The SBA approves the guarantee and the contractor gets the bond. The contractor must also pay certain fees to the SBA.

Full information on SBA loan programs may be obtained at the SBA field offices listed below.

ALABAMA
908 South 20th Street, Room 202
Birmingham, Alabama 35205
(205) 254–1344

ALASKA
1016 West 6th Avenue, Suite
200, Anchorage Legal Center
Anchorage, Alaska 99501
(907) 272–5561

50½ Second Avenue
Fairbanks, Alaska 99701
(907) 452–1951

ARIZONA
112 North Central Avenue
Phoenix, Arizona 85004
(602) 261–3611

ARKANSAS
611 Gaines Street, Suite 900
Little Rock, Arkansas 72201
(501) 378–5871

CALIFORNIA
1130 O Street, Federal Building,
Room 4015
Fresno, California 93721
(209) 487–5000

350 South Figueroa Street,
6th Floor
Los Angeles, California 90071
(213) 688–2956

2800 Cottage Way
Sacramento, California 95825
(916) 484–4726

880 Front Street, Federal U.S.
Building, Room 4S33
San Diego, California 92188
(714) 293–5444

450 Golden Gate Avenue, Box
36044

San Francisco, California 94102
(415) 556–7487

211 Main Street
San Francisco, California 94105
(415) 556–7490

COLORADO
1405 Curtis Street, Executive
Tower Building, 22nd Floor
Denver, Colorado 80202
(303) 837–0111

721 19th Street, Room 426A
Denver, Colorado 80202
(303) 837–0111

CONNECTICUT
One Financial Plaza
Hartford, Connecticut 06103
(203) 244–3600

DELAWARE
844 King Street, Federal Building,
Room 5207
Wilmington, Delaware 19801
(302) 571–6294

DISTRICT OF COLUMBIA
1030 15th Street N.W., Suite 250
Washington, D.C. 20417
(202) 655–4000

FLORIDA
2222 Ponce de Leon Boulevard,
5th Floor
Coral Gables, Florida 33134
(305) 350–5521

400 West Bay Street, Federal
Building, Room 261, P.O. Box
35067
Jacksonville, Florida 32202
(904) 791–3782

1802 North Trask Street,
    Suite 203
Tampa, Florida 33602
    (813) 228–2594

701 Clematis Street, Federal
    Building, Room 229
West Palm Beach, Florida 33402
    (305) 659–7533

GEORGIA
1375 Peachtree Street N.E.
Atlanta, Georgia 30309
    (404) 881–4943

1720 Peachtree Street N.W.,
    6th Floor
Atlanta, Georgia 30309
    (404) 881–4325

GUAM
Ada Plaza Center Building
Agana, Guam 96910
    (671) 777–8420

HAWAII
1149 Bethel Street, Room 402
Honolulu, Hawaii 96813
    (808) 546–8950

IDAHO
216 North 8th Street, Room 408
Boise, Idaho 83702
    (208) 384–1096

ILLINOIS
219 South Dearborn Street,
    Federal Building, Room 838
Chicago, Illinois 60604
    (312) 353–0355

219 South Dearborn Street,
    Federal Building, Room 437
Chicago, Illinois 60604
    (312) 353–4528

One North, Old State Capital
    Plaza
Springfield, Illinois 62701
    (217) 525–4416

INDIANA
575 North Pennsylvania Street,
    New Federal Building,
    Room 552
Indianapolis, Indiana 46204
    (317) 269–7272

IOWA
210 Walnut Street, New Federal
    Building, Room 749
Des Moines, Iowa 50309
    (515) 284–4422

KANSAS
110 East Waterman Street, Main
    Place Building
Wichita, Kansas 67202
    (316) 267–6311

KENTUCKY
600 Federal Plaza, Federal
    Building, Room 188
Louisville, Kentucky 40202
    (502) 582–5971

LOUISIANA
1001 Howard Avenue, Plaza
    Tower, 17th Floor
New Orleans, Louisiana 70113
    (504) 589–2611

Fannin Street, U.S. Post Office
    and Courthouse Building
Shreveport, Louisiana 71101
    (318) 226–5196

MARYLAND
8600 LaSalle Road, Oxford
    Building, Room 630

Towson, Maryland 21204
 (301) 962–4392

MASSACHUSETTS
150 Causeway Street, 10th Floor
Boston, Massachusetts 02114
 (617) 223–3224

150 Causeway Street, 10th Floor
Boston, Massachusetts 02114
 (617) 223–3224

302 High Street, 4th Floor
Holyoke, Massachusetts 01040
 (413) 536–8770

MAINE
40 Western Avenue, Federal
 Building, Room 512
Augusta, Maine 04330
 (207) 622–6171

MICHIGAN
477 Michigan Avenue,
 McNamara Building
Detroit, Michigan 48226
 (313) 226–6075

540 West Kaye Avenue, Don H.
 Bottom University Center
Marquette, Michigan 49855
 (906) 225–1108

MINNESOTA
12 South 6th Street, Plymouth
 Building
Minneapolis, Minnesota 55402
 (612) 725–2362

MISSISSIPPI
111 Fred Haise Boulevard, Gulf
 National Life Insurance
 Building, 2nd Floor
Biloxi, Mississippi 39530
 (601) 435–3676

200 East Pascagoula Street,
 Providence Capitol Building,
 Suite 690
Jackson, Mississippi 39201
 (601) 969–4371

MISSOURI
911 Walnut Street, 23rd Floor
Kansas City, Missouri 64106
 (816) 374–3318

1150 Grande Avenue, 5th Floor
Kansas City, Missouri 64106
 (816) 374–5557

One Mercantile Center,
 Mercantile Tower, Suite 2500
St. Louis, Missouri 63101
 (314) 425–4191

MONTANA
618 Helena Avenue
Helena, Montana 59601
 (406) 449–5381

NEBRASKA
Nineteenth and Farnum streets,
 Empire State Building
Omaha, Nebraska 68102
 (402) 221–4691

NEVADA
301 East Stewart
Las Vegas, Nevada 89101
 (702) 385–6011

50 South Virginia Street,
 Room 308
Reno, Nevada 89505
 (702) 784–5234

NEW HAMPSHIRE
55 Pleasant Street, Room 213
Concord, New Hampshire 03301
 (603) 224–4041

NEW MEXICO
5000 Marble Avenue N.E., Patio
　Plaza Building
Albuquerque, New Mexico
　87110
　　(505) 766–3430

NEW JERSEY
1800 East Davis Street
Camden, New Jersey 08104
　(609) 757–5183

970 Broad Street, Room 1635
Newark, New Jersey 07102
　(201) 645–2434

NEW YORK
99 Washington Avenue, Twin
　Towers Building, Room 921
Albany, New York 12210
　(518) 472–6300

111 West Huron Street, Federal
　Building, Room 1311
Buffalo, New York 14202
　(716) 842–3240

180 State Street, Room 412
Elmira, New York 14901
　(607) 733–4686

425 Broad Hollow Road,
　Room 205
Melville, New York 11746
　(516) 752–1626

26 Federal Plaza, Room 3100
New York, New York 10007
　(212) 264–4355

26 Federal Plaza, Room 3214
New York, New York 10007
　(212) 264–1468

100 State Street, Federal Building
Rochester, New York 14614
　(716) 263–6700

100 South Clinton Street, Federal
　Building, Room 1073
Syracuse, New York 13202
　(315) 423–5370

NORTH CAROLINA
230 South Tryon Street
Charlotte, North Carolina 28202
　(704) 372–0711

215 South Evans Street, Room
　206
Greenville, North Carolina
　27834
　(919) 752–3798

NORTH DAKOTA
653 2nd Avenue North, Federal
　Building, Room 218
Fargo, North Dakota 58102
　(701) 237–5131

OHIO
550 Main Street, Federal Building
Cincinnati, Ohio 45202
　(513) 684–2814

1240 East 9th Street, Room 317
Cleveland, Ohio 44199
　(216) 522–4180

34 North High Street, Tonti
　Building
Columbus, Ohio 43215
　(614) 469–6860

OKLAHOMA
200 N.W. 5th Street, Federal
　Building, Suite 670
Oklahoma City, Oklahoma
　73102
　(405) 231–4301

OREGON
1220 S.W. Third Avenue, Federal
　Building

Portland, Oregon 97204
(503) 221–2682

PENNSYLVANIA
231 St. Asaphs Road, 1 Bala
Cynwyd Plaza, Suite 646,
West Lobby
Bala Cynwyd, Pennsylvania
19004
(215) 597–5888

231 St. Asaphs Road, 1 Bala
Cynwyd Plaza, Suite 400,
East Lobby
Bala Cynwyd, Pennsylvania
19004
(215) 597–5888

1500 North 2nd Street
Harrisburg, Pennsylvania
17102
(717) 782–3840

1000 Liberty Avenue, Federal
Building, Room 1401
Pittsburgh, Pennsylvania
15222
(412) 644–2780

20 North Pennsylvania Avenue,
Penn Place
Wilkes-Barre, Pennsylvania
18702
(717) 826–6497

PUERTO RICO
Chardon and Bolivia streets,
P.O. Box 1915
Hato Rey, Puerto Rico 00919
(809) 763–6363

RHODE ISLAND
57 Eddy Street, 7th Floor
Providence, Rhode Island 02903
(401) 528–1000

SOUTH CAROLINA
1801 Assembly Street, Room 131
Columbia, South Carolina 29201
(803) 765–5376

SOUTH DAKOTA
515 9th Street, Federal Building,
Room 246
Rapid City, South Dakota 57701
(605) 343–5074

8th and Main Avenue, National
Bank Building, Room 402
Sioux Falls, South Dakota 57102
(605) 336–2980

TENNESSEE
502 South Gay Street, Fidelity
Bankers Building, Room 307
Knoxville, Tennessee 37902
(615) 637–9300

167 North Main Street, Federal
Building, Room 211
Memphis, Tennessee 38103
(901) 521–3588

404 James Robertson Parkway,
Suite 1012
Nashville, Tennessee 37219
(615) 251–5881

TEXAS
3105 Leopard Street
Corpus Christi, Texas 78408
(512) 888–3011

1720 Regal Row, Regal Park
Office Building, Room 3C36
Dallas, Texas 75242
(214) 749–2531

1100 Commerce Street,
Room 300
Dallas, Texas 75670
(214) 749–3961

4100 Rio Bravo, Suite 300
El Paso, Texas 79901
(915) 543–7200

222 East Van Buran Street
Harlingen, Texas 78550
(512) 423–3011

500 Dallas Street, One Allen
Center
Houston, Texas 77002
(713) 226–4341

1205 Texas Avenue, 712 Federal
Office Building and
U.S. Courthouse
Lubbock, Texas 79401
(806) 762–7011

100 South Washington Street,
Federal Building, G12
Marshall, Texas 75670
(214) 935–5257

727 East Durango, Room A 513
San Antonio, Texas 78206
(512) 229–6250

UTAH
125 South State Street, Federal
Building, Room 2237
Salt Lake City, Utah 84138
(801) 524–5800

VERMONT
87 State Street, Federal Building,
Room 210
Montpelier, Vermont 05602
(802) 223–7472

VIRGINIA
400 North 8th Street, Federal
Building, Room 3015
Richmond, Virginia 23240
(804) 782–2617

VIRGIN ISLANDS
Veterans Drive, U.S. Federal
Office Building, Room 283
St. Thomas, Virgin Islands
00801
(809) 774–8530

WASHINGTON
710 2nd Avenue, Dexter Horton
Building, 5th Floor
Seattle, Washington 98104
(206) 442–1455

915 Second Avenue, Federal
Building, Room 1744
Seattle, Washington 98174
(206) 442–5534

Court House Building, Room 651
Spokane, Washington 99210
(509) 456–3777

WEST VIRGINIA
Charleston National Plaza,
Suite 628
Charleston, West Virginia 25301
(304) 343–6181

109 North 3rd Street, Lowndes
Building, Room 301
Clarksburg, West Virginia 26301
(304) 623–5631

WISCONSIN
500 South Barstow Street,
Federal Office Building and
U.S. Courthouse, Room B9AA
Eau Claire, Wisconsin 54701
(715) 834–9012

122 West Washington Avenue,
Room 713
Madison, Wisconsin 53703
(608) 252–5261

735 West Wisconsin Avenue,
   Continental Bank Building,
   Room 690
Milwaukee, Wisconsin 53233
   (414) 224–3941

WYOMING
100 East B Street, Federal
   Building, Room 4001
Casper, Wyoming 82601
   (307) 265–5550

It is not well known that SBA loans are available from a number of diverse financial institutions as well as from banks and SBA offices. Among the nonbank facilities now authorized to make SBA loans are Commercial Credit Corporation, units of Merrill Lynch, and International Telephone and Telegraph Corporation.

Although the others are starting out small with a very limited number of loans, Commercial Credit is in the market in a big way, granting more than $65 million in SBA loans through its ninety-six Control Data Business Centers. "We have established our centers primarily as a means of making small-business loans—as low as fifteen thousand dollars and as high as several million dollars—and as a means of getting closer to our customers," says Eugene S. Sirbaugh, president of Control Data Business Centers.

In addition to personal and business financing, the Control Data Business Centers offer management training programs designed to help borrowers make the most effective use of their funds. Courses include analyzing and interpreting financial statements, inventory control, cash management, short-term financing, problem analysis, and decision making. Building Your Own Business, a computerized course of basic business instructions, is also available. Those interested in taking the course may apply at local SBA offices for a voucher granting free admission to the thirty-hour program. "Our business has grown to a full-service, hot-air balloon facility offering flying lessons, balloon sales, and maintenance," says Mike Bundgaard, a partner in the Denver, Colorado, Life/Cycle Balloon School. "I felt I had to keep abreast of the company's growth by taking a refresher course in accounting and bookkeeping. The Control Data course, which I took at their local business center, has helped me to keep my management skills sharp."

The following is a listing of Control Data Business Centers:

ALABAMA

c/o The Service Bureau Company
301 Beacon Parkway West
Birmingham, Alabama 35209

Springhill Plaza Shopping Center
3412 Springhill Avenue Exit
Mobile, Alabama 33607

ARIZONA

2221 N. Scottsdale Road
Scottsdale, Arizona 85257

914 E. Camelback Road, Suite #3
Phoenix, Arizona 85014

CALIFORNIA

One Bay Plaza, Suite 330
1350 Old Bayshore Highway
Burlingame, California 94010

Hacienda Square, Suite C–E
700 N. Johnson Avenue
El Cajon, California 92020

Hirschmann Building, Suite 407
9550 Flair Drive
El Monte, California 91371

18831 Von Karman Avenue,
Suite 300
Irvine, California 92715

Commerce Square, Suite 814
6055 E. Washington Boulevard
Los Angeles, California 90040

Financial Plaza, Suite 770
500 Esplanade Drive
Oxnard, California 93030

273A S. Lake Avenue
Pasadena, California 91101

Arden Howe Plaza
1578 Howe Avenue
Sacramento, California 95825

2012 H Street, Suite 100
Sacramento, California 95814

3 Oakmead Terrace, Suite 111
1270 Oakmead Parkway
Sunnyvale, California 94086

13701 Burbank Boulevard
Van Nuys, California 91401

2224 Oak Grove Road
Walnut Creek, California 94598

COLORADO

1919 14th Street, Suites 602–604
Boulder, Colorado 80302

Western Federal Building,
Suite 405
101 N. Cascade Avenue
Colorado Springs, Colorado
80903

Tiffany Plaza
7400 E. Hampton
Denver, Colorado 80231

Building D
8000 E. Prentice Avenue
Englewood, Colorado 80111

220 Union Boulevard
Lakewood, Colorado 80228

CONNECTICUT
312 Farmington Avenue
Farmington, Connecticut 06032

DISTRICT OF COLUMBIA
c/o Control Data Learning
    Center
2101 L Street, N.W., Suite 900
Washington, DC 20037

FLORIDA
2460 Gulf to Bay Boulevard
Clearwater, Florida 33515

3247 Beach Boulevard
Jacksonville, Florida 32207

3813 E. Colonial Drive
Orlando, Florida 32803

4511 N. Himes Avenue,
    Suite 285
Tampa, Florida 33614

GEORGIA
11 Executive Park West, N.E.
Atlanta, Georgia 30329

180 Interstate North, Suite 115
Atlanta, Georgia 30339

3400 Woodale Drive, N.E.
Atlanta, Georgia 30326

2200 Northland Parkway, Suite
    100
Tucker, Georgia 30084

ILLINOIS
The Merchandise Mart, Suites
    136 and 138
Chicago, Illinois 60654

2001 Midwest Road, Suite 100
Oakbrook, Illinois 60521

1030 West Higgins Road
Park Ridge, Illinois 60088

1057–61 E. Golf Road
Schaumberg, Illinois 60195

INDIANA
c/o The Service Bureau
    Company, Suite 1212E
115 W. Washington Street
Indianapolis, Indiana 46204

The Ross Commons
500 W. Lincoln Highway
Merrillville, Indiana 46410

IOWA
United Central Bank Building,
    8th Floor
317 Sixth Avenue
Des Moines, Iowa 50309

KANSAS
Louisburg Square
9339 Santa Fe Drive
Overland Park, Kansas 66212

Executive Hills Office Park
11011 Antioch
Overland Park, Kansas 66210

1401 Topeka Avenue
Topeka, Kansas 66601

KENTUCKY
Triad East, Suite 150
10200 Linn Station Road
Louisville, Kentucky 40223

LOUISIANA
3601 Johnson Street
Lafayette, Louisiana 70502

1001 Howard Avenue, Suite 1003
New Orleans, Louisiana 70113

MAINE
46 Atlantic Place
South Portland, Maine 04106

MARYLAND
3002 Druid Park Drive
Baltimore, Maryland 21215

22 W. Padonia Road
Timonium, Maryland 21093

MASSACHUSETTS
677 Worchester Road
Natick, Massachusetts 48010

The 2nd Avenue Office Building
204 2nd Avenue
Waltham, Massachusetts 02154

MICHIGAN
Bingham Center Office Complex,
  Suite 2820
30800 Telegraph Road
Birmingham, Michigan 48010

MINNESOTA
5241 Viking Drive
Bloomington, Minnesota 55435

200 Medical Arts Building
324 W. Superior Street
Duluth, Minnesota 55802

6809 York Avenue South
Edina, Minnesota 55435

2393 North Fairview Avenue
Roseville, Minnesota 55113

MISSOURI
1100 Grand Avenue
Kansas City, Missouri 64106

Des Peres Square
12768 Manchester Road
St. Louis, Missouri 63130

Financial Center Office Park,
  Suite 120
1650 E. Battlefield Road
Springfield, Missouri 65804

8515 Delmar Boulevard
University City, Missouri
  63124

NEBRASKA
Embassy West, Suite 100
9140 West Dodge Road
Omaha, Nebraska 68114

NEW JERSEY
c/o American Credit Indemnity
141 S. Harrison Street
East Orange, New Jersey 07018

NEW MEXICO
City Centre, Suite 510E
6400 Uptown Boulevard, N.E.
Albuquerque, New Mexico
  87110

NEW YORK
666 Old Country Road, 1st Floor
  West
Garden City, New York
  11530

1350 Avenue of the Americas,
  4th Floor
New York, New York 10019

NORTH CAROLINA
Arnold Palmer Center
3726 Latrobe Drive
Charlotte, North Carolina
  28234

P.O. Box 1619
700 N. Eugene Street
Greensboro, North Carolina
  27401

OHIO

567 E. Turkeyfoot Lake Road,
    Suite A–9
Akron, Ohio 44319

Provident Tower, Suite 901
One E. Fourth Street
Cincinnati, Ohio 45202

Western Reserve Building
1468 W. 9th Street, Suite 100
Cleveland, Ohio 44113

6524 Busch Boulevard, Suite 102
Columbus, Ohio 43229

Talbot Tower
128 W. 1st Street
Dayton, Ohio 45402

29 E. Front Street
Youngstown, Ohio 44503

OKLAHOMA

6815 N. May
Oklahoma City, Oklahoma
    73116

OREGON

3651 Southwest Hall Boulevard
Beaverton, Oregon 97005

104 S.W. Clay
Portland, Oregon 97201

PENNSYLVANIA

Benjamin Fox Pavilion
Fox Croft Square
Jenkintown, Pennsylvania 19046

1617 John F. Kennedy Boulevard
Philadelphia, Pennsylvania
    19103

Philadelphia Stock Exchange
    Building, Suite 502
1900 Market Street

Philadelphia, Pennsylvania
    19103

c/o Control Data Learning
    Center
Center City Tower, Suite 1350
650 Smithfield Street
Pittsburgh, Pennsylvania
    15222

SOUTH CAROLINA

Landmark IV, Suite 206
3710 Landmark Drive
Columbia, South Carolina 29204

607 N. Main Street
Greenville, South Carolina
    29602

SOUTH DAKOTA

825 Columbus Street
Rapid City, South Dakota 55701

TEXAS

Caruth Plaza
Building J, Suite #183
9100 N. Central Expressway
Dallas, Texas 75231

14801 Quorum Drive, Suite 101
Dallas, Texas 75240

Plaza at the Quorum, Suite #280
15000 Quorum Drive
Dallas, Texas 75240

2707 Stemmons Freeway,
    Suite #100
Dallas, Texas 75207

2425 W. Loop South, Suite 105
Houston, Texas 77056

4538 Center View Drive,
    Suite 251
San Antonio, Texas 78228

UTAH
50 S. Main Street, Suite 940
Salt Lake City, Utah 84144

VIRGINIA
701 E. Franklin Street, Suite 1316
Richmond, Virginia 23219

WASHINGTON
Bellevue N. Shopping Center,
    Suite 7

1100 Bellevue Way, N.E.
Bellevue, Washington 98004

Parkway Plaza
17308 South Center Parkway
Tukwila, Washington 98188

WISCONSIN
790 N. Jackson
Milwaukee, Wisconsin 53202

2130 N. Mayfair Road
Wauwatosa, Wisconsin 53226

The following is a listing of Control Data Business and Technology Centers.

MINNESOTA
511 11th Avenue South
Minneapolis, Minnesota 55415

245 East Sixth Street
St. Paul, Minnesota 55101

OHIO
1946 North 13th Street
Toledo, Ohio 43624

SOUTH CAROLINA
701 East Bay Street
Charleston, South Carolina
    29403.

12

Small business investment companies (SBICs)

One of the richest sources of government-related loans is also one of the least known and least understood. It is the national network of Small Business Investment Companies (SBICs). SBICs are privately owned and privately operated investment companies that are licensed by the Small Business Administration to provide equity capital and long-term loans to small firms. Small businesses generally have difficulty obtaining long-term capital to finance their growth. Prior to 1958, there were few sources a small company could turn to for money once it had exhausted its secured line of credit from banks or the SBA. To help close this financing gap, Congress passed the Small Business Investment Act of 1958, which authorized the SBA to license, regulate, and help finance privately organized and privately operated SBICs.

Today SBICs are located in all parts of the country. As an industry, the SBICs have total assets of $1.5 billion, and additional funds are available to them through borrowings from the SBA and private sources. Over the years, SBICs have provided over $4 billion to sixty thousand small companies.

Many SBICs are owned by groups of local investors, some are publicly traded, and others are partially or wholly owned by commercial banks or are subsidiaries of other corporations. "Captive SBICs derive their private capital from a single corporate source (typically a bank, which can make equity investments in non-banking activities only through an SBIC subsidiary). . . . The captive SBICs, which behave more like classic venture capital companies, invest in riskier situations, and hope for handsomer returns." *

The terms of equity type investments are negotiated by the SBIC and the small business. Generally, interest rates are lower and collateral requirements less stringent—in fact, collateral may not even be required—than in the case of straight loans. Often the SBIC will subordinate its debenture or loan to other borrowings by the small firm, thereby strengthening the firm's credit standing with banks or other lenders. Sometimes amortization requirements will be deferred for the early years of the debt so as to give the small concern every chance for a good start.

The amount of equity sought by an SBIC when it finances a small firm depends on the percentage of the small business's total assets represented by the SBIC financing, the company's record of stability and growth, and a variety of other factors. A SBIC may offer several types of financing to a single small business. For example, it may purchase common stock in the business and simultaneously make a straight loan to it. If the company needs additional financing later, the SBIC might make a second loan, this time obtaining warrants to purchase additional common stock.

A major incentive for SBICs to risk their capital in small businesses is the chance to share in the profits if the businesses grow and prosper. Three types of investments are

* Stan Luxemberg, *Venture,* August 1981, page 44.

commonly used by the SBICs to give them an opportunity to participate in this growth:

Loans with warrants: In return for a loan, the small business issues warrants enabling the SBIC to purchase common stock in the company, usually at a favorable price, during a specified period of time.

Convertible debentures: The SBIC lends the small business money and in return receives a debenture. The SBIC can then either accept repayment of the loan or convert the debenture into an equivalent amount of common stock of the small business.

Common stock: The SBIC purchases common stock from the small business.

While most SBICs want an opportunity to share in the growth and potential profits of the small companies they finance, some will make loans that involve no equity features. The small business that obtains a straight loan usually must provide security, but this can take the form of a second mortgage, a personal guarantee, or some other type of collateral that may not be acceptable to banks or other conventional lending institutions.

The interest rate on a loan is determined by negotiation between the SBIC and the small business, subject of course to the state's legal limit, or that imposed by the SBA, whichever is lower. Collateral requirements, terms of repayment, and other stipulations of the loan agreement also are determined by negotiation, within the boundaries of the regulations.

The SBA generally considers a business "small," and therefore eligible for SBIC financing, if its net worth does not exceed $6 million and its average net income after taxes for each of the preceding two years is not more than $2 million. Businesses failing to qualify under these provisions may qualify under other criteria established under the SBA's business loan program.

In determining the size of a business, SBA also takes into account the size of any affiliates, including a parent company that can control the firm, and any other companies controlled by the same parent company. Firms operating under franchise agreements are considered small if they have the right to the profits and responsibility for any losses resulting from the operation. They must also meet the $6 million/$2 million formula.

SBICs invest in all types of manufacturing and service industries and a wide variety of other businesses, including construction, retail, and wholesale concerns. Many investment companies seek out small businesses offering new products or services because these firms usually have attractive growth potential. Some SBICs specialize in electronics companies, research and development firms, or businesses in other fields in which the SBIC management has special knowledge and competence. But most SBICs consider a wide variety of investment opportunitities.

An SBIC may invest up to 20 percent of its private capital in a single small business. For the smallest SBIC, the maximum loan or investment is $30,000; for the largest, it is several million dollars. In any event, several SBICs may participate in financing the same small business and thereby increase the maximum investment. An SBIC often will invest a negotiated amount in a small business and agree to advance additional funds after a specified period of time or after the small company has achieved pre-stated goals.

Since an SBIC's ultimate success is linked to the growth and profitability of its so-called portfolio companies—that is, those it has financed—many SBICs offer management services as a supplement to financing. These services can be as valuable as the financing itself. Virtually every growing company has identifiable management strengths and weaknesses. In many cases, weaknesses are not apparent until the company enters a period of rapid growth, the type that often follows a major financing.

SBICs will often look closely at the firm's overall operations. It may insist on improvements such as the installation of better accounting methods or inventory controls. Similarly, as part of the financing agreement, the small business may be required to furnish the SBIC with regular financial statements or progress reports.

The extent of management services offered varies with the individual SBIC. A large SBIC is usually staffed by an experienced and diversified management team. If desirable, a specialist from the SBIC may work with a portfolio company to iron out specific problems that arise during the company's growth. Other SBICs have one- or two-person staffs that divide their time between seeking new investments and working with portfolio companies. Many SBIC managers call in consultants to supplement their work with portfolio companies, while others draw on the talents of their own board members. Some SBICs that concentrate on well-secured loans do not offer management assistance.

Small-business persons who decide to look outside their own companies for venture capital may find only limited possibilities, unless they are able to make a public stock offering. If the company is not ready for such an offering, or if the person does not wish to go this route, then SBICs are one of the few sources of equity capital available and the only "institutional source." * What's more, even in periods of low activity by the private venture sector, the use of fed-

---

* SBICs are called an institutional source of financing because a businessperson in need of capital knows that each of the several hundred companies licensed by SBA operates under the same general rules.

eral leverage enables SBICs to continue to invest at a high rate.

Before entering the marketplace, applicants for SBIC financing should learn as much as possible about the SBICs in their area. Find out what types of investments they make, how much they have available for investment, whether they will be able to assist in obtaining additional financing down the road, whether they have contacts that would be helpful in a future public offering, and whether they offer management services.

Entrepreneurs taking advantage of SBIC financing and management assistance appear to grow more successful companies than the average small business. The following chart was prepared by the National Association of SBICs based on information supplied by the Federal Trade Commission, the Census Bureau, and Arthur D. Little, Inc.

A Comparison of the Growth of
SBIC Portfolio Companies with the Growth of
All Small Companies*

Year of Initial Financing:	Pre–1972		1972–1975		1976–1977	
	SBIC Portfolio Companies	All Small Companies**	SBIC Portfolio Companies	All Small Companies**	SBIC Portfolio Companies	All Small Companies**
Employment	384%	29%	155%	19%	48%	8%
Sales	896	76	386	27	81	16
Profits	1,165	144	553	25	52	53
Assets	694	48	188	24	92	13
Federal Corporate Taxes	739	135	652	63	85	57

* For SBICs, growth rates are measured from the year prior to SBIC financing to the most recent fiscal year. For small companies in general, the comparison is from 1970, 1973, and 1976, to 1978.

** For financial measures, manufacturing corporations with less than $5 million in assets. For employment, all corporations with less than one hundred employees. Percentages for employment and taxes for all small companies for 1978 were estimated based on historical data.

The National Association of SBICs suggests that applicants seeking money should search for those Small Business Investment Companies that are geographically convenient, have investment policies that are suitable to their needs, are willing to lend or invest in the applicant's industry, and will provide the amount of funds needed. The following list of the National Association of Small Business Investment Companies can help in this search:

Explanation of Codes

Preferred Limit for Loans or Investments
A—up to $100,000
B—up to $250,000
C—up to $500,000
D—up to $1 million
E—Above $1 million

Investment Policy
* —Will consider either loans or investments
** —Prefers to make long-term loans
*** —Prefers financings with right to acquire stock interest

Industry Preferences
1. Communications and movies
2. Construction and development
3. Natural resources
4. Hotels, motels, and restaurants
5. Manufacturing and processing
6. Medical and other health services
7. Recreation and amusements
8. Research and technology
9. Retailing, wholesaling, and distribution
10. Service trades
11. Transportation
12. Diversified

MESBIC—an SBIC that concentrates in placing its loans and investments with a small-business person who is socially or economically disadvantaged

ALABAMA

Coastal Capital Company
3201 Dauphin Street, Suite B
Mobile, Alabama 36606
(David C. De Laney, Investment Manager)
(205) 476–0700
C * 12

First SBIC of Alabama
3201 Dauphin Street, Suite B
Mobile, Alabama 36606
(David C. De Laney, President)
(205) 476–0700
C * 12

Western Financial Capital Corporation
306 Temple Avenue North
Fayette, Alabama 35555
(Fredric M. Rosemore, President)
(205) 932–3528
B * 6, 12

ARIZONA

American Business Capital Corporation
3550 N. Central, Suite 1305
Phoenix, Arizona 85012
(Leonard A. Frankel, President)
(602) 277–6259
A ** 12

ARKANSAS

First SBIC of Arkansas, Inc.
702 Worthen Bank Building
Little Rock, Arkansas 72201
(Fred C. Burns, President)
    (501) 378–1876
A *** 12

Kar-Mal Venture Capital, Inc.
610 Plaza West
Little Rock, Arkansas 72205
(Tommy Karam, President)
    (501) 661–0010
MESBIC B *** 9

Small Business Investment
    Capital, Inc.
10003 New Benton Highway
Little Rock, Arkansas 72203
(C. E. Toland, President)
    (501) 455–2234
A ** 9

CALIFORNIA

Bay Area Western Venture
    Capital Group, Inc.
383 Diablo Road, Suite 100
Danville, California 94526
(Jack Wong, Secretary/Treasurer)
    (415) 820–8079
MESBIC B *** 2, 8

Brantman Capital Corporation
P.O. Box 877
Tiburon, California 94920
(W. T. Brantman, President)
    (415) 435–4747
A *** 4,5,6,7,8,9,10,11,12

Brentwood Capital Corporation
11661 San Vicente Boulevard
Los Angeles, California 90049
(Timothy M. Pennington,
    General Partner); (Frederick J.

Warren, General Partner)
    (213) 826–6581
D *** 1,3,5,6,8,10,12

Builders Capital Corporation
2716 Ocean Park Boulevard
Santa Monica, California 90406
(Victor Indiek, President)
    (213) 450–0779
C * 2

Business Equity & Development
    Corporation
1411 W. Olympic Boulevard,
    Suite 200
Los Angeles, California 90015
(Ricardo J. Olivarez, President)
    (213) 385–0351
MESBIC B * 5,12

California Northwest Fund, Inc.
3000 Sand Hill Rd.
Menlo Park, California 94025
(Kirk L. Knight, Managing
    Director; Ken E. Joy, Managing
    Director; H. DuBose
    Montgomery, Managing
    Director)
    (415) 854–2940
D * 12
(Branch Office: NY)

California Partners
Two Palo Alto Square
Palo Alto, California 94304
(William H. Draper III, President)
    (415) 493–5600
A *** 8

Crocker Ventures, Inc.
#10 Montgomery Street
San Francisco, California 94104
(John M. Boyle, Vice-President)
    (415) 983–7024
B *** 1,5,8,11

Crosspoint Investment
Corporation
P.O. Box 10101
1015 Corporation Way
Palo Alto, California 94303
(Max S. Simpson, President)
(415) 964–3545
B *** 1,5,8

Developers Equity Capital
Corporation
9201 Wilshire Boulevard, Suite
204
Beverly Hills, California 90210
(Larry Sade, President)
(213) 278–3611
B * 2,4,6,11

Equitable Capital Corporation
855 Sansome Street, Suite 200
San Francisco, California 94111
(John C. Lee, President)
(415) 434–4114
MESBIC B * 12

First Interstate Capital, Inc.
707 Wilshire Boulevard, Suite
1850
Los Angeles, California 90017
(David B. Jones, President)
(213) 614–5903
D *** 12

Florists' Capital Corporation
10514 West Pico Boulevard
Los Angeles, California 90064
(Christopher M. Conroy,
President)
(213) 204–6956
D *** 9,12

Grocers Capital Company
2601 S. Eastern Avenue
Los Angeles, California 90040

(William Christy, President)
(213) 728–3322
B ** 9

HUB Enterprises, Ltd.
5874 Doyle Street
Emeryville, California 94608
(Richard Magary, General
Manager)
(415) 653–5707
MESBIC A * 2,5,6,8,10,12

Krasne Fund for Small Business,
Inc.
P.O. Box 5257
Beverly Hills, California 90210
(Clyde A. Krasne, President)
(213) 274–7007
A ** 2,12

Lasung Investment & Finance
Company, Inc.
3121 W. Olympic Boulevard,
#201
Los Angeles, California 90006
(Jung S. Lee, President)
(213) 384–7548
MESBIC A * 4

Lucky Star Investment Company
665 Grant Avenue
San Francisco, California 94108
(Sinclair Louie, President)
(415) 982–5729
C * 2,4,5,6,9,10

Marwit Capital Corporation
The Marwit Building
180 Newport Center Drive, Suite
200
Newport Beach, California 92660
(Martin W. Witte, President)
(714) 640–6234
D *** 1,2,4,5,6,8,10,12

MCA New Ventures, Inc.
100 Universal City Plaza
Universal City, California 91608
(Robert B. Braswell, Chairman
    and President)
    (213) 508–2937
MESBIC B * 1,5,7,12

Merrill, Pickard Capital
    Company
650 California Street, 31st Floor
San Francisco, California 94108
(Steven L. Merrill, Jeff Pickard)
    (415) 397–8800
E *** 1,5,6

Nelson Capital Corporation
    (Branch Office)
1901 Avenue of the Stars, Suite
    584
Los Angeles, California 90067
(Norman Tulchin, Chairman)
    (213) 556–1944
D ** 12
(Main Office: NY)

Novus Capital Corporation
5670 Wilshire Boulevard
Los Angeles, California 90036
(Errol M. Gerson, President)
    (213) 932–4051 or
    (213) 932–4077
C * 2

Oceanic Capital Corporation
350 California Street, Suite 2090
San Francisco, California 94104
(Robert C. Weeks, President)
    (415) 398–7677
C * 1,5,8

Opportunity Capital Corporation
100 California Street, Suite 714
San Francisco, California 94111

(J. Peter Thompson, President)
    (415) 421–5935
MESBIC B *** 1,3,5,6,9,12

Oxford Capital Corporation
3700 Wilshire Boulevard
Los Angeles, California
    90010
(Richard R. Lorenz, President)
    (213) 381–8743
B *** 12

Pan American Investment
    Company
350 California Street, #2090
San Francisco, California 94104
(Spencer W. Hoopes, President)
    (415) 398–7677
D *** 1,5,6,8

PBC Venture Capital, Inc.
P.O. Box 6008
1408 18th Street
Bakersfield, California 93386
(Richard Robins, Vice-President
    and Investment Manager)
    (805) 395–3555
B *** 1,5,8,12

San Joaquin Capital Corporation
P.O. Box 2538
Bakersfield, California 93303
(Chester W. Troudy, Executive
    Vice-President)
    (805) 323–7581
D *** 2,5

San Jose Capital Corporation
130 Park Center Plaza, Suite 132
San Jose, California 95113
(H. Bruce Furchtenicht,
    President)
    (408) 293–8052
B *** 1,5,6,8

Solid Capital Corporation
652 Kearny Street, Suites 1 & 2
San Francisco, California 94108
(Lusing Ty, Chief Financial
    Officer)
    (415) 434-3371
MESBIC A * 2,4,9,12

Space Ventures, Inc.
3901 MacArthur Boulevard,
    Suite 101
Newport Beach, California
    92660
(Leslie R. Brewer, General
    Manager)
    (714) 851-0855
MESBIC B ***
    1,2,4,5,7,8,9,10,11,12

TELACU Investment Company
1330 So. Atlantic Boulevard
Los Angeles, California 90022
(Gilberto Padilla, President)
    (213) 268-6745
MESBIC B * 5,9,10,12

Union Venture Corporation
445 S. Figueroa Street
Los Angeles, California 90071
(Brent T. Rider, President)
    (213) 687-6959
E *** 1,3,5,6,8,12

Unity Capital Corporation
362 30th Street "B"
San Diego, California 92104
(Frank W. Owen, President)
    (714) 295-6768
MESBIC C *** 2,4,5,9,12

WESTAMCO Investment
    Company
8929 Wilshire Boulevard, Suite
    400

Beverly Hills, California 90211
(Leonard G. Muskin, President)
    (213) 652-8288
B * 2,3,5,8,9,12

Washington Capital Corporation
    (Branch Office)
601 University Avenue
Campus Commons
Sacramento, California
    95825
D * 12
(Main Office: WA)

West Coast Venture Capital
10440 So. DeAnza Boulevard,
    Suite D-2
Cupertino, California
    95014
(Gary W. Kalbach, General
    Partner)
    (408) 996-2702
C *** 1,5,8

COLORADO

Central Investment Corporation
    of Denver (Branch Office)
7625 W. Fifth Avenue, Suite
    202N
Lakewood, Colorado 80226
(Blaine E. D'Arcey, General
    Manager)
    (303) 232-3018
D *** 12
(Main Office: Northwest Growth
    Fund, Inc., MN)

Colorado Growth Capital, Inc.
950 17th Street, #1630
Denver, Colorado 80202
(Nicholas H. C. Davis, President)
    (303) 629-0205
B * 1,3,7,8,9

Enervest, Inc.
7000 E. Belleview Avenue, #310
Englewood, Colorado 80111
(Mark Kimmel, President)
    (303) 771–9650
C *** 1,3,5,6,7,8,12

CONNECTICUT

Activest Capital Corporation
P.O. Box 76
Cornwall Bridge, Connecticut
  06754
(William N. Vitalis, President)
    (203) 672–6651
A * 2,4

Asset Capital & Management
  Corporation
608 Ferry Boulevard
Stratford, Connecticut
  06497
(Ralph Smith, President)
    (203) 375–0299
A * 1,2,6,9

Capital Resource Company of
  Connecticut
345 N. Main Street, Suite 304
West Hartford, Connecticut
  06117
(I. Martin Fierberg, President)
    (203) 232–1769
A * 12

The First Connecticut SBIC
177 State Street
Bridgeport, Connecticut
  06604
(James Breiner, Chairman; David
  Engelson, President)
    (203) 366–4726
D * 1,2,5,6,9,12
(Branch Office: NY)

Foster Management Company
1010 Summer Street
Stamford, Connecticut
  06905
(John H. Foster, President)
    (203) 348–4385
C *** 1,3,5,6,8,11

Manufacturers SBIC, Inc.
310 Main Street
East Haven, Connecticut 06512
(Louis W. Mingione, Executive
  Director)
    (203) 469–7901
A * 12

Marcon Capital Corporation
49 Riverside Avenue
Westport, Connecticut 06880
(Martin Cohen, President)
    (203) 226–7751
C ** 1,12

Regional Financial Enterprises,
  Inc.
1111 Summer Street
Stamford, Connecticut 06905
(Robert M. Williams, Chairman)
    (203) 356–1730
D * 1,3,5,6,8,12

Small Business Investment
  Company of Connecticut
c/o E&F Construction Company
505 Sylvan Avenue
Bridgeport, Connecticut 06604
(Kenneth F. Zarrilli, President)
    (203) 367–3282
A ** 12

DISTRICT OF COLUMBIA
Allied Capital Corporation
1625 I Street, NW
Washington, DC 20006

(George C. Williams, President;
David Gladstone, Executive
Vice-President)
(202) 331–1112
C * 1,2,4,5,6,8,9,11,12
(Branch Office: FL)

Broad Arrow Investment
Corporation (Branch Office)
1701 Pennsylvania Avenue, NW
Washington, DC 20006
(C. N. Bellm, President)
(202) 452–6680
MESBIC A * 5,9,12
(Main Office: NJ)

Capital Investment Company of
Washington
1010 Wisconsin Avenue, NW,
#900
Washington, D.C. 20007
(Jayrel Goldberg, President)
(202) 298–3214
A * 6,12

Columbia Ventures, Inc.
1828 L Street, NW
Washington, DC 20036
(Richard Whitney, President)
(202) 659–0033
FULLY INVESTED
(Branch Office: MS)

Continental Investors, Inc.
2020 K Street, NW, Suite 350
Washington, DC 20006
(Lac Thantrong, President)
(202) 466–3709
MESBIC A * 12

Fulcrum Venture Capital
Corporation
2021 K Street, NW, Suite 714
Washington, DC 20006

(Steven L. Lilly, President)
(202) 833–9590
MESBIC C * * * 1,5,8,9,11

Greater Washington Investors,
Inc.
1015–18th Street, NW
Washington, DC 20036
(Don A. Christensen, President
and Treasurer)
(202) 466–2210
B * * * 1,5,8,12

FLORIDA

Allied Capital Corporation
(Branch Office)
1614 One Financial Plaza
Ft. Lauderdale, Florida
33394
(George C. Williams, President;
Warren Miller, Regional Vice-
President)
(305) 763–8484
C * 1,2,4,5,6,8,9,11,12
(Main Office: DC)

CUBICO, Ltd.
7425 NW 79th Street
Miami, Florida 33166
(Anthony G. Marina, President)
(305) 885–8881
MESBIC B * 12

The First American Lending
Corporation
P.O. Box 1449
1200 N. Dixie Highway
Lake Worth, Florida
33460
(G. M. Caughlin, President)
(305) 582–3322
MESBIC A * 12

First Miami SBIC
1195 NE 125th Street
North Miami, Florida 33161
(Irve L. Libby, President)
    (305) 891–2534
B * 2,6,7,12

First Miami SBIC (Branch Office)
Suite 18-D
250 S. Ocean Boulevard
Boca Raton, Florida 33432
(Irve L. Libby, President)
    (305) 392–4424
B * 2,6,7,12

Gulf Coast Capital Corporation
P.O. Box 12790
70 N. Baylen Street
Pensacola, Florida 32575
(Oscar M. Tharp, President)
    (904) 434–1361
A *** 2,10

J & D Capital Corporation
12747 Biscayne Boulevard
North Miami, Florida 33181
(Jack Carmel, President)
    (305) 893–0303
C * 10,12

Market Capital Corporation
P.O. Box 22667
Tampa, Florida 33622
(E. E. Eads, President)
    (813) 248–5781
A *** 9,11

Massachusetts Capital
    Corporation (Branch Office)
1614 One Financial Plaza
Ft. Lauderdale, Florida 33394
(David Harkins, President;
    Warren Miller, Regional Vice-
    President)
    (305) 763–8484

B *** 1,3,5,6,10,11,12
(Main Office: MA)

The Quiet SBIC
105 E. Garden Street
Pensacola, Florida 32501
(Edward Gray III, Vice-President)
    (904) 434–5090
A * 12

Servico Business Investment
    Corporation
2000 Palm Beach Lakes
    Boulevard, Suite 1000
West Palm Beach, Florida 33409
(Gary O. Marino, President)
    (305) 689–5031
A * 12

Small Business Assistance
    Corporation
2612 W. 15th Street
Panama City, Florida 32401
(Charles S. Smith, President)
    (904) 785–9577
B * 4

Southeast SBIC, Inc.
100 S. Biscayne Boulevard
Miami, Florida 33131
(C. L. Hofmann, President)
    (305) 577–4680
C *** 1,5,6,8,12

Universal Financial Services, Inc.
225 NE 35th Street, Suite B
Miami, Florida 33137
(Norman N. Zipkin, CEO)
    (305) 573–6326
MESBIC A * 12

Venture Capital Corporation of
    America
4875 N. Federal Highway
Ft. Lauderdale, Florida 33308

(Richard A. Osias, President)
    (305) 772–1800
B *** 12

Verde Capital Corporation
6701 Sunset Drive, Suite 104
Miami, Florida 33143
(Jose Dearing, President)
    (305) 666–8789
MESBIC B * 1,2,5,11,12

GEORGIA
Affiliated Investment Fund, Ltd.
2225 Shurfine Drive
College Park, Georgia 30337
(Samuel Weissman, President)
    (404) 766–0221
A ** 9

CSRA Capital Corporation
P.O. Box 11045
1058 Claussen Road, Suite 102
Augusta, Georgia 30907
(Allen F. Caldwell, Jr., President)
    (404) 736–2236
B *** 2

Fidelity Capital Corporation
180 Interstate No. Parkway,
    Suite 400
Atlanta, Georgia 30339
(Alfred F. Skiba, President)
    (404) 955–4313
C * 1,2,5,11

Investor's Equity, Inc.
3517 First National Bank Tower
Atlanta, Georgia 30383
(Ronald W. White, Managing
    Director)
    (404) 523–3999
B *** 1,2,3,4,5,6,8

Peachtree Capital Corporation
Peachtree Center

1611 Gas Light Tower
Atlanta, Georgia 30303
(David W. Howe, President)
    (404) 522–9000
A *** 12

Southeastern Capital SBIC
100 Northcreek, Suite 600
3715 Northside Parkway, NW
Atlanta, Georgia 30327
(J. Ray Efird, President)
    (404) 237–1567
B *** 12

Sunbelt Funding Corporation
P.O. Box 7006
Macon, Georgia 31298
(Charles H. Jones, President)
    (912) 742–0177
MESBIC A * 12

HAWAII
Pacific Venture Capital, Ltd.
1505 Dillingham Boulevard
Honolulu, Hawaii 96817
(Dexter J. Taniguchi, President)
    (808) 847–6502
MESBIC A * 12

Small Business Investment
    Company of Hawaii, Inc.
1575 S. Beretania Street
Honolulu, Hawaii 96826
(James W. Y. Wong, Chairman)
    (808) 946–1171
A *** 2,12

IDAHO
First Idaho Venture Capital
    Company
P.O. Box 1739
Boise, Idaho 83701
(Jack J. Winderl, President)
    (208) 345–3460
B ** 12

ILLINOIS
Abbott Capital Corporation
120 S. LaSalle Street, Suite 1100
Chicago, Illinois 60603
(Richard E. Lassar, President)
    (312) 726–3803
C *** 5,6,8,10

Amoco Venture Capital
    Company
200 E. Randolph
Chicago, Illinois 60601
(L. E. Schaffer, President)
    (312) 856–6523
MESBIC B * 12

CEDCO Capital Corporation
180 N. Michigan Avenue,
    Suite 333
Chicago, Illinois 60601
(Frank B. Brooks, President;
    Joseph W. Miller, Vice-
    President)
    (312) 984–5971
MESBIC A *** 12

Chicago Community Ventures,
    Inc.
108 N. State Street, Suite 902
Chicago, Illinois 60602
(Phyllis George, President)
    (312) 726–6084
MESBIC B *** 12

Chicago Equity Corporation
One IBM Plaza, Suite 2424
Chicago, Illinois 60611
(Morris Weiser, President)
    (312) 321–9662
A *** 12

Claremont/LaSalle Corporation
29 S. LaSalle Street
Chicago, Illinois 60603

(Steven B. Randall, President)
    (312) 236–5888
D *** 1,3,5,6,7,8,12

Combined Opportunities, Inc.
300 N. State Street
Chicago, Illinois 60610
(E. Patric Jones, Assistant Vice-
    President)
    (312) 266–3091
MESBIC B * 1,5,12

Continental Illinois Venture
    Corporation
231 S. LaSalle Street, Suite 1617
Chicago, Illinois 60693
(John L. Hines, President)
    (312) 828–8021
E *** 1,3,5,6,8,9,11,12

First Capital Corporation of
    Chicago
One 1st National Plaza, Suite
    2628
Chicago, Illinois 60670
(John A. Canning, Jr., President)
    (312) 732–5400
E *** 12

Frontenac Capital Corporation
208 S. LaSalle Street
Chicago, Illinois 60604
(David A. R. Dullum, President)
    (312) 368–0047
C *** 1,5,6,8,12

Heizer Corporation
20 N. Wacker Drive
Chicago, Illinois 60606
(E. F. Heizer, Jr., Chairman)
    (312) 641–2200
E *** 1,3,5,6,7,8,11,12

Nelson Capital Corporation
    (Branch Office)

8550 W. Bryn Mawr Avenue,
    Suite 515
Chicago, Illinois 60631
(Irwin B. Nelson, President)
    (312) 693–5990
D ** 12
(Main Office: NY)

Tower Ventures, Inc.
Sears Tower, BSC 9–29
Chicago, Illinois 60684
(R. A. Comey, President)
    (312) 875–0583
MESBIC B * 12

United Capital Corporation of
    Illinois
United Center
State & Wyman Streets
Rockford, Illinois 61101
(Jack K. Ahrens, Vice-President)
    (815) 987–2179
C *** 1,5,6,8

The Urban Fund of Illinois, Inc.
300 N. State Street
Chicago, Illinois 60610
(E. Patric Jones, President)
    (312) 266–3050
MESBIC B * 12

Woodland Capital Company
1401 N. Western Avenue
Lake Forest, Illinois 60045
(James W. Erickson, President)
    (312) 295–6300
C *** 12

IOWA
R. W. Allsop Capital Corporation
1241 Park Place NE
Cedar Rapids, Iowa 52402
(Robert W. Allsop, President)
    (319) 393–6911

D *** 1,5,6,12
(Branch Offices: KS, WI, MO)

MorAmerica Capital Corporation
    300 American Building
Cedar Rapids, Iowa 52401
(Jerry M. Burrows, President)
    (319) 363–8249
D *** 12
(Branch Offices: MO, WI)

KANSAS
R. W. Allsop Capital Corporation
    (Branch Office)
35 Corporate Woods, Suite 229
9101 W. 10th Street
Overland Park, Kansas 66210
(Larry C. Maddox)
    (913) 642–4719
D *** 1,5,6,12
(Main Office: IA)

Kansas Venture Capital, Inc.
First National Bank Towers
One Townsite Plaza, Suite 1030
Topeka, Kansas 66603
(George L. Doak, President)
    (913) 233–1368
A *** 5

KENTUCKY
Equal Opportunity Finance, Inc.
9502 Williamsburg Plaza
Louisville, Kentucky 40222
(Frank P. Justice, Jr., President)
    (502) 423–1943
MESBIC A * 12

Financial Opportunities, Inc.
981 S. Third Street
Louisville, Kentucky 40203
(Gary J. Miller, General Manager)
    (502) 584–1281
A * 9

Mountain Ventures, Inc.
Box 628
911 N. Main Street
London, Kentucky 40741
(Frederick J. Beste III, President)
   (606) 878–6635
D *** 12

LOUISIANA
Business Capital Corporation
1732 Canal Street
New Orleans, Louisiana
   70112
(David R. Burrus, President)
   (504) 581–4002
MESBIC D * 12

CADDO Capital Corporation
820 Jordan Street, Suite 504
Shreveport, Louisiana
   71101
(Thomas L. Young, Jr., President)
   (318) 424–0505
D *** 3,5,12

Capital for Terrebonne, Inc.
P.O. Box 1868
1613 Barrow Street
Houma, Louisiana 70361
(Hartwell A. Lewis, President)
   (504) 868–3933
A ** 12

Commercial Capital, Inc.
200 Belle Terre Boulevard
Covington, Louisiana
   70433
(F. W. Pierce, President)
   (504) 892–4921 Ext. 261
A * 1,2,4,6,7,9,10,12

Branch Offices:
Commercial Capital, Inc.
c/o Northlake Insurance, Inc.

Bogue Falaya Plaza Shopping
   Center
Covington, Louisiana 70433

Commercial Capital, Inc.
c/o Central Progressive Bank
1809 W. Thomas
Hammond, Louisiana 70401

Dixie Business Investment
   Company
P.O. Box 588
Lake Providence, Louisiana
   71254
(Steve K. Cheek, President)
   (318) 559–1558
A ** 12

EDICT Investment Corporation
2908 S. Carrollton Avenue
New Orleans, Louisiana
   70118
(Gregory B. Johnson, Executive
   Vice-President)
   (504) 861–2364
MESBIC A ** 12

First SBIC of Louisiana
P.O. Box 1336
2852 Carey Street
Slidell, Louisiana 70459
(Alma O. Galle, President)
   (504) 561–0017 or
   (504) 561–2404
A * 12

First Southern Capital
   Corporation
P.O. Box 14205
Baton Rouge, Louisiana 70898
(John H. Crabtree, Chairman and
   President)
   (504) 769–3004
D *** 1,5,12

Louisiana Equity Capital
     Corporation
c/o Louisiana National Bank
P.O. Box 1511
Baton Rouge, Louisiana
     70821
(Charles A. Beard, Executive
     Vice-President)
     (504) 389–4421
C ** 5,9

Royal Street Investment
     Corporation
618 Baronne Street
New Orleans, Louisiana
     70113
(William D. Humphries,
     President)
     (504) 588–9271
B *** 12

Savings Venture Capital
     Corporation
6001 Financial Plaza
Shreveport, Louisiana 71130
(David R. Dixon, Executive Vice-
     President)
     (318) 686–9200
B ** 12

Venturtech Capital, Inc.
Republic Tower, Suite 602
5700 Florida Blvd.
Baton Rouge, Louisiana 70806
(E. M. Charlet, President)
     (504) 926–5482
B *** 1,6,8

MAINE
Maine Capital Corporation
One Memorial Circle
Augusta, Maine 04330
(Lloyd D. Brace, Jr., Vice-

President and Director of
     Finance)
     (207) 623–1686
B * 1,2,3,5,8,11,12

MARYLAND
Albright Venture Capital, Inc.
8005 Rappahannock Avenue
Jessup, Maryland 20794
(William A. Albright, President)
     (301) 799–7935
MESBIC A * 2,4,9,10,11,12

MASSACHUSETTS
Advent Capital Corporation
111 Devonshire Street
Boston, Massachusetts 02109
(David D. Croll, Chairman &
     CEO)
     (617) 725–2301
E * 1,3,5,6,8,12

Alta Capital Corporation
175 Federal Street
Boston, Massachusetts 02110
(William P. Egan, President)
     (617) 482–8020
D * 1,6,9,12

Atlas Capital Corporation
55 Court Street, Suite 200
Boston, Massachusetts 02108
(Herbert Carver, President)
     (617) 482–1218
B ** 12

Boston Hambro Corporation
One Boston Place
Boston, Massachusetts
     02106
(Edwin A. Goodman, President)
     (617) 722–7055
D * 1,2,3,5,6,8,12
(Branch Office: NY)

Chestnut Capital Corporation
111 Devonshire Street
Boston, Massachusetts 02109
(David D. Croll, Chairman and
    CEO)
    (617) 725–2302
E * 1,3,5,6,8,12

Cohasset Capital Corporation
4 Tupelo Road
Cohasset, Massachusetts 02025
(Grant Wilson, President)
    (617) 383–0758
A *** 1,12

Devonshire Capital Corporation
111 Devonshire Street
Boston, Massachusetts 02109
(David D. Croll, Chairman and
    CEO)
    (617) 725–2300
E * 1,3,5,6,8,12

First Capital Corporation of
    Boston
100 Federal Street
Boston, Massachusetts 02110
(George Rooks, President)
    (617) 434–2442
D *** 1,3,5,6,8,9

Massachusetts Capital
    Corporation
75 Federal Street
Boston, Massachusetts 01945
(David Harkins, President;
    Christopher Lynch, Vice-
    President)
    (617) 426–2488
B *** 1,3,5,6,10,11,12
(Branch Office: FL)

Massachusetts Venture Capital
    Corporation

59 Temple Place
Boston, Massachusetts 02111
(Charles Grigsby, President)
    (617) 426–0208
MESBIC B *** 12

New England Enterprise Capital
    Corporation
28 State Street
Boston, Massachusetts
    02106
(Z. David Patterson, Vice-
    President)
    (617) 742–0285
C *** 1,5,6,8,10,12

Schooner Capital Corporation
77 Franklin Street
Boston, Massachusetts 02110
(Vincent J. Ryan, Jr., President)
    (617) 357–9031
B *** 1,3

Transatlantic Capital
    Corporation
60 Batterymarch Street, Room
    728
Boston, Massachusetts 02110
(Bayard Henry, President)
    (617) 482–0015
C *** 1,5,6,8,10

UST Capital Corporation
40 Court Street
Boston, Massachusetts
    02108
(Stephen R. Lewinstein,
    President)
    (617) 726–7260
A * 1,2,3,5,6,8,11

W.C.C.I. Capital Corporation
791 Main Street
Worcester, Massachusetts 01610

(Deborah G. Nurse, Vice-
President)
(617) 791–0941
MESBIC A * * * 12

Worcester Capital Corporation
446 Main Street
Worcester, Massachusetts 01608
(W. Kenneth Kidd, Vice-
President)
(617) 853–7508
A * * * 5,8

MICHIGAN
DBT Capital Corporation
211 W. Fort Street
Detroit, Michigan 48231
(John D. Berkaw, President)
(313) 222–3907
C * * * 5,6,8,12

Doan Resources Corporation
110 East Grove
Midland, Michigan 48640
(Ian R. N. Bund, Vice-President)
(517) 631–2471
C * * * 1,5,6,8

Federated Capital Corporation
20000 W. Twelve Mile Road
Southfield, Michigan 48076
(Louis P. Ferris, Jr., President)
(313) 559–0554
A * * 12

Independence Capital Formation,
Inc.
Pierson Building, Suite 700
1505 Woodward Avenue
Detroit, Michigan 48226
(Walter M. McMurtry, Jr.,
President)
(313) 961–2470
MESBIC B * 1,5,8,9,11

Metro-Detroit Investment Company
18481 W. Ten Mile Road
Southfield, Michigan 48075
(William J. Fowler, President)
(313) 557–3818/19
MESBIC A * * 9

Michigan Capital & Service, Inc.
740 City Center Building
Ann Arbor, Michigan 48104
(Joseph F. Conway, President)
(313) 663–0702
C * * * 1,3,5,6,8,12

Motor Enterprises, Inc.
General Motors Building, Room
6–248
3044 W. Grand Boulevard
Detroit, Michigan 48202
(James Kobus, Manager)
(313) 556–4273
MESBIC B * * 5

Mutual Investment Company, Inc.
17348 W. Twelve Mile Road,
Suite 104
Southfield, Michigan 48076
(Timothy J. Taylor, Treasurer)
(313) 552–8515
MESBIC A * 9

PRIME, Inc.
1845 David Whitney Building
Detroit, Michigan 48226
(Jimmy N. Hill, President)
(313) 964–3380
MESBIC B * 12

Tyler Refrigeration Capital
Corporation
1329 Lake
Niles, Michigan 49120
(Gary J. Slock, Chairman)
(616) 683–1610
A * 2

MINNESOTA

Consumer Growth Capital, Inc.
430 Oak Grove
Minneapolis, Minnesota 55403
(John T. Gerlach, President)
    (612) 874–0694
C *** 1,4,5,10,12

Control Data Capital
    Corporation
8100 34th Avenue S.
Minneapolis, Minnesota 55440
(John F. Tracy, President)
    (612) 853–6537
B * 1,5,6,8,12

Eagle Ventures, Inc.
700 Soo Line Building
Minneapolis, Minnesota 55422
(Thomas N. Neitge, Vice-
    President)
    (612) 339–9694
C *** 1,5,6,7,8

First Midwest Capital
    Corporation
Chamber of Commerce Building,
    Suite 700
15 S. Fifth Street
Minneapolis, Minnesota 55402
(Alan K. Ruvelson, President)
    (612) 339–9391
B *** 1,5,6,8,9,10,12

Northland Capital Corporation
613 Missabe Building
Duluth, Minnesota 55802
(George G. Barnum, Jr.,
    President)
    (218) 722–0545
B *** 12

North Star Ventures, Inc.
NFC Building, Suite 1258

7900 Xerxes Avenue S.
Minneapolis, Minnesota 55431
(Terrence W. Glarner, Executive
    Vice-President and General
    Manager)
    (612) 830–4550
C *** 1,5,6,7,8,12

Northwest Growth Fund, Inc.
1730 Midwest Plaza Building
801 Nicollet Mall
Minneapolis, Minnesota 55402
(Robert F. Zicarelli, Chairman)
    (612) 372–8770
D *** 12
(Branch Offices: OR, CO)

Pathfinder Venture Capital Fund
7300 Metro Boulevard, Suite 585
Minneapolis, Minnesota 55435
(A. H. Greenshields, Partner)
    (612) 835–1121
E *** 1,5,6,8

P.R. Peterson Venture Capital
    Corporation
7301 Washington Avenue S.
Edina, Minnesota 55435
(P.R. Peterson, President)
    (612) 941–8171
A *** 6,8

Retailers Growth Fund, Inc.
5100 Gamble Drive, Suite 380
Minneapolis, Minnesota 55416
(Cornell M. Moore, Chairman
    and President)
    (612) 546–8989
A * 9

Shared Ventures, Inc.
4601 Excelsior Boulevard, Suite
    411
Minneapolis, Minnesota 55416

(Howard Weiner, President)
    (612) 925–3411
A * 12

MISSISSIPPI
Columbia Ventures, Inc. (Branch
    Office)
809 State Street
Jackson, Mississippi 39201
FULLY INVESTED
(Main Office: DC)

DeSoto Capital Corporation
8885 E. Goodman
Olive Branch, Mississippi
    38654
(William B. Rudner, President)
    (601) 895–4145
A *** 12

Invesat Corporation
162 E. Amite Street, Suite 204
Jackson, Mississippi 39207
(J. Thomas Noojin, President)
    (601) 969–3242
C * 12

Sun Delta Capital Access Center,
    Inc.
Box 588
819 Main Street
Greenville, Mississippi 38701
(Charles Bannerman, President)
    (601) 335–5291
MESBIC B * 12

Vicksburg Small Business
    Investment Company
First National Bank Building
P.O. Box 852
Vicksburg, Mississippi 39180
(David L. May, President)
    (601) 636–4762
A * 5,9,12

MISSOURI
R. W. Allsop Capital Corporation
    (Branch Office)
111 W. Port Plaza, Suite 600
St. Louis, Missouri 63141
(Robert L. Kuk)
    (314) 434–1688
D *** 1,5,6,12
(Main Office: IA)

Bankers Capital Corporation
4049 Pennsylvania, Suite 304
Kansas City, Missouri 64111
(Raymond E. Glasnapp,
    President)
    (816) 531–1600
A * 12

Intercapco West, Inc.
7800 Bonhomme
Clayton, Missouri 63105
(Thomas E. Phelps, President)
    (314) 863–0600
A *** 1,2,3,5,6,8,9,11,12

MorAmerica Capital
    Corporation (Branch Office)
Commerce Tower, Suite 2724A
911 Main Street
Kansas City, Missouri 64105
(Rex E. Wiggins, Regional Vice-
    President)
    (816) 842–0114
D *** 12
(Main Office: IA)

NEBRASKA
Community Equity Corporation
    of Nebraska
5620 Ames Avenue, Suite 109
Omaha, Nebraska 68104
(William C. Moore, President)
    (402) 455–7722
MESBIC A ** 12

NEVADA
Westland Capital Corporation
100 W. Grove Street, Suite 550
Reno, Nevada 89509
(Morton B. Phillips, Chairman)
    (702) 826–6307
B * 12

NEW HAMPSHIRE
Hampshire Capital Corporation
P.O. Box 468
48 Congress Street
Portsmouth, New Hampshire
    03801
(Philip G. Baker, President)
    (603) 431–1415
A * * * 5,9,12

NEW JERSEY
Broad Arrow Investment
    Corporation
P.O. Box 2231-R
Morristown, New Jersey 07960
(C. N. Bellm, President)
    (201) 766–2835
MESBIC A * 5,9,12
(Branch Office: DC)

Engle Investment Company
35 Essex Street
Hackensack, New Jersey 07601
(Murray Hendel, President)
    (201) 489–3583
A * 12
(Branch Office: NY)

Eslo Capital Corporation
485 Morris Avenue
Springfield, New Jersey 07081
(Leo Katz, President)
    (201) 467–2545
A * * 12

Lloyd Capital Corporation
77 State Highway #5
Edgewater, New Jersey 07020
(Solomon T. Scharf, President)
    (201) 947–6000
C * 2,4,6,9,12

Main Capital Investment
    Corporation
818 Main Street
Hackensack, New Jersey 07601
(Sam Klotz, President)
    (201) 489–2080
A * * * 1,2,3,4,7,10,12

Monmouth Capital Corporation
P.O. Box 335
125 Wyckoff Road
Eatontown, New Jersey 07724
(Eugene W. Landy, President)
    (201) 542–4927
B * 12

Quidnet Capital Corporation
909 State Road
Princeton, New Jersey
    08540
(Stephen W. Fillo, President)
    (609) 924–7665
C * * * 12

Rutgers Minority Investment
    Company
92 New Street
Newark, New Jersey 07102
(Louis T. German, President)
    (201) 648–5287
MESBIC A * 5,9

NEW MEXICO
Albuquerque SBIC
P.O. Box 487
Albuquerque, New Mexico
    87103

(Albert T. Ussery, President)
    (505) 247–4089
A *** 12

Associated Southwest Investors,
    Inc.
2425 Alamo SE
Albuquerque, New Mexico
    87106
(John R. Rice, President)
    (505) 842–5955
MESBIC B * 1,5,6,8,12

First Capital Corporation of New
    Mexico
8425 Osuna Road, NE
Albuquerque, New Mexico
    87112
(Shirley A. Williams, President)
    (505) 292–2300
A * 12

Fluid Capital Corporation
200 Lomas, NW, Suite 527
Albuquerque, New Mexico
    87102
(George T. Slaughter, President)
    (505) 243–2279
B * 2,12

The Franklin Corporation
    (Branch Office)
4209 San Mateo NE
Albuquerque, New Mexico
    87110
(Herman E. Goodman, President)
    (505) 243–9680
D *** 1,5,6,7,8,11,12
(Main Office: NY)

New Mexico Capital
    Corporation
2900 Louisiana Boulevard, NE,
    Suite 201

Albuquerque, New Mexico
    87110
(S.P. Hidalgo II, Executive Vice-
    President)
    (505) 884–3600
C * 12

Southwest Capital Investments,
    Inc.
8000 Pennsylvania Circle, NE
Albuquerque, New Mexico
    87110
(Martin J. Roe, President)
    (505) 265–9564
A * 5,10,12

Venture Capital Corporation of
    New Mexico
5301 Central Avenue, NE, Suite
    1600
Albuquerque, New Mexico
    87108
(Ben Bronstein, Chairman)
    (505) 266–0066
B *** 12

NEW YORK
AMEV Capital Corporation
Two World Trade Center, #9766
New York, New York
    10048
(Martin S. Orland, President)
    (212) 775–1912
D *** 1,4,5,6,7,9,10,12

Amistad DOT Venture Capital,
    Inc.
801 Second Avenue, Suite 303
New York, New York 10017
(Percy E. Sutton, Chairman and
    President)
    (212) 573–6600
MESBIC C * 5,8,11

BanCap Corporation
155 E. 42nd Street
New York, New York 10017
(William L. Whitely, President)
    (212) 687–6470
MESBIC B *** 1,3,5,12

Beneficial Capital Corporation
645 Fifth Avenue
New York, New York 10022
(John J. Hoey, President)
    (212) 752–1291
A * 3,12

Bohlen Capital Corporation
230 Park Avenue
New York, New York 10169
(Harvey Wertheim, President)
    (212) 867–9535
D *** 1,3,5,6,8

Boston Hambro Corporation
    (Branch Office)
17 E. 71st Street
New York, New York 10021
(Edwin A. Goodman, President)
    (212) 288–7778
D * 1,2,3,5,6,8,12
(Main Office: MA)

BT Capital Corporation
280 Park Avenue
New York, New York 10017
(James G. Hellmuth, President)
    (212) 692–4840
D * 12

California Northwest Fund, Inc.
    (Branch Office)
230 Park Avenue, 3rd Floor
New York, New York 10017
(Yung Wong, Managing Director)
    (212) 935–0997
D * 12
(Main Office: CA)

Central New York SIBC, Inc.
351 S. Warren Street
Syracuse, New York 13202
(Robert E. Romig, President)
    (315) 478–5026
FULLY INVESTED

Citicorp Venture Capital, Ltd.
399 Park Avenue, 20th Floor
New York, New York 10043
(William T. Comfort, Chairman)
    (212) 559–1127
C *** 12

Clinton Capital Corporation
35 Middagh Street
Brooklyn, New York 11201
(Mark Scharfman, President)
    (212) 858–0920
C *** 12

CMNY Capital Company, Inc.
77 Water Street
New York, New York 10005
(Robert Davidoff, Vice-President)
    (212) 437–7078
B *** 1,5,6,7,8,9,10,12

College Venture Equity
    Corporation
P.O. Box 791
1222 Main Street
Niagara Falls, New York
    14301
(Francis M. Williams, President)
    (716) 285–8455
A * 12

Cornell Capital Corporation
8-B Main Street
East Hampton, New York 11937
(Barry M. Bloom, President)
    (516) 324–0408
D * 4,12

EAB Venture Corporation
90 Park Avenue
New York, New York 10016
(Richard C. Burcaw, President;
    Mark R. Littell, Vice-President
    and Treasurer)
    (212) 437–4182
C * 1,3,5,6,8,10,12

Edwards Capital Corporation
215 Lexington Avenue
New York, New York 10016
(Edward H. Teitelbaum,
    President)
    (212) 686–2568
B * 12

Engle Investment Company
    (Branch Office)
135 W. 50th Street
New York, New York 10020
(Murray Hendel, President)
    (212) 757–9580
A * 12
(Main Office: NJ)

Equico Capital Corporation
1211 Avenue of the Americas,
    Suite 2905
New York, New York 10020
(Carlos R. Evering, Executive
    Vice-President)
    (212) 921–2290
MESBIC C *** 12

Equitable SBIC
350 Fifth Avenue, Suite 5805
New York, New York 10118
(David Goldberg, President)
    (212) 564–5420
A * 6

ESIC Capital, Inc.
110 E. 59th Street
New York, New York 10022
(George H. Bookbinder,
    President)
    (212) 421–1605
C ** 12

European Development Capital
    Corporation
230 Park Avenue
New York, New York
    10169
(Harvey Wertheim, President)
    (212) 867–9535
D *** 1,3,5,6,8

Exim Capital Corporation
290 Madison Avenue
New York, New York
    10017
(Victor Chun, President)
    (212) 683–3200
MESBIC A *** 5

Fairfield Equity Corporation
200 E. 42nd Street
New York, New York 10017
(Matthew A. Berdon, President)
    (212) 867–0150
B *** 1,5,7,9,10,12

Fifty-Third Street Ventures, Inc.
1 E. 53rd Street
New York, New York 10023
(Alan J. Patricof, Chairman)
    (212) 753–6300
D *** 1,3,5,6,8,12

The First Connecticut SBIC
    (Branch Office)
680 Fifth Avenue
New York, New York 10019
(James Breiner, Chairman; David
    Engelson, President)
(Main Office: CT)

First Wall Street SBIC, Inc.
767 Fifth Avenue, Suite 4403
New York, New York 10153
(John W. Chappell, President)
    (212) 355–6540
A *** 3

The Franklin Corporation
1 Rockefeller Plaza
New York, New York
    10020
(Herman E. Goodman, President)
    (212) 581–4900
D *** 1,5,6,7,8,11,12
(Branch Office: NM)

Fundex Capital Corporation
525 Northern Boulevard
Great Neck, New York
    11021
(Howard Sommer, President)
    (516) 466–8550 or
    (212) 895–7361
C ** 12

Hanover Capital Corporation
233 E. 62nd Street
New York, New York 10021
(Daniel J. Sullivan, President)
    (212) 752–5173
B * 12

Heller Capital Services, Inc.
200 Park Avenue
New York, New York 10166
(Jack A. Prizzi, Executive Vice-
    President)
    (212) 880–7198
E * 1,3,5,6,7,8,9,11,12

Ibero-American Investors
    Corporation
954 Clifford Avenue
Rochester, New York 14621

(Emilio Serrano, General
    Manager)
    (716) 544–7420
MESBIC A *** 5,9,12

Intercoastal Capital Corporation
380 Madison Avenue
New York, New York 10017
(Herbert Krasnow, President)
    (212) 986–0482
D * 1,2,4,5,6,7,10,11,12

Intergroup Venture Capital
    Corporation
230 Park Avenue
New York, New York 10169
(Ben Hauben, President)
    (212) 661–5428
A * 12

International Film Investors, Inc.
595 Madison Avenue
New York, New York 10022
(Neil Braun, Vice-President-
    Finance)
    (212) 310–1500
E *** 7

Irving Capital Corporation
1290 Avenue of the Americas,
    3rd Floor
New York, New York 10019
(J. Andrew McWethy, Executive
    Vice-President)
    (212) 922–8790
E *** 1,3,5,8,9

Japanese American Capital
    Corporation
120 Broadway
New York, New York 10271
(Stephen Huang, President)
    (212) 964–4077
MESBIC B * 2,4,12

Korean Capital Corporation
222–48 Birmington Parkway
Bayside, New York 11364
(Min ja OH, President)
   (212) 224–5891
MESBIC C * 12

Lincoln Capital Corporation
41 E. 42nd Street, Suite 1510
New York, New York 10017
(Martin Lifton, President)
   (212) 697–0610
C * 2,12

Medallion Funding Corporation
86 Glen Cove Road
East Hills, New York
   11576
(Alvin Murstein, President)
   (212) 682–3300
MESBIC A * 11

Medallion Funding Corporation
   (Branch Office)
205 E. 42nd Street, Room 2020
New York, New York 10017
(Alvin Murstein, President)
   (212) 682–3300
MESBIC A * 11
(Main Office: NY)

Midland Capital Corporation
110 William Street
New York, New York 10038
(Michael R. Stanfield, Managing
   Director; Robert B. Machinist,
   Managing Director)
   (212) 577–0750
E * 1,3,12

Minority Equity Capital
   Company, Inc. (MECCO)
275 Madison Avenue, Suite 1901
New York, New York 10016

(Patrick Owen Burns, President)
   (212) 686–9710
MESBIC C * * * 1,5,6,9,12

M & T Capital Corporation
One M & T Plaza
Buffalo, New York 14240
(Harold M. Small, President)
   (716) 842–4881
C * * * 12

Multi-Purpose Capital
   Corporation
31 S. Broadway
Yonkers, New York
   10701
(Eli B. Fine, President)
   (914) 963–2733
A * 1,2,3,4,5,6,7,8,9,10,11,12

Nelson Capital Corporation
591 Stewart Avenue
Garden City, New York
   11530
(Irwin B. Nelson, President)
   (516) 222–2555
D * * 12
(Branch Offices: CA, IL)

New Oasis Capital Corporation
114 Liberty Street, Suite 404
New York, New York
   10006
(James J. H. Huang, President)
   (212) 394–2804/5
MESBIC B * 12

Noro Capital Corporation
230 Park Avenue
New York, New York
   10169
(Harvey Wertheim, President)
   (212) 867–9535
D * * * 1,3,5,6,8

North Street Capital Corporation
250 North Street, TA-2
White Plains, New York 10625
(Ralph L. McNeal, Sr., President)
    (914) 683–6306
MESBIC A *** 1,5,11,12

NYBDC Capital Corporation
41 State Street
Albany, New York 12209
(Marshall R. Lustig, President)
    (518) 463–2268
A *** 5

Pioneer Investors
113 E. 55th Street
New York, New York 10022
(James G. Niven, President)
    (212) 980–9090
C *** 1,3,5,6,8

Rand SBIC, Inc.
2600 Rand Building
Buffalo, New York 14203
(Donald A. Ross, President and
    CEO)
    (716) 853–0802
A * 12

Realty Growth Capital
    Corporation
575 Lexington Avenue
New York, New York 10022
(Lawrence A. Benenson,
    President)
    (212) 755–9044
A ** 11

Royal Business Funds
    Corporation
60 E. 42nd Street, Suite 2530
New York, New York 10165
(I. S. Goodman, Executive Vice-
    President)
    (212) 986–8463
E * 2,7

R & R Financial Corporation
1451 Broadway
New York, New York 10036
(Imre J. Rosenthal, President)
    (212) 790–1400
A * 12

Peter J. Schmitt Company, Inc.
678 Bailey Avenue
Buffalo, New York 14206
(Denis G. Riley, Manager)
    (716) 825–1111
A *** 5,8,9

Sherwood Business Capital
    Corporation
770 King Street
Port Chester, New York 10573
(Lewis R. Eisner, President)
    (914) 937–6000
B ** 12

Sherwood Business Capital
    Corporation (Branch Office)
230 Park Avenue
New York, New York 10169
(Lewis R. Eisner, President)
    (212) 661–2424
B ** 12

Small Business Electronics
    Investment Corporation
60 Broad Street
New York, New York 10004
(Stanley Meisels, President)
    (212) 952–7531
A ** 12

Southern Tier Capital
    Corporation
55 S. Main Street
Liberty, New York 12754
(Irving Brizel, President)
    (914) 292–3030
A * 2,4,9,12

Sprout Capital Corporation
140 Broadway
New York, New York 10005
(L. Robert Johnson, President)
   (212) 943-0300
D *** 1,3,5,6,8,9

Tappan Zee Capital Corporation
120 North Main Street
New City, New York 10956
(Jack Birnberg, Executive Vice-
   President)
   (914) 634-8890
C ** 12

Taroco Capital Corporation
120 Broadway
New York, New York 10271
(David Chang, President)
   (212) 964-4210
MESBIC B * 2,4,5,6,7,8,9,10

Telesciences Capital
   Corporation
135 E. 54th Street
New York, New York 10022
(George E. Carmody, President)
   (212) 935-2550
B *** 1,8

TLC Funding Corporation
200 E. 42nd Street
New York, New York 10017
(Philip G. Kass, President)
   (212) 682-0790
B ** 1,4,5,7,9,10,11

Transportation SBIC, Inc.
122 E. 42nd Street, 46th Floor
New York, New York 10168
(Melvin L. Hirsch, President)
   (212) 986-6050
MESBIC A ** 11

Van Rietschoten Capital
   Corporation

230 Park Avenue
New York, New York 10169
(Harvey Wertheim, President)
   (212) 867-9535
D *** 1,3,5,6,8

Vega Capital Corporation
10 E. 40th Street
New York, New York
   10016
(Victor Harz, President)
   (212) 685-8222
C * 12

Watchung Capital Corporation
111 Broadway, Room 2002
New York, New York 10006
(Thomas S. T. Jeng, President)
   (212) 227-4597
MESBIC A * 2,4

Winfield Capital Corporation
237 Mamaroneck Avenue
White Plains, New York
   10605
(Stan Pechman, President)
   (914) 949-2600
C * 12

Wood River Capital Corporation
767 Fifth Avenue, 27th Floor
New York, New York 10053
(Richard M. Drysdale, President)
   (212) 750-9420
D *** 1,5,6,8,12

NORTH CAROLINA
Delta Capital, Inc.
202 Latta Arcade
320 S. Tryon Street
Charlotte, North Carolina
   28202
(Alex Wilkins, President)
   (704) 372-1410
C *** 12

Heritage Capital Corporation
2290 First Union Plaza
Charlotte, North Carolina 28282
(J. Randolph Gregory, President)
    (704) 334–2867
C *** 12

Kitty Hawk Capital, Ltd.
2195 First Union Plaza
Charlotte, North Carolina 28282
(Walter Wilkinson, President)
    (704) 333–3777
B *** 1,5,6,9,12

Vanguard Investment Company,
Inc.
309 Pepper Building
Winston-Salem, North Carolina
27101
(James F. Hansley, President)
    (919) 724–3676
MESBIC B * 1,5,6,11,12

NORTH DAKOTA
First Dakota Capital Corporation
52 Broadway
Fargo, North Dakota 58102
(David L. Johnson, Vice-
    President)
    (701) 237–0450
A *** 12

OHIO
Clarion Capital Corporation
The Chesterfield
1801 E. 12th Street, Room 201
Cleveland, Ohio 44114
(Peter Van Oosterhout,
    President)
    (216) 687–1096
D *** 2,3,5,12

Dycap, Inc.
88 E. Broad Street, Suite 1980
Columbus, Ohio 43215

(A. Gordon Imhoff, President)
    (614) 228–6641
A * 1,3,6,12

Glenco Enterprises, Inc.
1464 E. 105th Street
Cleveland, Ohio 44106
(Lewis F. Wright, Jr., Vice-
    President)
    (216) 721–1200
MESBIC A *** 12

Greater Miami Investment
    Service, Inc.
3131 S. Dixie Drive, Suite 505
Dayton, Ohio 45439
(Emmett B. Lewis, President)
    (513) 294–6124
A *** 5,8

Gries Investment Company
2310 Terminal Tower Building
Cleveland, Ohio 44113
(Robert D. Gries, President)
    (216) 861–1146
B *** 12

Intercapco, Inc.
One Erieview Plaza
Cleveland, Ohio 44114
(Robert B. Haas, Executive Vice-
    President)
    (216) 241–7170
C *** 12

National City Capital
    Corporation
National City Center
1900 E. Ninth Street
Cleveland, Ohio 44114
(Michael Sherwin, President)
    (216) 575–2491
C *** 12

Tamco Investors SBIC, Inc.
P.O. Box 1588

375 Victoria Road
Youngstown, Ohio 44501
(Nathan H. Monus, President)
    (216) 792–3811
A * 9

Tomlinson Capital Corporation
3055 E. 63rd Street
Cleveland, Ohio 44127
(Donald R. Calkins, Vice-
    President)
    (216) 271–2103
A *** 12

OKLAHOMA

Alliance Business Investment
    Company
500 McFarlin Building
11 E. 5th Street
Tulsa, Oklahoma 74103
(Barry M. Davis, President)
    (918) 584–3581
C *** 3,5,11,12
(Branch office: TX)

Bartlesville Investment
    Corporation
P.O. Box 548
Bartlesville, Oklahoma
    74003
(J. L. Diamond, President)
    (918) 333–3022
A *** 2,3,12

First Oklahoma Investment
    Capital Corporation
P.O. Box 25189
Oklahoma City, Oklahoma
    73125
(Gary Bunch, Sr., Vice-President)
    (405) 272–4338
B *** 12

Investment Capital, Inc.
P.O. Box 1071

300 N. Harrison
Cushing, Oklahoma 74023
(James J. Wasson, President)
    (918) 225–5850
B * 12

Oklahoma Capital Corporation
2200 Classen Boulevard,
    Suite 540
Oklahoma City, Oklahoma
    73106
(William T. Daniel, Chairman)
    (405) 525–5544
A * 6

Southwest Venture Capital,
    Inc.
1920 First Place
Tulsa, Oklahoma 74103
(D. J. Rubottom, President)
    (918) 583–4663
A * 8,11,12

Utica Investment Corporation
1924 S. Utica
Tulsa, Oklahoma 74104
(David D. Nunneley, President)
    (918) 749–9976
A *** 12

OREGON

Cascade Capital Corporation
    (Branch Office)
3018 First National Tower
1300 S.W. 5th Avenue
Portland, Oregon
    97201
(Wayne B. Kingsley, Vice-
    President)
    (503) 223–6622
D *** 12
(Main Office: Northwest Growth
    Fund, Inc., MN)

Northern Pacific Capital
   Corporation
P.O. Box 1530
Portland, Oregon 97207
(John J. Tennant, Jr., President)
   (503) 245–3147
B *** 5,11

Washington Capital Corporation
   (Branch Office)
1335 S.W. Fifth Avenue
Portland, Oregon 97201
   (503) 243–1850
D * 12
(Main Office: WA)

PENNSYLVANIA

Alliance Enterprise Corporation
2000 Market Street, 2nd Floor
Philadelphia, Pennsylvania
   19103
(Richard H. Cummings, Jr.,
   President)
   (215) 972–4230
MESBIC B *** 1,5

American Venture Capital
   Company
Blue Bell W, Suite 122
Blue Bell, Pennsylvania
   19422
(Knute C. Albrecht, President)
   (215) 278–8905
B *** 12

Central Capital Corporation
P.O. Box 3959
1097 Commercial Avenue
Lancaster, Pennsylvania
   17604
(Robert A. Rupel, Vice-President)
   (717) 569–9650
B * 12

Greater Philadelphia Venture
   Capital Corporation, Inc.
225 S. 15th Street, Suite 920
Philadelphia, Pennsylvania
   19102
(Wilson E. DeWald, Vice-
   President)
   (215) 732–3415
MESBIC B *** 12

Osher Capital Corporation
Wyncote House
Township Line Road and
   Washington Lane
Wyncote, Pennsylvania
   19095
(L. Cantor, President)
   (215) 624–4800
C *** 5,6,8,9,10,12

TDH Capital Corporation
P.O. Box 234
Two Radnor Corporate Center
Radnor, Pennsylvania 19087
(J. Mahlon Buck, Jr., President)
   (215) 297–9787
C *** 12

PUERTO RICO

CREDI-I-F.A.C., Inc.
Banco Cooperativo Plaza, Suite
   1001
Avenue Ponce de Leon #623
Hato Rey, Puerto Rico 00917
(Manuel L. Prats, Investment
   Advisor)
   (809) 765–0070
MESBIC A * 12

First Puerto Rico Capital, Inc.
P.O. Box 816
52 McKinley Street
Mayaguez, Puerto Rico 00708

(Eliseo E. Font, President)
     (809) 832–9171
MESBIC B ** 12

North America Investment
   Corporation
P.O. Box 1831
Hato Rey, Puerto Rico 00918
(Santiago Ruiz Betancourt,
   President)
     (809) 754–6177
MESBIC B * 1,5,9,12

Venture Capital Puerto Rico, Inc.
Banco Cooperativo, Suite 602
Hato Rey, Puerto Rico 00917
(Manuel L. Prats, President)
     (809) 751–8040 or
     (809) 751–8138
MESBIC A * 12

RHODE ISLAND
Industrial Capital Corporation
111 Westminster Street
Providence, Rhode Island 02903
(A. A. T. Wickersham, President)
     (401) 278–6770
C *** 12

Narragansett Capital
   Corporation
40 Westminster Street
Providence, Rhode Island
   02903
(Arthur D. Little, Chairman)
     (401) 751–1000
E *** 1,5,6,12

SOUTH CAROLINA
Carolina Venture Capital
   Corporation
P.O. Box 3110
Hilton Head Island, South
   Carolina 29928

(Thomas H. Harvey III, President)
     (803) 842–3101
B * 1,2,4,7,8,12

Charleston Capital Corporation
P.O. Box 30895
Charleston, South Carolina
   29407
(I. J. Futeral, Vice-President)
     (803) 723–6464
A *** 2,9,10

Reedy River Ventures
P.O. Box 8931
Greenville, South Carolina
   29604
(John M. Sterling, President)
     (803) 233–2374
B *** 12

TENNESSEE
Chickasaw Capital Corporation
P.O. Box 387
67 Madison
Memphis, Tennessee 38147
(Wayne J. Haskins, President)
     (901) 523–6404
MESBIC A ** 12

C & C Capital Corporation
531 S. Gay Street, 14th Floor
Knoxville, Tennessee
   37901
(T. Wendell Holliday, President)
     (615) 637–0521
A *** 12

Financial Resources, Inc.
Sterick Building, Suite 2800
Memphis, Tennessee 38103
(Milton C. Picard, Chairman)
     (901) 527–9411
A * 12

Tennessee Equity Capital
    Corporation
4515 Poplar Avenue, Suite 222
Memphis, Tennessee 38117
(Richard Kantor, President)
    (901) 761–3410
MESBIC E *** 12

TEXAS
Alliance Business Investment
    Company (Branch Office)
2660 South Tower, Pennzoil
    Place
Houston, Texas 77002
(Leon Davis, Chairman)
    (713) 224–8224
C *** 3,5,11,12
(Main Office: OK)

Allied Bancshares Capital
    Corporation
808 Travis
Houston, Texas 77002
(D. Kent Anderson, President)
    (713) 224–6611
C * 3,5,10,12

Bow Lane Capital Corporation
2411 Fountainview, Suite 250
Houston, Texas 77079
(Stuart Schube, President)
    (713) 977–8882
D *** 12

Brittany Capital Corporation
2424 LTV Tower
Dallas, Texas 75201
(Robert E. Clements, President)
    (214) 742–5810
A *** 1,3,6,8

Capital Marketing Corporation
P.O. Box 225293

9004 Ambassador Row
Dallas, Texas 75222
(Nathaniel Gibbs, Chairman)
    (214) 638–1913
D ** 9

CSC Capital Corporation
12900 Preston Road, Suite 700
Dallas, Texas 75230
(William R. Thomas, President)
    (214) 233–8242
C *** 1,3,5,6,7,8,9,11,12

Diman Financial Corporation
13601 Preston Road, 717E
Dallas, Texas 75240
(David S. Willis, President)
    (214) 233–7610
A * 2,3,5,8

Energy Assets, Inc.
1800 S. Tower Pennzoil Place
Houston, Texas 77002
(L. E. Simmons, Vice-President)
    (713) 236–9999
A * 3

Energy Capital Corporation
953 Esperson Building
Houston, Texas 77002
(Herbert F. Poyner, Jr., President)
    (713) 236–0006
E *** 3

First City Capital Corporation
One West Loop S., Suite 809
Houston, Texas 77027
(William E. Laden, President)
    (713) 623–6151
A *** 12

First Dallas Capital Corporation
P.O. Box 83385
Dallas, Texas 75283

(Eric C. Neuman, President)
(214) 744–8050
D *** 1,3,5,11

Great American Capital
  Investors
1006 Holliday
Wichita Falls, Texas 76301
(Albert Dillard, President)
(817) 322–5554
A *** 12

The Grocers SBIC
3131 E. Holcombe Boulevard
Houston, Texas 77021
(Milton Levit, President)
(713) 747–7913
A ** 9

Livingston Capital, Ltd.
5701 Woodway
Houston, Texas 77057
(J. Livingston Kosberg, President)
(713) 977–4040
D *** 12

Mapleleaf Capital Corporation
7500 San Felipe, Suite 100
Houston, Texas 77063
(Edward B. Scott, President)
(713) 975–8060
D ** 3,8

Mercantile Dallas Corporation
P.O. Box 222090
Dallas, Texas 75222
(J. Wayne Gaylord, Sr., Vice-
  President)
(214) 741–1469
E * 3,5,12

MESBIC Financial Corporation
  of Dallas
7701 N. Stemmons Freeway,
  Suite 850

Dallas, Texas 75247
(Walter W. Durham, President)
(214) 637–0445
MESBIC C *** 12

MESBIC Financial Corporation
  of Houston
717 Travis, Suite 600
Houston, Texas 77061
(Richard Rothfeld, President)
(713) 228–8321
MESBIC B * 12

MESBIC of San Antonio, Inc.
2300 W. Commerce
San Antonio, Texas 78207
(William A. Fagan, Jr.)
(512) 225–4241
MESBIC A *** 1,4,5,11

Permian Basin Capital
  Corporation
P.O. Box 1599
303 W. Wall
Midland, Texas 79702
(Douglas B. Henson, President)
(915) 685–2000
A *** 5,12

Rainbow Capital Corporation
1470 One Allen Center
Houston, Texas 77002
(W. A. Anderson, Jr., President)
(713) 757–0461
A * 2,3,5,11

Red River Ventures, Inc.
2050 Houston Natural Gas
  Building
Houston, Texas 77002
(Thomas H. Schnitzius,
  President)
(713) 658–9806
B *** 1,3,5,6

Republic Venture Group, Inc.
P.O. Box 225961
Dallas, Texas 75265
(Robert H. Wellborn, Vice-
   President)
      (214) 653–5078
D *** 12

Retail Capital Corporation
13403 Northwest Freeway, Suite
   160
Houston, Texas 77040
(William J. Boschma, President)
      (713) 462–8517
A ** 9

Rice Country Capital, Inc.
P.O. Box 215
100 Commerce
Eagle Lake, Texas 77434
(William H. Harrison, Jr.,
   President)
      (713) 234–2506
A * 12

Rust Capital, Ltd.
605 Brazos, Suite 300
Austin, Texas 78701
(Jeffrey C. Garvey, Executive
   Vice-President)
      (512) 479–0055
C * 1,5,12

San Antonio Venture Group, Inc.
2300 W. Commerce
San Antonio, Texas 78207
(William A. Fagan, Jr., President)
      (512) 223–3633
A *** 1,3,4,5,6,11

Southwestern Venture Capital of
   Texas, Inc.
113 S. River Street
La Plaza Building, Suite 108

Seguin, Texas 78155
(J. A. Bettersworth, President)
      (512) 379–2258
B * 2,3,5,12

Texas Capital Corporation
2424 Houston Natural Gas
   Building
Houston, Texas 77002
(W. Grogan Lord, Chairman)
      (713) 658–9961
C *** 12

Trammell Crow Investment
   Company
2001 Bryan Tower, #3900
Dallas, Texas 75201
(Henry Billingsley, President)
      (214) 747–0643
A ** 2

TSM Corporation
444 Executive Center Boulevard,
   Suite 237
El Paso, Texas 79902
(Joe Justice)
      (915) 533–6375
A * 12

West Central Capital
   Corporation
440 Northlake Center, Suite 206
Dallas, Texas 75238
(Howard W. Jacob, President)
      (214) 348–3969
A *** 2,4,5,6,12

Zenith Capital Corporation
5150 Shepherd, Suite 218
Houston, Texas 77018
(Andrew L. Johnston, Secretary-
   Treasurer)
      (713) 692–6121
A * 12

VERMONT
Mansfield Capital Corporation
Box 986
Mountain Road
Stowe, Vermont 05672
(Stephen H. Farrington,
    President)
    (802) 253–9400
A * 2,9,11,12

Vermont Investment Capital,
    Inc.
Route 14, Box 84
South Royalton, Vermont 05068
(Harold Jacobs, President)
    (802) 763–8878
A * 12

VIRGINIA
East West United Investment
    Company
6723 Whittier Avenue,
    Suite 206-B
McLean, Virginia 22101
(Doug Bui, President)
    (703) 821–6616
MESBIC A ** 4,12

Inverness Capital Corporation
424 N. Washington Street
Alexandria, Virginia 22314
(Harry Flemming, President)
    (703) 549–5730
C *** 12

Metropolitan Capital
    Corporation
2550 Huntington Avenue
Alexandria, Virginia
    22193
(Fred Scoville, President)
    (703) 960–4698
A *** 12

Norfolk Investment Company,
    Inc.
201 Granby Mall Building, Suite
    515
Norfolk, Virginia 23510
(Kirk W. Saunders, President)
    (804) 623–1042
MESBIC B * 5,9,12

Tidewater Small Business
    Investment Corporation
1106 Maritime Tower
234 Monticello Avenue
Norfolk, Virginia 23510
(Robert H. Schmidt, Chairman)
    (804) 627–2315
B ** 5

Virginia Capital Corporation
P.O. Box 1493
Richmond, Virginia
    23212
(Robert H. Pratt, President)
    (804) 644–5496
B *** 12

WASHINGTON
Capital Resource Corporation
1001 Logan Building
Seattle, Washington 98101
(Theodore M. Wight, General
    Manager)
    (206) 623–6550
D *** 1,5,6,7,8,12

Northwest Capital Investment
    Corporation
P.O. Box 3500
1940 116th Avenue, NE
Bellevue, Washington 98009
(Dale H. Zeigler, President)
    (206) 455–3049
D *** 12

Seafirst Capital Corporation
Fourth and Blanchard Building
Seattle, Washington 98121
(Steven G. Blanchard, Vice-
  President and General
  Manager)
  (206) 583-3278
C * 5,9

Washington Capital Corporation
1417 Fourth Avenue
Seattle, Washington 98101
(James F. Aylward, President;
  David A. Kohls, Vice-
  President)
  (206) 682-5400
D * 12
(Branch Offices: OR, CA, WA)

Washington Capital Corporation
  (Branch Office)
North 920 Washington
Spokane, Washington 99201
  (509) 326-6940
D * 12
(Main Office: WA)

Washington Trust Equity
  Corporation
Washington Trust Financial
  Center
Spokane, Washington 99210
(Alan Bradley, President)
  (509) 455-4106
C * 12

WISCONSIN
R. W. Allsop Capital Corporation
  (Branch Office)
P.O. Box 1368
815 E. Mason Street, Suite 1501
Milwaukee, Wisconsin
  53201

(Gregory B. Bultman)
  (414) 271-6510
D *** 1,5,6,12
(Main Office: IA)

Bando-McGlocklin Investment
  Company, Inc.
13555 Bishops Court, Suite 225
Brookfield, Wisconsin 53005
(Salvatore L. Bando, President)
  (414) 784-9010
B ** 5,9

CERTO Capital Corporation
6150 McKee Road
Madison, Wisconsin 53711
(Howard E. Hill, President)
  (608) 271-4500
A ** 9

MorAmerica Capital
  Corporation (Branch Office)
710 N. Plankinton Avenue, Suite
  333
Milwaukee, Wisconsin
  53203
(H. Wayne Foreman, Regional
  Vice-President)
  (414) 276-3839
D *** 12
(Main Office: IA)

SC Opportunities, Inc.
1112 7th Avenue
Monroe, Wisconsin 53566
(Robert L. Ableman, Vice-
  President and Secretary)
  (608) 325-3134
MESBIC A *** 9

77 Capital Corporation
3060 First Wisconsin Center
777 E. Wisconsin Avenue
Milwaukee, Wisconsin 53202

(Sheldon B. Lubar, President)
    (414) 291–9000
C * 3,5,8,12

Super Market Investors, Inc.
P.O. Box 473
Milwaukee, Wisconsin 53201
(John W. Andorfer, President)
    (414) 453–8200
A ** 9

WYOMING

Capital Corporation of
    Wyoming, Inc.
P.O. Box 612
145 S. Durbin, Suite 201
Casper, Wyoming 82602
(Larry McDonald, Executive
    Vice-President)
    (307) 234–5438
A * 12

Additional information is available by writing to the National Association of SBICs at 618 Washington Building, Washington, D.C. 20005 or calling (202) 638–3411.

Bear in mind that most SBICs are small and will not take over a $1 million financing singlehandedly. Most loans in their portfolio are in the $100,000 to $300,000 range. However, larger sums can be obtained through syndicated deals where one SBIC acts as the "lead investor" and convinces other SBICs to invest along with it. This way, the borrower can raise several millions of dollars. Explore this approach with the SBICs you contact.

A special group of SBICs, called Minority Enterprise Small Business Investment Companies, provide debt and equity financing for small firms that are at least 51 percent owned by socially or economically disadvantaged people. The following are members of the American Association of Minority Enterprise Small Business Investment Companies.

ALABAMA

First Alabama Capital
    Corporation
3201 Dauphin Street, Suite B
Mobile, Alabama 36606
(David C. DeLaney, President)
    (205) 476–0700

ARKANSAS

Capital Management Services,
    Inc.
4801 North Hills Boulevard
North Little Rock, Arkansas
    72116
(David Loy Hales, President and
    General Manager)
    (501) 758–4553

Kar-Mal Venture Capital, Inc.
Plaza W. Office Building, Suite 610
Little Rock, Arkansas 72205
(Thomas Karam, President)
(501) 661–0010

CALIFORNIA

Asian American Capital Corporation
1191 West Tennyson Road, Suite 5
Hayward, California 94546
(John F. Louie, General Manager)
(916) 444–6778

Associates Venture Capital Corporation
632 Kearney Street
San Francisco, California 94108
(Walter Strycker, Vice President)
(415) 397–0351

Bay Area Western Venture Capital Group, Inc.
383 Diablo Road, Suite 100
Danville, California 94526
(Jack Wong, President)
(415) 820–8079

Beauham Minority Investment Corporation
2 Commercial Boulevard
Novato, California 94947
(Gerald E. Webb, President)
(415) 479–4310

Business Equity & Development Corporation
1411 West Olympic Boulevard
Los Angeles, California 90015
(Ricardo J. Olivarez, President)
(213) 385–0351

Equitable Capital Corporation
419 Columbus Avenue
San Francisco, California 94133
(John C. Lee, President)
(415) 982–4028

First California Business and Development Corporation
3901 MacArthur Boulevard, Suite 101
Newport Beach, California 92660
(Leslie R. Brewer, President)
(714) 851–0855

HUB Enterprises, Ltd.
5874 Doyle Street
Emeryville, California 94608
(Richard Magary, General Manager)
(415) 653–5707

Lucky Star Investment Company
677 Grant Avenue
San Francisco, California 94108
(Sinclair Louie, President)
(415) 397–8272

MCA New Ventures, Inc.
100 Universal City Plaza, Room 5073H
Universal City, California 91608
(Robert Braswell, President)
(213) 508–2937

Milestone Capital Corporation
5401 Mission Street
San Francisco, California 94112
(Zoilo R. Inacay, President)
(415) 586–5702

Minority Enterprise Funding, Inc.
7171 Patterson Drive
Garden Grove, California 92641
(Howard D. Balshan, President)

Myriad Capital, Inc.
8820 Sepulveda Boulevard, #109
Los Angeles, California 90045
(Chuang Lin, President)
   (213) 641–7936

Opportunity Capital Corporation
   of California
100 California Street, Suite 714
San Francisco, California 94111
(Peter Thompson, President)
   (415) 421–5935

Pacific Capital Fund, Inc.
500 Airport Boulevard, #400
Burlingame, California 94010
(Victor H. Gallego, President)
   (405) 342–0748

Positive Enterprise, Inc.
399 Arguello Street
San Francisco, California 94118
(Kwork Szeto, President)
   (415) 386–6600

Sam Woong Investment
   Company
1625 West Olympic Boulevard,
   Suite 1007
Los Angeles, California 90037
(Masoa Aoki, President)
   (213) 232–5194

Solid Capital Corporation
652 Kearney Street, 1 & 2
San Francisco, California 94108
(Kirby Kwok, President)
   (415) 434–3371

Sun Capital Corporation
3360 Geary Boulevard, Suite 304
San Francisco, California
   94118
(John Sun, President)
   (415) 751–6868

TELACU Investment Company,
   Inc.
1330 South Atlantic Boulevard
Los Angeles, California 90022
(Gill Padilla, President)
   (213) 268–6745

Unity Capital Corporation
3620 30th Street, #B
San Diego, California 92104
(Frank W. Owen, President)
   (714) 295–6768

YFY Capital Corporation
533 Jackson Street
San Francisco, California 94133
(Richard Lim, President)
   (415) 433–5346

Yosemite Capital Investment
   Company
448 Fresno Street
Fresno, California 93706
(J. Horace Hampton, President)
   (209) 485–2430

CONNECTICUT
Cominvest of Hartford, Inc.
18 Asylum Street
Hartford, Connecticut 06103
(Vern Mendez, General Manager)
   (202) 246–7259

DISTRICT OF COLUMBIA
Broadcast Capital, Inc.
1771 N Street, N.W., Suite 420
Washington, D.C. 20036
(Samuel Ewing, Jr., President)
   (202) 293–3574

Continental Investors
2020 K Street, N.W., Suite 350
Washington, D.C. 20006
(Lac Thantrong, President)
   (202) 466–3709

D.C. Investment Company
1420 NY Avenue, N.W., 3rd
    Floor
Washington, D.C. 20005
(Abe Beaton, Vice-President)
    (202) 628–0303

Fulcrum Venture Capital
    Corporation
2021 K Street, N.W., Suite 701
Washington, D.C. 20006
(Stephen L. Lilly, President)
    (202) 833–9580

Minority Broadcast Investment
    Company
1220 19th Street, N.W., Suite 501
Washington, D.C. 20036
(Walter Threadgill, President)
    (202) 293–2977

SYNCOM Capital Corporation
1625 Eye Street, N.W.
Washington, D.C. 20006
(Herbert P. Wilkins, President)
    (202) 293–9428

FLORIDA

Allied Investment Developers,
    Inc.
9999 N. E. 2nd Avenue, Room
    304
Miami Shores, Florida 33138
(Robert V. Milberg, President)

Broward Venture Capital
660 South Federal Highway,
    Suite 300
Pompano Beach, Florida 33062
(William Lackey, President)
    (305) 463–3399

CUBICO Limited, Inc.
7425 N. W. 79th Street
Miami, Florida 33166

(Anthony G. Marina, President)
    (305) 885–8881

FEYCA Investment Company
1830 N. W. 7th Street
Miami, Florida 33127
(Felipe de Diego, President)
    (305) 643–1822

First American Lending Bank of
    Palm Beach County
1200 North Dixie Highway
Lake Worth, Florida 33460
(Robert J. Zammit, President)
    (305) 582–3322

First BDJ Financial Service
4747 Worth Ocean Boulevard,
    #215
Ft. Lauderdale, Florida 33308
(John Rhodes, President)
    (305) 782–9494

Jets Venture Capital
2721 Park Street
Jacksonville, Florida 32205
(Larry Barnett, President)
    (904) 384–3477

Metro Capital Corporation
5403 Aloha Place
Holiday, Florida 33590
(Harris E. Long, President)
    (813) 938–2851

SAFECO Capital Corporation
8770 S. W. 8th Street
Miami, Florida 33174
(Rene J. Leonard, President)
    (305) 551–0809

Universal Financial Services
225 N.E. 35th Street
Miami, Florida 33137
(Norman Zipkin, President)
    (305) 573–6326

Venture Opportunities
  Corporation
444 Brickel Avenue, Suite 750
Miami, Florida 33131
(A. Fred March, President)
  (305) 358–5800

Verde Capital Corporation
6701 Sunset Drive, Suite 104
South Miami, Florida 33143
(Jose Dearing, President)
  (305) 666–0195

GEORGIA
Sun Belt Funding Corporation
P.O. Box 7006
2720 Riverside Drive
Macon, Georgia 31298
(Charles H. Jones, President)
  (912) 742–0177

HAWAII
Pacific Venture Capital, Ltd.
1505 Dillingham Boulevard
Honolulu, Hawaii 96817
(Dexter Taniguchi, President)
  (808) 847–6502

ILLINOIS
AMOCO Venture Capital
  Company
200 E. Randolph Drive
Chicago, Illinois 60601
(Gordon Stone, President)
  (312) 856–6523

CEDCO Capital Corporation
180 North Michigan Avenue
Chicago, Illinois 60601
(Frank B. Brooks, President)
  (312) 984–5950

Chicago Community Ventures,
  Inc.

108 North State Street, Suite 902
Chicago, Illinois 60602
(Phyllis George, Vice-President)
  (312) 726–6084

Combined Opportunties, Inc.
300 North State Street
Chicago, Illinois 60610
(Peter H. Ross, Vice-President)
  (312) 266–3091

The Neighborhood Fund, Inc.
1950 East 71st Street
Chicago, Illinois 60610
(James Fletcher, President)
  (312) 684–8074

The Urban Fund of Illinois
300 North State Street
Chicago, Illinois 60610
(E. Patrick Jones, President)
  (312) 266–3050

Tower Ventures, Inc.
Sears Tower, BSC 9–29
Chicago, Illinois 60684
(Robert Comey, Vice-President
  and General Manager)
  (312) 875–0583

KANSAS
Central Systems Equity
  Corporation
350 West Douglas
Wichita, Kansas 67202
(Clarence E. Wesley, President)
  (316) 265–7771

KENTUCKY
Equal Opportunity Finance, Inc.
P.O. Box 1915
Louisville, Kentucky 40201
(Franklin Justice, Jr., Vice-
  President)
  (606) 329–3333

LOUISIANA
Business Capital Corporation
1732 Canal Street
New Orleans, Louisiana
    70112
(David R. Burrus, President)
    (504) 581–4002

Edict Investment Corporation
2908 S. Carrollton Avenue
New Orleans, Louisiana 70118
(Roger Morin, President)
    (504) 861–2364

Louisiana Venture Capital
    Corporation
315 North Street
Natchitoches, Louisiana 71457
(Ben D. Johnson, President)
    (318) 352–4404

NIA
Century Venture Capital
    Corporation
c/o Doley Securities
616 Baronne Street, Suite 720
New Orleans, Louisiana 70113
(Harold Doley, Jr., Vice-
    President)
    (504) 561–1128

SCDF Investment Corporation
1006 Surrey Street
Lafayette, Louisiana
    70501
(Albert McKnight, President)
    (318) 232–9206

MARYLAND
Albright Venture Capital, Inc.
8005 Rappahannock Avenue
Jessup, Maryland 20794
(William A. Albright, President)
    (301) 490–4441

MASSACHUSETTS
Massachusetts Venture Capital
    Company
59 Temple Place
Boston, Massachusetts 02111
(Charles T. Grigsby, President)
    (617) 426-0208

WCCI Capital Corporation
791 Main Street
Worcester, Massachusetts 02111
(George R. Sherwin, President)
    (617) 791–3259

MICHIGAN
Dearborn Capital Corporation
P.O. Box 1729
Dearborn, Michigan 48121
(R.C. Chambers, President)
    (313) 337-8577

Inner City Capital Access
    Center, Inc.
1505 Woodward Avenue, 7th
    Floor
Detroit, Michigan 48202
(Walter McMurtry, President)
    (313) 961–2470

Independence Capital Formation,
    Inc.
1505 Woodward Avenue, 7th
    Floor
Detroit, Michigan 48202
(Walter M. McMurtry, Jr.,
    President)
    (313) 961–2470

Metro Detroit Investment
    Company
18481 West Ten Mile Road, Suite
    202
Southfield, Michigan
    48075

(William Fowler, President)
    (313) 557–3818

Motor Enterprises, Inc.
6–248 General Motors Building
3044 Grand Boulevard
Detroit, Michigan 48226
(James Kobus, Manager)
    (313) 566–4273

Mutual Investment Company, Inc.
17348 North 12 Mile Road
Southfield, Michigan 48076
(Jack Najor, President)
    (313) 552–8515

Pooled Resources Investing in Minority Enterprises, Inc.
1845 David Whitney Building
Detroit, Michigan 48226
(Jimmy Hill, President)
    (313) 964–3380

MINNESOTA
Control Data Community Ventures, Inc.
8100 34th Avenue, South, 13th Floor
Bloomington, Minnesota 55440
(Philip Bifulk, Vice-President)
    (612) 853–5114

MISSISSIPPI
Sun Delta Capital Access Center, Inc.
P.O. Box 588
819 Main Street
Greenville, Mississippi 38701
(Charles Bannerman, President)
    (601) 335–5291

NEBRASKA
Community Equity Corporation of Nebraska

5620 Ames Avenue, Room 109
Omaha, Nebraska 68104
(Herbert Patten, President)
    (402) 455–7722

NEW JERSEY
Rutgers Minority Investment Company
Ackerson Hall, 3rd Floor
180 University Avenue
Newark, New Jersey 07102
(Louis German, President)
    (201) 648-5621/27

NEW MEXICO
Associated Southwest Investors, Inc.
2425 Alamo, Southeast
Albuquerque, New Mexico 87106
(John Rice, General Manager)
    (505) 842–5955

NEW YORK
American Asian Capital Corporation
79 Wall Street, Room 907
New York, New York 10005
(Howard H. Lin, President)
    (212) 422–6880

Amistad DOT Venture Capital, Inc.
801 Second Avenue
New York, New York 10017
(Percy E. Sutton, President)
    (212) 573–6600

BanCap Corporation
155 East 42nd Street, Suite 305
New York, New York 10017
(William L. Whitely, President)
    (212) 687–6470

Brooklyn Capital Corporation
1476 39th Street
Brooklyn, New York
   11218
(Isaac Raitport, President)
   (212) 436–1803

CEDC MESBIC, Inc.
106 Main Street
Hempstead, New York
   11550
(John L. Kearse, President)
   (516) 292–9710

CVC Capital Corporation
666 Fifth Avenue
New York, New York 10019
(Joerg G. Klebe, President)
   (202) 246–1980

Capital Investment and
   Management Corporation
3 Pell Street, Suite 300
New York, New York 10013
(Rose Chal, Manager)
   (212) 964–2480

Cohen Capital Corporation
8 East 36th Street
New York, New York 10016
(Edward H. Cohen, President)
   (212) 689–9030

Equico Capital Corporation
1290 Avenue of the Americas,
   Suite 3400
New York, New York 10036
(Duane E. Hill, President)
   (212) 554–4090

Exim Capital Corporation
290 Madison Avenue
New York, New York 10017
(Victor Chun, President)
   (202) 679–5036

HBR Capital Corporation
1775 Broadway
New York, New York 10019
(Eric Boswell, Manager)
   (212) 247–8040

Hop Chung Capital Investment,
   Inc.
21 Mott Street
New York, New York 10013
(Brock Lee Hor, Manager)
   (212) 267–2727

Ibero American Investors
   Corporation
Chamber of Commerce Building
55 Saint Paul Street
Rochester, New York 14604
(Domingo Garcia, President)
   (716) 262–3440

Intergroup Funding Corporation
230 Park Avenue, Suite 206
New York, New York 10169
(Ben Hauber, President)
   (212) 661–5428

Japanese American Capital
   Corporation
120 Broadway
New York, New York 10271
(Stephen C. Huang, President)
   (212) 964–4077

King Small Business Investment
   Corporation
4444 River Road
Tonawanda, New York
   14150
(Neil Ritz, President)
   (716) 875–1833

Korean Capital Corporation
222–48 Birmington Parkway
Bayside, New York 11364

(Minja Oh, President)
(212) 224–5891

Medallion Funding Corporation
86 Glencove Road
East Hill, New York 11577
(Alvin Mustein, President)
(516) 621–4336

Merit Funding, Inc.
One Battery Park Plaza
New York, New York 10004
(Roger Cohen, President)
(212) 344–6254

Minority Equity Capital
Company, Inc.
275 Madison Avenue, Suite 1901
New York, New York 10016
(Patrick Owen Burns, President)
(212) 686–9710

New Oasis Capital Corporation
114 Liberty Street
New York, New York 10006
(James Haung, President)
(212) 349–2804

North American Funding
Corporation
177 Canal Street
New York, New York 10013
(Franklyn Wong, Vice-President
and General Manager)
(212) 266–0080

North Street Capital Corporation
250 North Street
White Plains, New York 10625
(Ralph McNeal, President)
(914) 683–6306

ODA Capital Corporation
82 Lee Avenue
Brooklyn, New York 11211

(Phillip Klein, Executive
Director)
(212) 963–0604

Pan Pac Capital Corporation
195 Hudson Street
New York, New York 10013
(In Ping Jack Lee, President)
(212) 966–2296

Pierre Funding Corporation
270 Madison Avenue, #1608
New York, New York 10017
(Elias Debbas, President)
(212) 689–9361

Rainbow Bridge Capital
Corporation
4544 19th Street
Flushing, New York 11358
(Baldwin T. Ching, President)
(212) 357–5062

Situation Ventures Corporation
502 Flushing Avenue
Brooklyn, New York 11205
(Sam Hollander, President)
(212) 855–1835

Square Deal Venture Capital
Lincoln Corner, Jefferson Avenue
New Square, New York 10977
(Victor Ostricher, President)
(212) 964–6877

Transportation SBIC, Inc.
34 Wendwood Drive
Glenhead, New York 11545
(Melvin L. Hirsh, President)
(212) 986–6050

Watchung Capital Corporation
111 Broadway, Room 2002
New York, New York 10006
(Thomas S.T. Jeng, President)
(212) 227–4597

NORTH CAROLINA
Vanguard Investment Company,
   Inc.
Pepper Building, Suite 305
Fourth and Liberty Streets
Winston-Salem, North Carolina
   27101
(James F. Hansley, President)
   (919) 724-3676

OHIO
Center City Minority Enterprise
   Investment Company
40 South Main Street
Dayton, Ohio 45402
(Claude Patmon, General
   Manager)
   (513) 461-6164

Glenco Enterprises, Inc.
1464 E. 105th Street, Suite 101
Cleveland, Ohio 44106
(Lewis Wright, Vice-President)
   (216) 721-1200

PENNSYLVANIA
Alliance Enterprise Corporation
2000 Market Street, 2nd Floor
Philadelphia, Pennsylvania
   19103
(Richard Cummings, President)
   (215) 972-4230

Greater Philadelphia Venture
   Capital Corporation, Inc.
920 Lewis Tower Building
225 South Fifteenth Street
Philadelphia, Pennsylvania
   19102
(Wilson DeWald, General
   Manager)
   (215) 732-3415

PUERTO RICO
Credi-IFAC, Inc.
623 Ponce De Leon Avenue,
   Suite 1001
Hato Rey, Puerto Rico 00917
(Manuel L. Prats, Manager)
   (809) 765-0070

First Puerto Rico Capital, Inc.
54 West McKinley Street
Mayaguez, Puerto Rico 00708
(Eliseo E. Font, President)
   (809) 833-2929

North American Investment
   Corporation
P.O. Box 1831, Hato Rey Station
Hato Rey, Puerto Rico 00919
(Santiago Ruiz Bentacourt)
   (809) 754-6177

Venture Capital Puerto Rico, Inc.
Executive Building, Suite 1204
623 Ponce De Leon Avenue
Hato Rey, Puerto Rico 00917
(Manuel Prats, Manager)
   (809) 763-0581

TENNESSEE
Chickasaw Capital Corporation
P.O. Box 387
Memphis, Tennessee 33231
(Wayne Haskins, President)
   (901) 523-6404

Tennessee Equity Capital
   Corporation
4515 Poplar Avenue
Memphis, Tennessee 38117
(Richard Kantor, President)
   (615) 373-4502

Tennessee Venture Capital
107-4th Avenue, Room 622
Nashville, Tennessee 37219

(Wendle Knox, President)
   (615) 244–6935

TEXAS

MESBIC Financial Corporation
   of Dallas
7701 N. Stemmons Freeway,
   Suite 850
Dallas, Texas 75247
(Walter W. Durham, President)
   (214) 637–0445

MESBIC Financial Corporation
   of Houston
717 Travis, Suite 600
Houston, Texas 77002
(Richard Rothfeld, President)
   (713) 228–8321

MESBIC of San Antonio
2300 West Commerce Street
San Antonio, Texas 78207
(Juan Patlan, President)
   (512) 225–4241

Southern Orient Capital
   Corporation
2419 Fannin, Suite 200
Houston, Texas 77220
(Min H. Liang, President)
   (713) 225–3369

VIRGINIA

East West United Investment
   Company
6723 Whittier Avenue, Suite
   205B
McLean, Virginia 22101
(Doug Bui, Chairman)
   (703) 821–6616

Norfolk Investment Company,
   Inc.
515 Granby Mall Building
201 Granby Street
Norfolk, Virginia 23510
(Kirk Saunders, President)
   (804) 622–0013

Professional Capital Corporation
1121 Arlington Boulevard,
   Suite 56
Arlington, Virginia 22209
(Bentley V. Plummer, President)
   (703) 528–0302

WASHINGTON

MESBIC of Washington, Inc.
201 Broad Street
Seattle, Washington 98121
(Dale Durden, President)
   (206) 447–2900

WEST VIRGINIA

LICO MESBIC Investment
   Company
106½ South Fayette Street
Beckley, West Virginia 25801
(James A. Parker, General
   Manager)
   (304) 252–5942

WISCONSIN

SC Opportunities, Inc.
1112 Seventh Avenue
Monroe, Wisconsin 53566
(Robert Ableman, Vice-
   President)
   (608) 328–8400

13

Farmers home administration loans

Talk of lenders and investors always conjures up images of Wall Street, the nation's capital, and big-city banks. But the folks in rural America, located far from the major money centers, need financing, too. They need loans for everything from houses to grazing land. One credit agency—the Farmers Home Administration, or FmHA—addresses these needs, offering a smorgasbord of excellent loan and financing programs. If you think this is limited to money for feedstock or milking machines, think again. One FmHA program provides funds for nonfarm enterprises (on family farms), including camping and mining facilities, tennis courts, and riding stables.

Farmers Home Administration (FmHA) is the credit agency for agriculture and rural development throughout the United States.

The FmHA's history of financial and technical assistance in rural America goes back forty-five years. Today, the agency serves a broader purpose than the 1930s singular effort to make loans to Depression-stricken farm families. Although it is still a source of credit for building stronger family farms (in 1980 farm credit accounted for nearly one-half of all resources administered by the FmHA), the FmHA has created additional programs to benefit families and com-

156

munities throughout the rural population by helping to provide housing, modern water and sewer systems, essential community facilities, and job/economy programs designed to boost business and industry in those areas.

The localized financing system developed by the FmHA over the years is a major advantage to rural people. Approximately eight thousand permanent full-time employees direct FmHA resources from forty-six state offices, three hundred district offices, and more than eighteen hundred county offices serving every county in the country, as well as Guam, Puerto Rico, and the Virgin Islands.

FmHA loans and grants supplement the amount of credit and capital directly available from commercial lenders in rural areas. In most programs, the agency makes loans to qualified applicants who can find no other sources of financing at acceptable terms. The money loaned by the FmHA comes from collections on previous loans or from private investors through the sale of government securities. In guaranteed loan-making, funds are supplied directly to borrowers by commercial lenders, with the FmHA minimizing the lender's risk.

The following are among the major financial services the FmHA provides.

FARMER PROGRAMS

Farm-Ownership Loans

Farm-ownership loans enable family farmers lacking other sources or credit to buy, improve, or enlarge their farming operations. Family-size farms operated by individuals, partnerships, cooperatives, or corporations are eligible for insured or guaranteed loans, secured by mortgage on the farm real estate. Loan limits are $200,000 for insured loans and $300,000 for guaranteed loans. Insured loans may be repaid in up to forty years, and interest rates are set periodically, based on the cost of government borrowing. In the case of guaranteed loans, repayment terms and interest rates are negotiated between borrower and lender.

Farm-ownership loans can be used to construct, improve, or repair farm homes and farm-service buildings, drill wells, and otherwise improve on-farm water supplies, provide drainage systems, install pollution-control measures, develop energy-conservation measures, develop and improve farmland, clear and level land, establish and improve farm forests, carry out basic land-treatment practices, provide facilities to produce fish under controlled conditions, refinance debts, and finance nonfarm enterprises that will help farmers supplement their farm incomes.

Nonfarm enterprises that may be financed on family farms include camping and swimming facilities, tennis courts, riding stables, vacation rental cottages, lakes and ponds for boating and fishing docks, nature trails, picnic grounds, repair shops, roadside markets, souvenir shops, craft and woodworking or metalworking facilities, and small grocery stores or service-station facilities.

Farm-Operating Loans

Insured or guaranteed, these loans are usually secured by chattel mortgages for feed, seed, fertilizer, livestock, machinery, or other elements of production. Family farmers and ranchers lacking other sources of production financing are eligible. Limits $100,000 for insured loans and $200,000 for guaranteed loans. Terms usually range from one to seven years, according to the purpose of the loan, and interest rates are fixed periodically with the advice of the U.S. Treasury.

The FmHA considers a limited-resource farmer as one

with a low income who operates or will operate a family farm and who, with special help and a low-interest loan, will be able to make loan payments and have an adequate living. Among limited-resource farmers are:

Beginning farmers, especially young farmers, who have training or farm experience and adequate ability, but who do not have the income and other resources needed to enter into a successful farm operation.

Owners or operators of family farms who need low-interest loans to make essential adjustments in their operations. These persons include tenants who have an opportunity to buy a farm, operators who may be forced out of farming without FmHA credit, or operators who need to change farming practices because of economic or other conditions.

Disadvantaged farmers, including minorities or those with very limited resources, low incomes, indebtedness beyond their present ability to repay, inadequate financial or production management and credit, limited education, and an unsatisfactory level of living.

The interest rate varies for farm-ownership and farm-operating loans made to limited-resource farmers. During the beginning years of the loan, farmers repay the loan at a reduced rate. Afterwards, they pay whatever interest rate they can afford for both types of loans, as long as it is not less than 5 percent and not more than the full rate ordinarily charged for FmHA farm loans.

Insured or Guaranteed Emergency Loans

These loans cover farming losses inflicted by natural disaster.

Economic Emergency Loans

These loans are designed to help farmers overcome economic hardships caused by credit scarcity or cost/price squeezes beyond their control.

Other Farmer Programs

Loans to nonprofit associations for irrigation and drainage systems and grazing ranges, to Indian tribal organizations to buy up privately owned land lying within reservation boundaries, and loans for aquaculture are covered by other farmer loan programs.

HOMEOWNER LOANS

Individual Homeownership Loans

These insured loans go to families with low or moderate incomes, as well as to senior citizens, who need adequate housing. The maximum term for repayment is thirty-three years; interest rates are adjustable and are determined by formula. Interest supplement benefits may reduce interest to as low as 1 percent for low-income borrowers. FmHA housing credit is available to eligible applicants in rural towns of not more than twenty thousand. The FmHA also guarantees up to 90 percent repayment of housing loans made by private commercial lenders to borrowers of "above-moderate" income. In the case of the guaranteed loan, the interest rate is negotiated between the borrower and the commercial lender, and a small downpayment is required. A very-low-income homeowner whose house is severely deficient may be eligible for a low-interest loan for repairs needed to make the house safe and adequate for habitation and to remove health hazards. The loan limit is $7,500. Grants or grant/loan combinations are available to help very-low-income elderly homeowners (sixty-two years of age or older) make necessary repairs to their homes. The amount of grants of grant/loan combinations cannot exceed $7,500.

Loans for Rental Housing

Loans for rental housing in rural areas are available to provide living units for persons with low or moderate incomes, and for those persons sixty-two years of age or older. Loans may be made for housing in open country and in communities with a population up to twenty thousand people, but applicants in towns of ten thousand to twenty thousand inhabitants should check with their local FmHA office to see whether the agency can serve them.

Loans of this sort are made primarily for the construction, purchase, or repair of apartment-style housing, which usually consists of duplexes, garden-type, or similar multi-unit dwellings. The housing must be modest in size, design, and cost, but adequate to meet the tenant's needs.

Funds may also be used to :

Buy and improve the land on which the buildings are to be located

Provide streets, and water or waste-disposal systems

Supply appropriate recreation and service facilities

Install laundry facilities and equipment

Landscape, which could include lawn seeding, shrubbery and tree planting, and other measures aimed at making the housing an attractive addition to the community

The loans can be made to individuals, trusts, associations, partnerships and limited-partnerships, state and local public agencies, consumer cooperatives, and profit and nonprofit corporations. Prospective borrowers should have the ability and experience to operate and manage rental housing projects successfully. They must also be unable both to finance the housing with personal resources and, with the exception of state and local public agencies, to obtain credit from other sources on conditions and terms that would permit them to rent units to eligible families or individuals—a stipulation to which prospective borrowers must agree. If the borrower is a profit or limited-profit organization, the assets of the individual members are considered in determining whether other credit is available.

The maximum repayment period is fifty years for projects designed for senior citizens and forty years for all other projects. Applicants are required to provide initial operating capital equal to at least 2 percent of the cost of the project. For nonprofit organizations and state and local public agencies, the 2 percent operating capital may be included in the loan as part of the development cost.

Before a loan can be approved, applicants must prepare detailed plans, specifications, and cost estimates; they must also be responsible for complete architectural services, including inspections during construction. The Farmers Home Administration reviews the plans and inspects the construction as it progresses.

Mutual Self-Help Housing Loans

These loans are made to families who wish to work together to build their own homes with financial and technical assistance from the FmHA.

Congregate Housing Loans

These loans offer senior citizens and handicapped persons semi-independent living quarters, which may include central dining facilities, housekeeping help, limited health-care units, and other centralized services.

Other Housing Programs

Other housing programs include two-year loans to nonprofit developers of improved rural homesite areas, loans and grants for development of adequate farm labor housing, grants to qualified organizations to help low-income families accomplish "self-help" home-building projects, grants for counseling of homeowners and technical assistance in the development of new single-family homes, and home weatherizing improvements with simplified financing through FmHA and rural electric cooperatives or other utility companies.

BUSINESS AND INDUSTRY LOANS

These loans are available in rural areas, with priority given to towns with populations of twenty-five thousand or less. Business and industry loans can be used to accomplish the following:

Finance business and industry construction, conversion, acquisition, and modernization

Finance, purchase, and develop land, easements, equipment, facilities, machinery, supplies and materials, pollution controls, and aquaculture

Refinance a business and provide working capital

Business and industry loans are characterized by the following:

Sufficient collateral so that repayment of the loan will be reasonably assured. The integrity and ability of the project management and the soundness of the project are prime considerations.

A minimum of 10 percent equity in cash or other assets provided by the applicant as reasonable assurance of a successful project

Fixed or variable interest rates which are determined between the lender and borrower

The repayment schedule for guaranteed loans is, for the most part, controlled by the lender; however, FmHA has imposed certain limitations on their guaranteed loans: final maturity will not exceed thirty years for land, buildings, and permanent fixtures; fifteen years for machinery or equipment, or the life of the machinery, equipment, whichever is shorter; and seven years maximum for working capital.

Apply for financing at the following FmHA state office locations:

ALABAMA
Aronov Building, Room 717
474 South Court Street
Montgomery, Alabama 36104

ALASKA
P.O. Box 1289
Palmer, Alaska 99645

ARIZONA
Federal Building, Room 3433
230 North First Avenue
Phoenix, Arizona 85025

ARKANSAS
5529 Federal Office Building
700 West Capitol
Little Rock, Arkansas 72201

CALIFORNIA
459 Cleveland Street
Woodland, California 95695

COLORADO
#1 Diamond Plaza, Room 231
2490 West 26th Avenue
Denver, Colorado 80211

DELAWARE, DISTRICT OF COLUMBIA, MARYLAND
Robscott Building
151 East Chestnut Hill Road, Suite 2
Newark, Delaware 19713

FLORIDA
Federal Building, Room 214
401 S.E. 1st Avenue
Gainesville, Florida 32602

GEORGIA
Stephens Federal Building
355 East Hancock Avenue
Athens, Georgia 30601

HAWAII
345 Kekuanaoa Street
Hilo, Hawaii 96720

IDAHO
Federal Building, Room 429
304 N. Eighth Street
Boise, Idaho 83702

ILLINOIS
2106 W. Springfield Avenue
Champaign, Illinois 61820

INDIANA
Suite 1700
5600 Crawforsville Road
Indianapolis, Indiana 46224

IOWA
Federal Building, Room 873
210 Walnut
Des Moines, Iowa 50309

KANSAS
444 SE Quincy Street
Topeka, Kansas 66683

KENTUCKY
333 Waller Avenue
Lexington, Kentucky 40504

LOUISIANA
3727 Government Street
Alexandria, Louisiana 71301

MAINE
USDA Office Building
Orono, Maine 04473

MASSACHUSETTS, CONNECTICUT, RHODE ISLAND
358 North Pleasant Street
Amherst, Massachusetts 01002

MICHIGAN
Room 209
1405 South Harrison Road
East Lansing, Michigan 48823

MINNESOTA
252 Federal Office Building and U.S. Courthouse
St. Paul, Minnesota 55101

MISSISSIPPI
Milner Building, Room 830
Jackson, Mississippi 39201

MISSOURI
555 Vandiver Drive
Columbia, Missouri 65201

MONTANA
Federal Building
P.O. Box 850
Bozeman, Montana 59715

NEBRASKA
Federal Building, Room 308
100 Centennial Mall North
Lincoln, Nebraska 68508

NEW JERSEY
1 Vahlsing Center
Robbinsville, New Jersey 08691

NEW MEXICO
Federal Building, Room 3414
517 Gold Avenue, S.W.
Albuquerque, New Mexico
   87102

NEW YORK, VIRGIN ISLANDS
U.S. Courthouse and Federal
   Building, Room 871
100 South Clinton Street
Syracuse New York, 13202

NORTH CAROLINA
Room 514
310 New Bern Avenue
Raleigh, North Carolina
   27601

NORTH DAKOTA
Federal Building, Room 208
Third and Rosser
Bismarck, North Dakota 58501

OHIO
Federal Building, Room 507
200 North High Street
Columbus, Ohio 43215

OKLAHOMA
USDA Agricultural Center
   Building
Stillwater, Oklahoma 74074

OREGON
Federal Building, Room 1590
1220 S.W. 3rd Avenue
Portland, Oregon 97204

PENNSYLVANIA
Federal Building, Room 728
P.O. Box 905
228 Walnut Street
Harrisburg, Pennsylvania
   17108

PUERTO RICO
Federal Building
Carlos Chardon Street
Hato Rey
San Juan, Puerto Rico
   00918

SOUTH CAROLINA
240 Stoneridge Road
Columbia, South Carolina
   29221

SOUTH DAKOTA
Huron Federal Building, Room
   208
200 4th Street, S.W.
Huron, South Dakota 57350

TENNESSEE
538 U.S. Court House Building
801 Broadway
Nashville, Tennessee 37203

TEXAS
W. R. Poage Building
101 South Main
Temple, Texas 76501

UTAH, NEVADA
Federal Building, Room 5311
125 South State Street
Salt Lake City, Utah
   84138

VERMONT, NEW HAMPSHIRE
P.O. Box 588
141 Main Street
Montpelier, Vermont
   05602

VIRGINIA
Federal Building, Room 8213
400 North Eighth Street
Richmond, Virginia 23240

WASHINGTON
Federal Office Building, Room
319
301 Yakima Street
Wenatchee, Washington 98801

WEST VIRGINIA
Federal Building, Room 320
75 High Street
Morgantown, West Virginia
26505

WISCONSIN
1st Financial Plaza, Suite 209
1305 Main Street
Stevens Point, Wisconsin 54481

WYOMING
Federal Building, Room 1005
100 East B Street
Casper, Wyoming 82601

NATIONAL OFFICE
U.S. Department of Agriculture
Farmers Home Administration
Washington, DC 20250

14

First national unfriendly

Bank commercials. They're all alike. Cherubic faces smiling like Santa's elves as they rush here and there to help depositors with every little thing.

"Lovely day, Ms. Jones."

"Good morning, Mr. Smith. How wonderful to see you."

How wonderful to see your money, they mean. Banks love to watch it flowing in, but the elves can suddenly turn into surly gnomes when they're asked to let a few bucks flow the other way. Anyone who's ever approached a local bank officer for a loan knows that all too well. An icy chill descends from on high as loan applicants—hard-working, wage-earning, model citizens—are made to feel like destitute panhandlers, as though what they are doing is shameful. Clearly, First National Gifts and Smiles becomes First National Unfriendly.

Thus is born the widespread notion that banks hate to lend money. But, as we have noted, this is a misconception. Bankers embrace deposits only because they can then turn around and make loans based on this inflow. Bank earnings are, in fact, determined in part by the spread between the interest paid to depositors and the higher interest charged to borrowers. So why the cold shoulder to loan applicants? Because routine small business and personal loans aren't all that profitable per transaction and because the demand for them exceeds the supply of funds the banks commit to them. But walk back to the branch vice-president's office or to the bank's headquarters downtown and you'll find a different attitude in the lending department. When the big loans—those extended to corporations and wealthy individuals—are up for grabs, there's cutthroat competition among the banks to snare the prospective borrower. With a little more paperwork than required by an auto loan, the banks can earn $100,000-plus interest rather than $1,000. That's why they compete for the larger loans and why, curious as it may seem to the man on the street, the more you ask from First National, the friendlier it can get. Of course, prospective borrowers must be considered prudent risks, but much of that has to do with image. How you approach the bank says a lot. One important rule is to detour the middle managers—the so-called platform officers—and deal directly with the branch manager. (Use the procedures outlined in the first three chapters, and you are likely to get a hearing at the top.) This accomplishes two major objectives with one fell swoop: it removes the application from the nitpickers who are inundated with hordes of small-loan seekers and who seem to take perverse pleasure in saying no, and it puts the decision in the hands of an individual authorized to make or influence big-loan decisions. And big loans are what you are after.

The greatest problem with most bank lending is that it tends to be relatively inflexible. More than other cash sources, banks base most of their lending decisions on financial criteria, such as the applicant's debt-to-worth ratio, that are difficult for most individuals and small businesses to satisfy. Still, by learning as much as possible about bank lending and by utilizing our special borrowing and leveraging procedures, we can tap these financing sources even if only to a limited extent.

*   *   *

The following types of loans, typical of commercial banks, are offered by the Bank of America: *

SHORT-TERM LOANS. Granted for less than a year, short-term loans are a primary source of funds for a small business's day-to-day financial needs. All types of companies use these loans to take advantage of supplier discounts, boost inventory, or increase production for seasonal sales peaks. Short-term loans are usually self-liquidating; that is, they are repaid when the receivables or inventory financed are converted to cash.

The basic short-term vehicle is the *commercial loan*, repayable in a lump sum after three to six months. It is normally unsecured (*i.e.*, made without any specific collateral), although the bank relies upon the firm's financial statement to determine the borrower's credit-worthiness and will draw upon the business's assets should the business fail to meet the loan terms. Stocks and bonds, time certificates of deposit (TCDs), the cash value of life insurance, or a personal guarantee may be accepted as evidence of the borrower's ability to repay the loan.

If the loan exceeds a specified amount, usually $100,000, some banks require that the borrower maintain a reserve of cash in a bank account. The size of this "compensating balance" will depend on several variables; in some cases, the balance may be a combination of 10 percent of the credit committed plus 10 percent of the credit in use. However, most banks will accept fees or additional interest as a substitute for compensating balances.

* Bank of America, NT & SA, "Financing Small Business," *Small Business Reporter*, 14, no. 10 (1980).

When a major part of a company's working capital is tied up in unpaid accounts, or when more credit is needed than the bank will extend in an unsecured loan, accounts receivable financing may be the answer. Receivables financing gives the company a cash injection that grows along with its sales yet protects the banker with an asset that can be readily liquidated.

An accounts receivable loan turns unpaid invoices into ready cash. The bank advances the borrower between 65 and 80 percent of the eligible receivables' value as ordered goods are shipped. (Generally, banks do not finance receivables that are ninety days past due.) The borrower usually grants an interest in the receivables to the bank as security for the loan and sends customers' payments to the bank; the bank then credits the loan with the agreed-upon percentage and deposits the remainder in the borrower's account. Receivables loans form a revolving line of credit in which funds are continually advanced, repaid, and readvanced. Interest is paid only on outstanding balances. The receivables line is usually contracted for a year, reviewed by the lender, and, if approved, renewed for an additional year.

Inventory financing, or commodities loans—a second type of revolving credit—are secured by the raw materials, work in progress, or finished goods that constitute the firm's inventory. Because inventory is less easily liquidated than receivables, banks usually advance only up to 50 percent of the inventory's value. Inventory financing is effectively combined with receivables financing to build inventory for peak selling seasons. The inventory loan is paid off by receivables advances that are in turn repaid when the accounts are collected.

An established borrower of known profitability may qualify for an unsecured line of credit. Banks usually extend a line of credit for one year, promising to lend the borrower up to a set amount. Like a receivables or inventory line, the unsecured line is usually revolving; that is, the business can repeatedly borrow, repay, and borrow again all or part of the credit available.

INTERMEDIATE AND LONG-TERM LOANS.   Intermediate and long-term loans extend for more than a year and are used for business start-ups, the purchase of facilities and equipment, construction, real estate improvement, or for added working capital. Term loans are repaid monthly or quarterly, and are intended to be repaid from profits.

Unsecured term loans are usually granted only to firms with profit histories and whose current or projected financial data demonstrate that profits will be sufficient to repay the loan. If a term loan is extended for a business start-up, most banks require the entrepreneur to contribute at least 50 percent of the venture's cost.

The term loan usually requires a written agreement that, among other things, limits the company's other debts, dividends, and principals' salaries. In addition, the agreement may specify a percentage of company profits to be used to accelerate repayment of the loan. Violation of this agreement constitutes a default. (A compensating balance may also be required.)

Term loans may be supported by personal guarantees, stocks and bonds, or, sometimes, partially secured by equipment. Intermediate or long-term loans that are fully secured by equipment or real estate are separate loan vehicles.

Equipment loans can enable a business to purchase new equipment or can provide funding for the company that cannot qualify for unsecured credit. With an unsecured term loan a business could cover 100 percent of its equipment costs, but most banks limit their equipment loans to between 60 and 80 percent of the equipment's value. The loan is usually repaid monthly over one to five years or the length of the equipment's usable life.

Real-estate financing, or *commercial* or *industrial mortgages,* are offered by most banks. The commercial mortgage is usually made for up to 75 percent of the property value and amortized over a set period, usually from ten to twenty-five years. Banks also provide residential mortgages and real-estate refinancing.

Equipment leasing has become a financing tool for more and more banks. They generally write equipment leases for a minimum of three years, extending up to 80 percent of the equipment's useful economic life, possibly as long as fifteen years.

SPECIALIZED CREDIT VEHICLES. These serve retailers who sell expensive items such as cars, boats, and mobile homes. In *flooring,* the bank finances the retailer's purchase of big-ticket items and holds a security interest until the merchandise is sold and the loan is paid off. The bank collects monthly interest on the amount advanced, and the retailer repays principal as each item is sold. A flooring line may be renewed annually.

Indirect collection financing is used to help retailers sell big-ticket items on an installment basis. As in accounts receivable financing, installment sales contracts are turned into ready cash when the bank advances between 70 and 80 percent of their value as the item is sold. The retailer repays the advance with interest as the consumer pays each installment. This is another annually renewable line of credit.

"The interest rates for all of our loans are based on the borrower's risk profile, the terms of the loan, and the current costs of money," says Donna Diehl, an assistant vice-president with the Pleasant, California, branch of the Bank of America. "Most are pegged to float with the prime. The era of a set interest rate is ending. With today's volatile economy, banks must have floating rates in order to assure that they will be profitable throughout the loan period."

BANK LOAN CRITERIA.   Generally, bankers require the most information from first-time borrowers. Unsecured loans require more proof of repayment ability than secured loans, and the loan package usually becomes more detailed as the size of the loan or its term is increased. Bankers view a loan package with three main criteria in mind:

They look for borrowers with experience in the business they propose to enter. Like investors, bankers view management as their "security" in making a commitment.

They check the borrower's personal credit record. Most lending officers advise applicants to establish credit through local stores or credit cards before seeking a bank loan.

Bankers investigate the business's ability to repay the loan. Depending on the type of financing requested, the banker will pay particular attention to different aspects of the business.

When a bank considers a short-term loan, it studies the firm's liquidity, that is, its working capital available to meet short-term debt. If a firm's current working-capital situation is strong, its inventory turns swiftly, and accounts are collected on time, then the business will be a good prospect for short-term credit.

When considering intermediate or long-term loans, lending officers search for proof of business profitability. Therefore, for equipment loans, equipment leasing, real-estate loans, and especially the high-risk unsecured term loans, bankers require long-term profit-and-loss projection as well as cash-flow projections to document the business's ability to pay off the debt, together with some historical profit-and-loss information that would indicate that those projections are realistic. Projections should be explained and backed up with facts. Lending officers compare projections to published industry standards so that overestimated earnings or underestimated costs will be quickly noticed.

Borrowers should strive to establish and maintain relationships with their bankers. Business owners who avoid the banker until they need money may find that a loan is harder to get because the lender is unfamiliar with the history of the business.

*   *   *

If a loan cannot be justified solely on the basis of the borrower's financial statements, one of the following pledges of security may bridge the gap.

GUARANTORS.   A guarantor is one who guarantees the payment of a note by signing a guaranty commitment. Both private and government lenders often require guarantees from officers of corporations in order to assure continuity of effective management. Sometimes, a manufacturer will act as guarantor for one of his customers.

WAREHOUSE RECEIPTS.   Banks also take commodities as security by lending money on a warehouse receipt. Such a receipt is usually delivered directly to the bank and shows that the merchandise used as security either has been placed in a public warehouse or has been left on the borrower's premises under the control of a bonded employee. Such loans are generally made on staple or standard merchandise that can be readily marketed. The typical warehouse-receipt loan is for a percentage of the estimated value of the goods used as security.

TRUST RECEIPTS AND FLOOR PLANNING.   Merchandise such as automobiles, appliances, and boats has to be displayed to be sold; and the only way many small marketers can afford such displays is to borrow money. Such loans are often secured by a note and a trust receipt, which is the legal paper for floor planning. It is used for serial-numbered merchandise. When a borrower signs one, he or she (1) acknowledges receipt of the merchandise, (2) agrees to keep the merchandise in trust for the bank, and (3) promises to pay the bank as the goods are sold.

CHATTEL MORTGAGES. If you buy equipment such as a cash register or a delivery truck, you may want to get a chattel mortgage loan. In exchange, you give the bank a lien on the equipment you are buying. The bank evaluates the present and future market value of the equipment being used to secure the loan and determines whether the borrower had adequately protected the chattel. For instance, does the borrower have the necessary fire, theft, property damage, and public liability insurance on the equipment?

REAL ESTATE. Real estate is another form of collateral for long-term loans. When taking a real-estate mortgage, the bank ascertains the location of the real estate, its physical condition, its foreclosure value, and the amount of insurance carried on the property.

STOCKS AND BONDS. If stocks and bonds are used as collateral, they must be marketable. As a protection against market declines and possible expenses of liquidation, banks usually lend no more than 75 percent of the market value of high-grade stock. On federal government or municipal bonds, they may be willing to lend 90 percent or more of the market value. The bank also may ask the borrower for additional security or payment whenever the market value of the stocks or bonds drops below the bank's required margin.

Bank loans can carry a hidden danger. When a small business signs for a loan, more than the company name is at stake. The owner's home, car, and bank account may also be on the line. Pledging personal assets as collateral can help to win over reluctant lenders but may also pose serious problems should the owner die before the loan is repaid. Creditors may claim all or part of the estate, leaving the business insolvent and the heirs penniless.

"The lending institution will, invariably, require the owner to sign the loan agreement twice—once as an officer of the corporation and once as an individual," says an executive with the Million Dollar Round Table, a professional association of life insurance agents. "The second signature personally obligates the business owner for the loan. It's as if he has personally borrowed the money: all of the assets of the owner may be reached by the bank to satisfy the loan."

The risks of this double jeopardy can be reduced by purchasing a life insurance policy for the amount of the owner's personal exposure on business loans. This way the insurer provides the proceeds for the debt balances, leaving the business intact and the family in a stronger financial position. It is a way of insulating companies and estates from sudden loss.

"Having insurance—or informing bankers at the outset that insurance will be purchased—can also help in the search for business financing," says Bruce M. Dayton, chairman of Multi-Financial Services, Inc., financial advisers. "Bankers tend to be wary of small-business loans, especially if the companies are highly leveraged or lack substantial assets. An insurance policy often calms their fears by providing a source of funds to cover the balance. The loans may come a lot easier."

The business owner need not dig into his own pocket for the policy premium. With one strategy, the corporation pays a tax-deductible "guarantor's fee," which may be applied toward the insurance. The fee is in recognition of the owner's risks in personally signing for the loan.

Under this procedure, the corporation pays the guaran-

tor's fee. The guarantor, in turn, purchases life insurance
with the fee. At death, the insurance pays off the bank loan
and releases the estate from liability. The loan is canceled
by the bank, increasing the corporation's book value.

One problem with this method is that the value of the
business is restored to its pre-loan level, thus boosting the
estate taxes. Payment of the loan with life insurance proceeds may, for example, result in a $200,000 increase in the
value of the company's stock.

For this reason, experts have devised the "substitute
creditor" method to keep the value of the corporation, and
therefore its stock, from rising when the bank loan is satisfied.

"In this way, the fee is paid to the guarantor," the Round
Table executive adds. "The spouse, preferably with her own
funds, purchases life insurance on the life of the guarantor
in the amount of the loan. The spouse is the beneficiary. The
intention is to keep the proceeds out of the estate of the
guarantor. The spouse then enters into an agreement with
the lender that obligates the spouse to buy and the bank to
sell the note to the spouse for the value of the note at the
time of the sale."

Should the guarantor die, the agreement between the
spouse and the lender becomes effective. The note is not
paid off. The spouse, who owns the note and is now a creditor of the corporation, can release the guarantor's liability
and allow settlement of the estate. But the value of the corporation does not increase because the note remains outstanding. The proceeds are excluded from the estate, so there
is no estate-tax increase.

Because this procedure may not serve the best interests
of every borrower, it is best to work closely with tax and
legal professionals in selecting and implementing guarantor
insurance plans. Only experts can steer through the complex
maze of laws, regulations, and business needs. Have them
look into it for you.

One organization that helps applicants succeed in snaring bank loans is the Center for Entrepreneurial Managment. This nonprofit, nongovernmental organization is run expressly for the self-employed, bringing insight and information to those going it alone.

"The fact that you're independent doesn't mean you have to be alone," says Joseph Mancuso, president of the CEM. "That's the basic thrust of our service. Entrepreneurs are generally isolated from one another, and, as such, they keep working on problems others before them have tackled and solved. But because they don't share information, they don't know that the answers are already available. They keep reinventing the wheel. This leads to the loss of valuable time."

The CEM seeks to acquaint entrepreneurs with state-of-the-art developments in finance and general management. A yearly membership fee of $96 brings the following services:

Newsletter: Published monthly, the *Entrepreneurial Manager's Newsletter* covers a range of topics relating to current and long-term business operations. The emphasis is on tips and facts designed to raise money, cut costs, locate reputable services, and expand markets.

Research service: Members seeking hard-to-find information on virtually any business topic can turn to the CEM for research assistance. Staffers will attempt to track down the data—including lists of lenders or venture capitalists—copy it, and send it off by mail. Charges are limited to the costs of photocopying.

Referrals: Need an attorney specializing in public offerings on limited partnerships? How about a CPA with experience serving loan applicants? The CEM routinely taps its files for the names of reputable professionals, agents, and suppliers in cities across the nation.

Seminars: The CEM hosts a national program of seminars related primarily to financing strategies. Experts address small groups on venture captial, government loans, private placements, and going public. Rates for the seminars, which are not included in the CEM membership fee, range from $200 to $300 per session. Lists of topics and locations are available in advance from the CEM at 83 Spring Street, New York, New York 10012.

"One man who attended a recent seminar was, at the time, employed by a major business," Mancuso adds. "After hearing our ideas, he took $200,000 of his own capital, borrowed another $800,000, and bought out one of his employer's divisions. He's now self-employed and quite successful. Most of our services produce good feedback from the membership."

Dr. Richard Hallisey, a dentist and real-estate investor, agrees. "Both my dental practice and real-estate activities are businesses. To manage them properly, I need current and accurate information. Although I don't use all of the CEM's materials, there are usually several items a month I can profit from."

It may come as a surprise to many that banks themselves offer a wide range of financial services that can be profitable to money seekers whether or not loans are authorized. The old image of the stiff, formal banker propped behind a huge mahogany desk is as dated as the bowler hat. Today's bankers roll up their sleeves, pitch in, and play an active role in customer affairs.

The following are among the major banking services:

Consulting: Banks can be a good source of free management consulting. Leading banks are staffed with an impressive array of business experts, including economists, accountants, tax attorneys, and planners. These specialists can bring a team approach to solving business problems and to establishing growth strategies. In many cases, bank customers can tap all of this high-priced talent simply by asking for it.

"We often get involved in a small company's overall operations through the loan application process," says the executive vice-president of a prominent national bank. "We do a comprehensive analysis to see if the firm is creditworthy. Sometimes we find that the firm is too highly leveraged and that it is basing its plans and programs on erroneous assumptions. We'll work with management to set up accurate and sophisticated guidelines for current borrowing and long-term growth."

Real estate: When entrepreneurs first decide to build their own stores, offices, or factories, they enter the complex world of commercial real estate. Banks can help to smooth out the rough spots and avoid the pitfalls by providing advice and counsel from contract to construction. Many banks retain a sizable staff of real-estate professionals who can help the inexperienced conduct surveys and appraisals, select the best locations, secure funds, and structure financing. This can reduce both the risks and the costs of building business facilities.

Accounting and payroll services: A growing number of banks now offer automated accounting services that do everything from preparing payrolls to providing general ledgers and balance sheets. This reduces the volume of paperwork, thus freeing the owner to concentrate on managerial functions. The cost is based on the type of services performed. Borrowers can use these services to keep tabs on cash needs, make long-term projections, and produce documentation for loan applications.

Forums and seminars: Banks are now sponsoring forums and seminars on loan sources, financial trends, tax rulings, mergers, and acquisitions. These seminars—a form of continuing education—can keep owner-managers up-to-date on money-making and money-saving opportunities.

Personal cash-flow management: Individuals can receive assistance planning for fluctuations in annual income. When business patterns bring sharp changes in earnings, cash-management techniques can be used to regulate the flow. Typically, the strategy calls for short-term investments in surplus periods and borrowing during the slow months.

Investment-management services: Individuals can also receive help formulating investment strategies, selecting investment vehicles, and managing portfolios. A mix of stocks, bonds, and money-market instruments is put together to reflect the investor's needs, objectives, and preferred degree of risk. For clients with oil and mineral holdings, some banks will maintain records reflecting gross revenue, production tax, units of production, operating expenses, cash flow, depreciation, and depletion.

"We would never presume to tell customers how to run their businesses—that's their specialty," says the manager of the personal trust division of a leading bank. "But the truth is that they are often so wrapped up in business affairs that they ignore their personal finances. That's where we come in. Investments demand constant supervision, including buying and selling at the most opportune time, and we provide that through our portfolio management service.

"Clients can choose between nondiscretionary accounts, where they make the key decisions on securities purchases and sales, or discretionary accounts, where we call the shots. Either way, the clients' objectives guide the strategy, and we assume the burden of account administration."

Commercial valuation services: These services compute and document an individual's net worth. Putting an accurate dollar value on personal holdings, including business interests, can be crucial for borrowing money.

Estate planning and administrative services: These broad and diverse services include the preparation of wills and the supervision of family trusts. In so-called living trusts, banks manage personal interests during one's lifetime, design strategies for the tax-wise transfer of assets after death, and continue to administer the estate for as long as necessary.

Tax-planning services: High-income individuals can be assisted in the selection of appropriate investments and tax shelters, the scheduling of income for the lowest tax bite, and the preparation of tax returns. The emphasis is on year-round planning rather than crisis sessions held only when taxes are due.

Some banking services are offered for set fees; others are based on a percentage of the dollar amount of the assets managed. In most cases, the larger the account, the lower the percentage. The best approach is to compare the range of services, fees, and professional reputation of various banks. Ask for references, and have an attorney review all contracts and agreements.

15

Investment bankers

Behind the national network of Main Street bankers doing business in thousands of local branches, there is another layer of American bankers that few people ever see or hear about. These bankers are part of the complex and somewhat mysterious world of investment banking—a world that every prospective borrower should explore.

Here, without checking accounts, savings plans, or credit cards, most of the biggest deals in corporate finance are planned and implemented. Investment bankers specialize in raising substantial sums of money, and they can be the single most important contact for investors or entrepreneurs wishing to raise $1 million or more. Although investment bankers are often associated with the blue chip names of the *Fortune* 500, most serve a wide range of clients, from sole proprietors to IBM. They are superb at shaping sophisticated financial strategies—strategies that may take your ideas from drawing board to marketplace.

Two accountants who make it their business to keep close tabs on the investment banking community—and who have shepherded thousands of clients through investment banks—are Al Bernikow, a partner in the small business practice of Touche Ross, and Harvey Braun, the CPA firm's partner in charge of client services. Bernikow and

Braun, who often work as a team, suggest that entrepreneurs look to investment bankers for the following services:

Raising debt and equity capital through public markets, limited partnerships, and private placements with pension funds and insurance companies. Investment bankers will recommend the best sources of funds for the venture's needs, will structure the financing, and will make contact with lenders and investors.

"Experienced investment bankers have built up an intricate network of money sources that they can tap for virtually every kind of money requirement," Bernikow notes. "For example, they know of wealthy individuals in the U.S. and overseas who are loaded with cash and who are eager to invest in specific kinds of deals. The bankers know which proposals to bring to them."

Serving as marriage brokers between two or more companies. Merger and acquisition divisions of investment banks find the partners for the union, determine the firms' market values, and structure the financing for the transaction. Because active bankers maintain files of entrepreneurs looking to buy, sell, or merge, they are in the unique position of bringing both sides together. Those individuals seeking to raise money through the sale of a business or wanting to finance the purchase of a company will fare better working through the bankers than going it alone.

Engaging in a wide range of money-management activities, including the handling of personal investments for wealthy individuals. Related to this is the bankers' function as both syndicators and marketers of tax-sheltered investment programs in real estate, oil and gas, leasing, and research and development projects. Borrowers seeking to raise money through these deals or wanting to shelter some of their profits from past transactions will find investment bankers to be particularly adroit at both ends of the market.

Braun offers the following caveat to those selecting an investment banker: "Don't make the mistake of thinking that all investment bankers are alike. They definitely are not. While one may be eager and qualified to handle your deal, another may be disinterested or inexperienced in the specific type of transaction. The success of the deal can hinge on finding the ideal banker to handle it.

"Size of the investment bank is the most important criterion. There's a wide spectrum in the investment banking community with the likes of a Morgan Stanley at one end and a small venture-capital firm at the other. The banks at the upper end of the spectrum will not handle smaller deals. The dollar volume has to be great enough—certainly in the tens of millions—for them to earn what they consider an adequate profit. Smaller deals go to the smaller banks."

Adds Bernikow, "The other major factors to consider are expertise in a particular type of transaction—some banks are good at leverage buyouts, others at real-estate syndications—and industry specialization. If a company or individual is in the real-estate field, it's a plus to work with a bank that has a good track record in real estate.

"One of our clients is now trying to sell a money-losing division. The firm has value, however, because of its underlying assets. But only an investment banker with experience in the company's field could recognize that. The client found just such a bank."

The best approach is to interview several bankers, comparing their operating styles, fees, and proposals for handling your business. Check this shoppers' guide to seven major investment banks that do not limit their services to the Fortune 500.

DREXEL BURNHAM LAMBERT: Aggressive firm; develops innovative financing strategies for small business (bonds, subordinated debt); major underwriter of public financing for cash-starved companies ($1–$10 million net income); active in wide range of venture capital projects; stays away from debt financing for service firms.

LADENBURG THALMANN: Its niche is serving smaller companies (specializes in public offerings of from $3 to $35 million); active with high-tech clients in computer hardware and telecommunications; prefers companies with seasoned management and solid string of earnings; reluctant to do startups or limited partnerships.

BEAR STEARNS: Well-respected name; excellent reputation with corporate financial executives and professional investors; serves mid-size to large companies with growth aspirations; minimum $5 million for public offerings; among the best at structuring leveraged buyouts; not a good match for the smallest firms.

DONALDSON LUFKIN & JENRETTE: Entrepreneurially oriented; relishes venture capital deals; known for creative financing capabilities; fond of high-tech clients in energy field; strong in mergers and acquisitions; tries to identify today the Fortune 500 companies of the 1990s—and prefers to work with them.

SMITH BARNEY HARRIS UPHAM: Covers the field from emerging companies to multinational giants; wide sweep of services from run-of-the-mill equity offerings to creative debt deals; fine banking name with strong track record and emphasis on research; excellent securities distribution capabilities; could be too stuffy for some smaller firms.

LAIDLAW ADAMS & PECK: Classy operation for smaller clients; specializes in emerging and mid-range companies with minimum of $4 million in annual sales; looks for financing candidates that have distinct market niche in their field as well as solid management; works with a wide cross-section of industries; old world flavor.

A.G. BECKER: Prestigious firm; fine reputation for securities distribution; specialists in services to financial institutions (banks, leasing and finance companies); looks for clients with good management (good ideas alone not enough here); little taste for startups; known to be savvy risk takers.

The following firms are members of the Securities Industry Association, a trade group representing more than five hundred investment banks, securities brokers and dealers, and other firms involved in raising money through public and private offerings. Use this as a starting point for contacting investment bankers.

ALABAMA
Birmingham
First Birmingham Securities
  Corporation
Hendrix, Mohr & Yardley, Inc.
Perry (Berney) & Company,
  Inc.
Sterne, Agee & Leach, Inc.

Montgomery
Frazer Lanier Company, Inc.
  (The)

ARIZONA
Phoenix
Hobson (R. M.), Inc.

ARKANSAS
Little Rock
Hill, Crawford & Lanford, Inc.
Raney (T. J.) & Sons, Inc.
Stephens, Inc.

CALIFORNIA
Beverly Hills
Cantor, Fitzgerald & Company,
  Inc.
MacDonald, Krieger & Bowyer,
  Inc.

Burbank
Mauney Company

Long Beach
University Securities
  Corporation

Los Angeles
Bateman Eichler, Hill Richards,
  Inc.
Crowell, Weedon & Company
Morgan, Olmstead, Kennedy &
  Gardner, Inc.
Seidler, Arnett & Spillane, Inc.
Wagenseller & Durst, Inc.
Wedbush, Noble, Cooke, Inc.

San Diego
First Affiliated Securities, Inc.

San Francisco
Anderson (C.D.) & Company,
   Inc.
Birr, Wilson & Company, Inc.
Cazenove, Inc.
Davis, Skaggs & Company, Inc.
Edelstein, Campbell &
   Company, Inc.
Hambrecht & Quist
Larkin (Emmett A.) Company
Montgomery Securities
Pacific Securities, Inc.
Robertson, Colman, Stephens &
   Woodman
Rowe & Pitman, Inc.
Shaw, Hooker & Company
Stone & Youngberg
Sutro & Company, Inc.
Swift (Henry F.) & Company
Van Kasper & Company, Inc.
Wulff Hansen & Company

COLORADO
Denver
Boettcher & Company
Coughlin and Company, Inc.
Gerwin and Company
Hanifen, Imhoff & Samford,
   Inc.

CONNECTICUT
Bridgeport
Carreau, Smith, Inc.

Greenwich
Gintel & Company

Hartford
Advest, Inc.
Conning & Company

DISTRICT OF COLUMBIA
Washington
Ferris & Company, Inc.
Folger Nolan Fleming Douglas,
   Inc.
Johnston, Lemon & Company,
   Inc.
Sade & Company
Walsh (Julia M.) & Sons, Inc.

FLORIDA
Ft. Lauderdale
Werbel-Roth Securities, Inc.

Hialeah Gardens
Loosemore, Loosemore &
   Company

Jacksonville
Ewing (Allen C.) & Company

Lakeland
Allen & Company of Florida,
   Inc.

Miami
First Equity Corporation of
   Florida

Orlando
Leedy Corporation (The)
Leedy, Wheeler & Alleman,
   Inc.

St. Petersburg
Hough (William R.) & Company
Raymond, James & Associates,
   Inc.

Tampa
Nix (H. G.) Inc.
Williams (Jerry), Inc.

Winter Park
Lewis (M. G.) & Company,
   Inc.

GEORGIA

Atlanta

First Southeastern Company

Henderson, Few & Company

Jared, Mulcay & Company, Inc.

Jolley (Lex) & Company, Inc.

Knox (W. L.) & Company

Norris & Hirshberg, Inc.

Robinson-Humphrey Company, Inc. (The)

Macon

Essex Company

Savannah

Johnson, Lane, Space, Smith & Company, Inc.

ILLINOIS

Aurora

Oberweis Securities, Inc.

Chicago

Altorfer, Podesta, Woolard & Company

Bacon, Whipple & Company

Becker (A. G.), Inc.

Billings and Company

Blair (William) & Company

Brown (Clayton) Associates

Channer Newman Securities Company

Chicago Corporation (The)

Collins (Julien) & Company

Freehling & Company

Harris Associates, Inc.

Hickey & Company

Hickey (Jerome) Associates, Inc.

Horowitz (G. A.) & Company, Inc.

Howe, Barnes & Johnson, Inc.

Hummer (Wayne) & Company

Illinois Company, Inc. (The)

Keeley Investment Corporation

Kemper Financial Services, Inc.

Mesirow & Company

Noyes (David A.) & Company

Nuveen (John) & Company, Inc.

Rodman & Renshaw, Inc.

Rose & Company Investment Brokers, Inc.

Rothschild Securities Corporation

Van Kampen Filkin & Merritt, Inc.

Vick (M. B.) & Company

Vincent (Burton J.), Chesley & Company

Homewood

Inland Securities Company, Inc.

Rolling Meadows

Ziegler Securities, Inc.

INDIANA

Fort Wayne

Headford & Company, Inc.

Indianapolis

City Securities Corporation

Raffensperger, Hughes & Company, Inc.

Traub and Company, Inc.

Muncie

Brown (K. J.) & Company, Inc.

IOWA

Cedar Rapids

Securities Corporation of Iowa

Council Bluffs

McIntosh & Company, Inc.

Des Moines

Dickinson (R.G.) & Company

Sioux City
Pecaut & Company

KANSAS
Atchison
Exchange National Bank of
Atchison (The)

Topeka
Beecroft, Cole & Company
Seltsam, Hanni & Company,
Inc.

Wichita
First Securities Company of
Kansas, Inc.
Mid-Continent Municipal
Investments, Inc.

KENTUCKY
Louisville
Hilliard (J. J. B.), Lyons (W. L.),
Inc.
Johnston, Brown, Burnett &
Knight, Inc.

LOUISIANA
New Orleans
Dinkins (Ladd) & Company
Hattier, Sanford & Reynoir
Howard, Weil, Labouisse,
Friedrichs, Inc.
Scharff & Jones, Inc.
Whitney National Bank of New
Orleans

MARYLAND
Baltimore
Baker, Watts & Company
Brown (Alex.) & Sons
Legg Mason Wood Walker, Inc.

Lutherville
Salkin, Welch and Company, Inc.

MASSACHUSETTS
Boston
Adams, Harkness & Hill, Inc.
Berg & Company, Inc.
Burgess & Leith, Inc.
Colonial Management
Associates, Inc.
Eaton & Howard, Vance Sanders,
Inc.
First New England Securities
Corporation
Moors & Cabot, Inc.
Moseley, Hallgarten, Estabrook
& Weeden, Inc.
Putnam (F. L.) & Company, Inc.
State Street Bank and Trust
Company
Trusteed Funds, Inc.
Wainwright (H. C.) & Company

MICHIGAN
Detroit
First Heritage Corporation
First of Michigan Corporation
Manley, Bennett, McDonald &
Company
Roney (Wm. C.) & Company
Smith, Hague & Company, Inc.

Grand Rapids
Shaine (H. B.) & Company, Inc.

Southfield
Harris (M. L.) & Company

Traverse City
Seward Corporation

MINNESOTA
Minneapolis
Craig-Hallum, Inc.
Dain Bosworth, Inc.
Kinnard (John G.) & Company,
Inc.

Miller & Schroeder Municipals, Inc.

Piper, Jaffray & Hopwood, Inc.

MISSISSIPPI

Columbus

Chandler Securities Corporation

Jackson

Brown, Geary & McInnes, Inc.

Kroeze, McLarty & Duddleston

MISSOURI

Kansas City

Baum (George K.) & Company, Inc.

Christopher (B. C.) & Company

Stepp (A. F.) Investments, Inc.

Stern Brothers & Company

Zahner and Company

St. Louis

Burns, Pauli & Company, Inc.

Edwards (A. G.) & Sons, Inc.

Glynn (J. A.) & Company

Heitner Corporation (The)

Jones (Edward D.) & Company

McCourtney-Breckenridge & Company

Newhard, Cook & Company, Inc.

Rowland (R.) & Company, Inc.

Scherck, Stein & Franc, Inc.

Simon (I. M.) & Company

Smith, Moore & Company

Stifel, Nicolaus & Company, Inc.

Stix & Company, Inc.

Weinrich-Zitzmann-Whitehead, Inc.

MONTANA

Great Falls

Davidson (D. A.) & Company, Inc.

NEBRASKA

Lincoln

First Mid America, Inc.

Omaha

Chiles, Heider & Company, Inc.

Kirkpatrick, Pettis, Smith, Polian, Inc.

NEW HAMPSHIRE

Manchester

Carr (Robert C.) & Company, Inc.

NEW MEXICO

Albuquerque

Quinn & Company, Inc.

NEW JERSEY

Bloomfield

Weller (J. W.) & Company, Inc.

Jersey City

Freeman Securities Company, Inc.

Herzog, Heine, Geduld, Inc.

Reaves (W. H.) & Company, Inc.

Princeton

Sword (Wm.) & Company, Inc.

Red Bank

Underhill Securities Corporation

Summit

Printon, Kane & Company

West Orange

Ryan, Beck & Company

Willingboro

Wegard (L. C.) & Company, Inc.

NEW YORK

Albany

First Albany Corporation

King (C. L.) & Associates, Inc.

Buffalo
Trubee, Collins & Company

Chappaqua
Bennett (William N.) Securities, Inc.
Wasserman (Peter J.)

Harrison
Lieber & Company

Manhasset
C.V.B. Brokerage, Inc.
Cullen (T. W.), Jr. & Company, Inc.

New York
ABD Securities Corporation
Adler, Coleman & Company
Allen & Company, Inc.
Allsopp (David) and Associates, Inc.
American Securities Corporation
Ames (A. E.) & Company, Inc.
Arnhold and S. Bleichroeder, Inc.
Ashley (O.H.) & Company, Inc.
Asiel & Company
Atlantic Capital Corporation
Bache Halsey Stuart Shields, Inc.
Baer Securities Corporation
Baird, Patrick & Company, Inc.
Balis & Zorn, Inc.
Basle Securities Corporation
Bear, Stearns & Company
Beauchamp & Company
Bernstein (Sanford C.) & Company, Inc.
Bodkin, Satloff & Company
Brimberg & Company
Brown Brothers Harriman & Company
Bruan, Gordon & Company

Bruns, Nordemann, Rea & Company
Bullock (Calvin), Ltd.
Burns Fry and Timmins, Inc.
Bush (J.) & Company, Inc.
Carr Securities Corporation
Chapdelaine & Company, Inc.
Chase Manhattan Bank, N.A. (The)
Clarke (G.X.) & Company
Clarke (Richard W.) Corporation
Coleman & Company
Conklin, Cahill & Company
Corroon, Lichtenstein & Company
Cowen & Company
Creem & Creem
Cullen (Eugene)
Cutter & Dixon
Daiwa Securities America, Inc.
Daniels & Bell, Inc.
de Cordova, Cooper & Company
Deltec Securities Corporation
De Simone, Lerman, Ruggiero & Company
Dillon, Read & Company, Inc.
Discount Corporation of New York
Doft & Company, Inc.
Dominick & Dominick, Inc.
Dominion Securities, Inc.
Donaldson, Lufkin & Jenrette Securities Corporation
Dreskin & Company, Inc.
Dretzin (Michael B.)
Drexel Burnham Lambert, Inc.
Dritz Goldring Wohlreich, Inc.
Eberstadt (F.) & Company, Inc.
Einhorn & Company
Ernst & Company

EuroPartners Securities
  Corporation
Evans & Company, Inc.
Faherty & Faherty, Inc.
Fahnestock & Company
Finkle (S.M.) & Company
First Boston Corporation (The)
First Investors Corporation
First Manhattan Company
Fleming (Robert), Inc.
Foster & Company
Fowler & Rosenau
Frank (Walter N.) & Company
Fried (Albert) & Company
Furman Selz Mager Dietz &
  Birney, Inc.
Gay & Company
Gengler Brothers
Gengler Brothers, Inc.
Gilder, Gagnon & Company,
  Inc.
Glickenhaus & Company
Goldbert (H. L.) & Company
Goldman, Sachs & Company
Goldstein (M. E.) & Company,
  Inc.
Granger & Company
Greenshields & Company, Inc.
Gruntal & Company
Haberman Brothers
Hamershlag, Kempner &
  Company
Harman (Richard S.) & Company
Haupt, Andrews, Fraiman & Hug
Henderson Brothers, Inc.
Herling (Irwin)
Herold (Bernard) & Company,
  Inc.
Herzfeld & Stern
Hoenig & Strock, Inc.
Homans & Company

Hutton (E. F.) & Company, Inc.
Ingalls & Snyder
Jacobson (Benjamin) & Sons
Josephthal & Company, Inc.
Kahn Brothers & Company, Inc.
Kalb, Voorhis & Company
Kaufman (Irving G.) & Company,
  Inc.
Kaufmann, Alsberg & Company
Keefe, Bruyette & Woods, Inc.
Kenny (J.J.) Company, Inc.
Kidder, Peabody & Company,
  Inc.
Kleinwort, Benson, Inc.
Kormendi, Byrd Brothers, Inc.
LaBranche & Company
Ladenburg, Thalmann &
  Company, Inc.
Laidlaw Adams & Peck, Inc.
Lanston (Aubrey G.) &
  Company, Inc.
Lasker, Stone & Stern
Lawrence (Cyrus J.), Inc.
Lazard Freres & Company
Lebenthal & Company, Inc.
Lehman Brothers Kuhn Loeb,
  Inc.
Lepercq, De Neuflize &
  Company, Inc.
Lewco Securities Corporation
Lief, Werle & Company
Lipper Analytical Distributors,
  Inc.
Lord, Abbett & Company
Lynch, Jones & Ryan
Mabon, Nugent & Company
Madoff (Bernard L.)
Marcus & Company
Marcus Schloss & Company, Inc.
McKenna, Cloud & Company
McLeod Young Weir, Inc.

Meehan (M. J.) & Company
Melhado, Flynn & Associates, Inc.
Merrill Lynch, Pierce, Fenner & Smith, Inc.
Midland Doherty, Inc.
Mitchel, Schreiber, Watts & Company, Inc.
MKI Securities Corporation
Moore & Schley, Cameron & Company
Morgan Stanley & Company, Inc.
Muir (John) & Company
Murphey, Marseilles & Smith
Nesbitt Thomson Securities, Inc.
Neuberger & Berman
New Court Securities Corporation
New Japan Securities International, Inc.
Newman (Robert M.), Jr. & Company
Nick (J. F.) & Company
Nikko Securities Company International, Inc. (The)
Nomura Securities International, Inc.
Oppenheimer & Company, Inc.
Paine, Webber, Jackson & Curtis, Inc.
Pearson (A.E.), Inc.
Peck (Andrew) Associates, Ltd.
Perta Capital Corporation
Phelan, Silver, Vesce, Barry & Company
Pollock (Wm. E.) & Company, Inc.
Purcell, Graham & Company, Inc.
Ramirez (Samuel A.) & Company, Inc.

Reynders, Gray & Company, Inc.
Robb, Peck, McCooey & Company, Inc.
Ross Stebbins, Inc.
Rothenburg, Stuart Company
Rothschild (L. F.), Unterberg, Towbin
Ruane, Cunniff & Company, Inc.
Salomon Brothers
Schapiro (M. A.) & Company, Inc.
Scholl & Levin
Seligman Securities, Inc.
Shaw & Adrian
Shaw & Company
Shearson Loeb Rhoades, Inc.
Sheldon (Donald) & Company, Inc.
Sherman, Dean & Company, Inc.
Shilling (A. Gary) & Company, Inc.
Shoenberg, Hieber, Inc.
Shufro, Rose & Ehrman
Silberberg, Rosenthal & Company
Sims (Herbert J.) & Company, Inc.
Sinclair Securities Company
Smith Barney, Harris Upham & Company, Inc.
Spear, Leeds & Kellogg
Sprague & Nammack
Standard & Poor's Securities, Inc.
Sterling, Grace & Company, Inc.
Stern Brothers
Stern (E. H.) & Company, Inc.
Stern & Kennedy
Stern, Lombardi & Company
Stillman, Maynard & Company
Stokes, Hoyt & Company

Strasbourger Pearson Tulcin Wolff, Inc.
Streicher (J.) & Company
Stuart Brothers
Swiss American Securities, Inc.
Thomson McKinnon Securities, Inc.
Tompane (A. B.) & Company
Transaction Management Corporation
Travers, Dear & Fernandez
Tucker, Anthony & Day (R. L.), Inc.
U.B.S. Securities, Inc.
Ultrafin International Corporation
Urisko (J.C.) & Company, Inc.
Valentine Securities, Inc.
Viner (Edward A.) & Company, Inc.
Wagner, Stott & Company
Ware & Keelips
Weiss, Peck & Greer
Wellington & Company
Wertheim & Company
Witter (Dean) Reynolds, Inc.
Wood Gundy, Inc.
Wreszin, Prosser, Romano & Company
Wurtzburger (Jon A.)
Yamaichi International (America), Inc.
Ziebarth, Geary & Company

Rochester
Sage, Rutty & Company, Inc.

NORTH CAROLINA
Charlotte
Interstate Securities Corporation

Greensboro
Independence Securities of N.C., Inc.
Lewis (McDaniel) & Company
McMillion/Eubanks, Inc.

Raleigh
Carolina Securities Corporation

OHIO
Cincinnati
Bartlett & Company
Conners & Company, Inc.
Finn (John) & Company, Inc.
Gradison & Company, Inc.
Seasongood & Mayer

Cleveland
Baker & Company, Inc.
Financial America Securities, Inc.
McDonald & Company
Prescott, Ball & Turben

Columbus
Ohio Company (The)
Sweney Cartwright & Company
Vercoe & Company, Inc.

Youngstown
Butler, Wick & Company

OKLAHOMA
Oklahoma City
Edwards (R. J.), Inc.
Oppenheim (Leo) & Company, Inc.

OREGON
Portland
Adams, Hess, Moore & Company
Atkinson & Company
Belford, Hammerbeck, Inc.
Black & Company, Inc.

Blakely, Strand & Williams,
Inc.
Jones (June S.) Company
Paulson Investment Company
Somers, Grove & Company,
Inc.

PENNSYLVANIA
Allentown
York (Warren W.) & Company,
Inc.

Bala Cynwyd
Pennsylvania Group, Inc. (The)

Philadelphia
Boenning & Scattergood, Inc.
Butcher & Singer, Inc.
Collings (C. C.) and Company,
Inc.
Delaware Management
Company, Inc.
Dougherty (A. Webster) &
Company, Inc.
Elkins & Company
Hopper Soliday & Company,
Inc.
Janney Montgomery Scott, Inc.
Newbold's (W.H.) Son &
Company, Inc.
Smith (E. W.) Company

Pittsburgh
Arthurs, Lestrange & Short
Covato/Lipsitz, Inc.
Cunningham, Schmertz &
Company, Inc.
Federated Securities Corporation
Hefren-Tillotson, Inc.
Masten (A. E.) & Company, Inc.
McKee (C. S.) & Company, Inc.
Parker/Hunter, Inc.
Thomas & Company, Inc.

PUERTO RICO
San Juan
Government Development Bank
for Puerto Rico

RHODE ISLAND
Providence
Carolan & Company, Inc.
Miller & George

SOUTH CAROLINA
Greenville
Norris (Edgar M.) & Company

TENNESSEE
Knoxville
Benton & Company
Cumberland Securities
Company, Inc.

Memphis
Morgan, Keegan & Company,
Inc.
UMIC, Inc.

Nashville
Bradford (J. C.) & Company
Cherokee Securities Company
(The)
Equitable Securities Corporation
Wiley Brothers, Inc.

TEXAS
Dallas
Eppler, Guerin & Turner, Inc.
First Southwest Company
Institutional Equity Corporation
May, Cullum, Ragland &
Brittain, Inc.
Rauscher Pierce Refsnes, Inc.
Schneider, Bernet & Hickman,
Inc.
Southwest Securities, Inc.
Weber, Hall, Sale & Associates,
Inc.

Houston
Porcari, Fearnow & Ace, Inc.
Rotan Mosle, Inc.
Underwood, Neuhaus &
    Company, Inc.
Westcap Corporation (The)

San Antonio
Allison (M. E.) & Company,
    Inc.

VIRGINIA
Lynchburg
Strader & Company, Inc.

Norfolk
Investment Corporation of
    Virginia

Richmond
Anderson & Strudwick, Inc.
Branch, Cabell & Company
Cecil, Waller & Sterling,
    Inc.
Craigie, Inc.
Davenport & Company of
    Virginia, Inc.
Scott & Stringfellow, Inc.
Wheat, First Securities,
    Inc.

WASHINGTON
Seattle
Campbell, Waterman, Inc.
Foster & Marshall, Inc.
Grande & Company, Inc.
Interpacific Investor Services,
    Inc.

Spokane
Murphey Favre, Inc.
Northwest Securities, Inc.
Richards, Merrill & Peterson,
    Inc.

WEST VIRGINIA
Wheeling
Hazlett, Burt & Watson, Inc.

WISCONSIN
Baird (Robert W.) & Company,
    Inc.
Blunt Ellis & Loewi, Inc.
Milwaukee Company (The)

West Bend
Ziegler (B. C.) and Company

MANITOBA
Winnipeg
Richardson Securities of Canada

ONTARIO
Toronto
Ames (A. E.) & Company, Ltd.
Bell Gouinlock, Ltd.
Equitable Securities, Ltd.
McLeod Young Weir, Ltd.
Pitfield Mackay Ross, Ltd.
Wood Gundy, Ltd.

QUEBEC
Montreal
Levesque, Beaubien, Inc.
Nesbitt Thomson Securities, Ltd.
Royal Bank of Canada
Tasse & Associes, Limitee

16

Venture capital

Working with investment bankers is a learning experience: It encourages prospective borrowers to look beyond borrowing as a means of raising money. This broadened outlook is important today because more people need more money for more projects than ever before. They need to tap every possible source.

Yes, the American dream is alive and well and flourishing in thousands of basements, garages, and workshops across the nation. Here, home inventors, chemists, biologists, architects, engineers, artists, and filmmakers are burning the midnight oil in an effort to develop tomorrow's Xerox, Polaroid, and *Gone With the Wind.* Those who will move from unknowns to Horatio Algers will need more than talent, skill, and unfailing commitment. They will need dollars.

Dollars for research, for raw materials, for parts, for actors, for production, for promotion, for distribution, and for the million and one expenses it takes to bring an idea, a blueprint, a screenplay, or a prototype to market. Wheelbarrows of dollars. Millions for the lowest-budget films. Tens of millions for the simplest products. Hundreds of millions for high technology.

One financing source that specializes in funding the

American dream, that provides vaults of cash to transport workshop entrepreneurs to executive suites, is venture capital; and venture capitalists are the high priests of high-risk financing, at the opposite end of the spectrum from the tight-vested commercial bankers.

> Venture capital is often thought of as "the early-stage financing of relatively small, rapidly growing companies." Although historically this has been the main thrust of venture capital, and it remains so, venture capital investments today cover a broad spectrum of interests. Venture capitalists provide seed, startup, early-stage development, and rounds of expansion financing to companies that have already demonstrated the viability of their business but do not yet have access to public or credit-oriented institutional funding.*

Venture capitalists do not finance the kinds of projects others avoid like the plague out of the goodness of their hearts. Angels of mercy they are not. In fact, there is no sector of the financial community that is as hard-nosed or as tough-minded as venture capitalists. Why then do they throw their support to the least-bankable of money seekers? Simply because they are in the financing business not to earn a respectable yield on their dollars but to reap the enormous rewards that are possible with the long-shot ventures. Because venture-capital clients typically cannot raise all or part of the cash they need through traditional sources, they must accept the venturists' financing terms. And this is another reason why venture capitalists take on the high risks. In exchange for their money, they expect a substantial equity interest in the company, film, product, or invention they back—an interest that will make them rich should the venture succeed.

* Stanley E. Pratt in *Guide to Venture Capital Sources*, 5th ed. (Wellesley Hills, Mass.: Capital Publishing Corp., 1981), p. 7.

Most venture capitalists want more than a piece of the action: they expect to play a major role in the management of the firm they invest in. With so much of their money at stake, they intend to call some of the shots. For this reason, it is not unusual for money seekers who are first led to venture capitalists to make an abrupt about-face when they hear the kind of terms they'll have to accept. But this can be a mistake.

"All too many people who desperately need to raise money and who stand to achieve great success if they get the needed funds stay away from venture capitalists because of ego problems," says a CPA with a Big Eight accounting firm. "That is, they don't want to share ownership with outsiders. They feel strongly that because the venture is their idea, their baby, no one else should make decisions about it or share in the profits. Call this a case of living by blind, stubborn, stupid principles. Do you know what most of these people wind up with? Nothing. By holding out for the ideal, by refusing to give up some interest in their ventures, they wind up with no venture at all. Just an empty dream.

"Successful borrowers—successful people of all stripes —know that there are always trade-offs. You give something to get something. You bargain, negotiate, bluff, seize, accommodate, sue, threaten, compromise—but you don't sit back waiting for everything to come your way just as you want it. When my clients need financing and venture capital is the only available source, I tell them to take all they can get."

Venture-capital firms are formed both as limited partnerships and as corporations, and are funded by wealthy individuals and families (such as the Rockefellers and Whitneys), pension funds, insurance companies, endowments, and bank trust departments. In addition, most Small Business Investment Corporations (SBICs) are venture-capital firms. (They differ from others in that they are obligated to comply with certain government regulations.)

Although venture capitalists differ greatly in their funding policies, procedures, and guidelines, all are extremely discriminating in the kinds of deals they'll take on. In spite of the fact that they extract stringent terms from their clients, they are overwhelmed with many more solicitations than they can or choose to accept. Those that get the nod are those that inspire the most confidence in the financiers. The image-building techniques discussed in the first three chapters are especially important in the search for venture funds. Even though venture capitalists are sophisticated financial experts with a keen eye for reading business plans, they are also part gamblers, always on the lookout for hot deals that may soar to the top regardless of what the balance sheet shows.

The supply of funds in the venture-capital pipeline varies with prevailing economic conditions and with tax laws that favor or discourage long-term business investments. Presently, the market is very strong, with a record amount of capital up for grabs.

> Although there is now a smaller number of active industry participants than at the beginning of the last decade, the surviving core is experienced in venture investment disciplines and is well capitalized. A dramatic expansion of the venture capital industry began in 1978 under the impetus of the 1978 capital gains reduction and is continuing today. With an estimated $4.5 billion in committed capital, the industry has at least 50 percent more resources than it did only three or four years ago. In addition to the recent expansion of the organized venture capital industry with its professional managers, there has been a resurgence of virtually all aspects of business development investment. A blend of classic startup and early-stage investors, generalists providing expansion financing, and specialists for specific industries . . . now makes

venture capitalists an attractive source of financing for
more entrepreneurs and managers than ever before.*

"A record amount of venture capital will be available in
1982," adds Stanley Pratt, publisher of the *Guide to Venture
Capital Sources.* "1981's total was $5.8 billion—double that
of previous years—and the upward trend will continue. This
abundant supply of cash can be traced to political and economic factors. First, legal changes have substantially reduced the maximum capital gains tax. This encourages
investors and entrepreneurs to accept risk. Second, a number of outstanding venture capital successes, like Apple
Computer and Federal Express, have produced a bandwagon
effect. And finally, the knowledge that there is more money
available has drawn out more business people in search of
it."

Today's aggressive corps of venture capitalists favors
investments in computers, communications, instrumenta-
tion and measurement devices, software, genetics, and ro-
botics. "But we are not limited to that," says Anthony M.
Lamport, managing partner of the Lambda Fund, a venture-
capital firm affiliated with Drexel Burnham Lambert, investment bankers. "One of our more successful ventures is
Collagen, Inc., a firm that makes a substance used in plastic
surgery. Our initial investment of five hundred thousand
dollars in the company is worth more than two million dollars."

The deal has proven to be equally beneficial to Collagen's management. "Our company would never have seen
the light of day without venture-capital funding," says Collagen President Howard Palefsky. "When four physicians
founded this corporation, they were out to develop an un-
tested product that would need government approval before
it could be marketed. That is much too risky a proposition

* Pratt, *Guide to Venture Capital Sources,* p. 9.

for the banks. Only venture capitalists will finance projects with that much uncertainty attached to them."

The breakdown, by source, of 1980's $4.5 billion of venture-capital funds is as follows:

Independent, private venture-capital firms	$1.8 billion
SBICs	$1.4 billion
Venture-capital subsidiaries of large financial institutions and industrial corporations	$1.3 billion

Venture-capital firms typically make five to ten new commitments annually, with investments ranging from $100,000 to several million dollars. Applicants most likely to get the green light for venture capital are those who can provide evidence of solid management, a promising product or service with a well-defined market niche, and the makings of a major enterprise in a growth industry. The best way to impress venturers is to make the initial contact through a prominent banker, CPA, or business attorney. A respected go-between can assure the venture capitalist that the applicant is a legitimate prospect for high-risk investment. This will help nail down an initial interview. If there is interest, the venture capitalist will invite the prospect back within two weeks so that the business plan can be examined. Because this document is so crucial to venture-capital financing, money seekers are advised to work with experienced CPAs in drawing up sophisticated business plans. Be assured that venture capitalists will dissect every aspect of the plan, testing and questioning the entrepreneur on his or her statistics, goals, assumptions, and projections. They will visit the place of business, test the prototype, and do everything possible to make certain that they are aware of all the risks. This review process is likely to take between two months and a year, depending on the complexity of the investment and the stage of development of the product or service. Should the outcome be positive, money will flow to the entrepreneur soon thereafter.

Venture capitalists usually take a 30 to 60 percent equity stake in the businesses they fund through common stock or preferred stock convertible into common shares. The instruments differ in their liquidity, equity participation, ability to influence a managerial decision, and order of claims should the company be liquidated. Just which is best for the party seeking to raise money is best determined with the advice of a CPA and with an eye on the entrepreneur's overall personal and business affairs. The wisest course is to be flexible and to abandon the "family jewels syndrome," which can get in the way of making any deal at all.

> Another major problem for venture investors is the entrepreneur who tries to hold out for the largest amount of equity at the lowest terms. Don't create this sort of obstacle. Any number of valid projects have never gotten off the ground because the entrepreneur simply did not understand the wager of capital—the percentage of equity that venture capitalists themselves view as a fair compensation for their risk. A few equity percentage points here and there in early-stage developments are relatively insignificant, but unreasonable negotiations can affect future relationships. Once the company begins to show progress, it is always possible to get options, to borrow money, and buy stock at low prices, buy a percentage of the venture capitalists' positions, or take a number of steps that would create major capital gains potential. This is a critical decision that must be made, and the good entrepreneur must know when he is fairly close to the best deal he can get and settle for that.*

The most comprehensive source of information on this financing mini-industry is the *Guide to Venture Capital*

* Alan Patricof in Pratt, *Guide to Venture Capital Sources*, p. 112.

Sources, 5th ed. (Wellesley Hills, Mass.: Capital Publishing Corp., 1981). The volume, which sells for $75, contains vital information on more than five hundred venture-capital firms in the United States and Canada. Listings include the venture-capital firm's name, address, and telephone; executives to contact for financing proposals; partners' names; and the firm's industry and project preference, and general size of its investments.

Many leading capital firms belong to the National Venture Capital Association. The following are members of that organization and may be contacted in the pursuit of venture funding.

Adler and Company
280 Park Avenue
New York, New York
    10017
    (212) 986–3010

Advanced Technology Ventures
50 Broad Street, Suite 1637
New York, New York 10004
    (212) 344–0622

Allen & Company, Inc.
711 Fifth Avenue
New York, New York 10022
    (212) 832–8000

R.W. Allsop & Associates
Corporate Center East
2750 First Ave., N.E., Suite 210
Cedar Rapids, Iowa 52402
    (319) 363–8971
Overland Park, Kansas—
    (913) 642–4719
St. Louis, Missouri—
    (314) 434–1688
Milwaukee, Wisconsin—
    (414) 271–6510

Allstate Insurance Company
Allstate Plaza, Building E-2
Northbrook, Illinois 60062
    (312) 291–5681

American Research and
    Development
One Beacon Street, Suite 3128
Boston, Massachusetts 02108
    (617) 523–6411

Ampersand Associates
100 Federal Street, 31st Floor
Boston, Massachusetts
    02101
    (617) 423–8230

Anatar Investments, Inc.
Gas Light Tower, Suite 2218
235 Peachtree Street, N.E.
Atlanta, Georgia 30303
    (404) 588–0770

Anderson Investment Company
P.O. Box 426
49 Locust Avenue
New Canaan, Connecticut 06840
    (203) 966–5684

Asset Management Company
1411 Edgewood Drive
Palo Alto, California 94301
(415) 321–3131

Basic Search Company
1790 Stoney Hill Drive
Hudson, Ohio 44236
(216) 656–2442

Bessemer Venture Partners L.P.
630 Fifth Avenue
New York, New York 10111
(212) 708–9300

Boston Hambro Corporation
One Boston Place
Boston, Massachusetts 02106
(617) 722–7055
                    also
17 East 71st Street
New York, New York 10021
(212) 288–7778

Brentwood Associates
11661 San Vicente Boulevard
Los Angeles, California
    90049
(213) 826–6581

Broventure Company, Inc.
Two Hopkins Plaza, Suite 1010
Baltimore, Maryland 21201
(301) 727–4520

Bryan and Edwards
3000 Sand Hill Road, Building 2,
    Suite 260
Menlo Park, California 94025
(415) 854–1555
                    also
235 Montgomery Street
San Francisco, California 94104
(415) 421–9990

Burr, Egan, Deleage & Company,
    Inc.
175 Federal Street
Boston, Massachusetts 02110
(617) 482–8020

Business Development Services,
    Inc.
3135 Easton Turnpike
Fairfield, Connecticut 06431
(203) 373–2067

Cable, Howse & Cozadd, Inc.
11201 S.E. 8th, Suite 163
Bellevue, Washington 98004
(206) 455–5522

Capital Partners International
    Ltd.
Westland House, 17c Curzon
    Street
London W1Y 7FE, England
01-629-9928
Telex—895 3393
CAPPTR G

Capital Southwest Corporation
12900 Preston Road, Suite 700
Dallas, Texas 75230
(214) 233–8242

Charles River Partnership
133 Federal Street, Suite 602
Boston, Massachusetts 02110
(617) 482–9370

Citicorp Venture Capital Ltd.
399 Park Avenue
New York, New York 10043
(212) 559–1117

Colorado Growth Capital, Inc.
950 17th Street, Suite 1730
Denver, Colorado 80202
(303) 629–0205 or
(303) 629–0206

Continental Capital Ventures
Bank of America Center, Suite
  2690
555 California Street
San Francisco, California 94104
  (415) 989–2020

Continental Illinois Venture
  Corporation
231 LaSalle Street, Suite 1617
Chicago, Illinois 60693
  (312) 828–8021

Curtin & Company, Inc.
2050 Houston Natural Gas
  Building
Houston, Texas 77002
  (713) 658–9806

Dillon, Read & Company, Inc.
46 William Street
New York, New York 10005
  (212) 285–5656

Doan Associates
110 East Grove Street
Midland, Michigan 48640
  (517) 631–2471

Drexel Burnham Lambert, Inc.
Lambda Fund
60 Broad Street
New York, New York 10004
  (212) 480–6011

DSV Partners III
221 Nassau Street
Princeton, New Jersey 08540
  (609) 924–6420 or
  (212) 586–0144

Eastech Associates
11 Beacon Street, Suite 614
Boston, Massachusetts 02108
  (617) 227–2702

Electro-Science Management
  Corporation
600 Courtland Street, Suite 490
Orlando, Florida 32804
  (305) 645–1188

Fiarfield Venture Management
  Company, Inc.
999 Summer Street
Stamford, Connecticut 06902
  (203) 358–0255

Faneuil Hall Associates
1 Boston Place
Boston, Massachusetts 02108
  (617) 723–1955

Fidelity Venture Associates, Inc.
82 Devonshire Street
Boston, Massachusetts 02109
  (617) 726–0450

First Capital Corporation of
  Boston
P.O. Box 2016
Boston, Massachusetts 02106
  (617) 434–2440

First Century Partnership II
c/o Smith Barney, Harris Upham
  & Company, Inc.
1345 Avenue of the Americas
New York, New York 10105
  (212) 399–6382

First Chicago Investment
  Corporation
One First National Plaza, Suite
  2628
Chicago, Illinois 60670
  (312) 732–8060

First Interstate Capital, Inc.
707 Wilshire Boulevard,
  Suite W 1850

Los Angeles, California 90017
    (213) 614–5903

First Midwest Capital
    Corporation
15 South 5th Street, Suite 700
Minneapolis, Minnesota 55402
    (612) 339–9391

First Venture Corporation
Venture Building
The Quarters
Bartlesville, Oklahoma 74003
    (918) 333–8820

Foster Management Company
1010 Summer Street
Stamford, Connecticut 06905
    (203) 348–4385

Frontenac Company
208 S. LaSalle Street, Suite 1900
Chicago, Illinois 60604
    (312) 368–0044

Golder, Thoma & Company
120 S. LaSalle Street
Chicago, Illinois 60603
    (312) 853–3322

Greylock Management
    Corporation
One Federal Street
Boston, Massachusetts 02110
    (617) 423–5525

Hambrecht & Quist
235 Montgomery Street
San Francisco, California 94104
    (415) 986–5500

Harvest Ventures, Inc.
230 Park Avenue, Suite 1260
New York, New York 10169
    (212) 867–9535

Heizer Corporation
20 N. Wacker Drive, Suite
    4100
Chicago, Illinois 60606
    (312) 641–2200

Heller Capital Services, Inc.
200 Park Avenue
New York, New York
    10166
    (212) 880–7047

Hewlett-Packard Company
3000 Hanover Street
Palo Alto, California 94304
    (415) 857–2314

The Hillman Company
2000 Grant Building
Pittsburgh, Pennsylvania
    15219
    (412) 281–2620

Hixon Venture Company/
    Southwest Venture Partners
341 Milam Building
San Antonio, Texas 78205
    (512) 225–3053

Idanta Partners
3344 North Torrey Pines Court,
    Suite 200
La Jolla, California 92037
    (714) 455–5280

Indiana Capital Corporation
5612 West Jefferson Boulevard
Fort Wayne, Indiana 46804
    (219) 432–8622

InnoVen Group
Park 80 Plaza West—One
Saddle Brook, New Jersey
    07662
    (201) 845–4900

Institutional Venture Associates
3000 Sand Hill Road, Building 2,
   Suite 290
Menlo Park, California
   94025
     (415) 854–0132

Institutional Venture Capital
   Fund
The First National Bank of
   Chicago
Trust Department, 15th Floor
Chicago, Illinois 60670
     (312) 732–4170

Institutional Venture Partners
3000 Sand Hill Road, Building
   No. 2, Suite 290
Menlo Park, California 94025
     (415) 854–0132

Intercapco, Inc.
One Erieview Plaza
Cleveland, Ohio 44114
     (216) 241–7170

InterWest Partners
235 Montgomery Street,
   Suite 520
San Francisco, California 94104
     (415) 391–1545

Kleiner, Perkins, Caufield &
   Byers
Four Embarcadero Center,
   Suite 3520
San Francisco, California 94111
     (415) 421–3110

Kohlberg Kravis Roberts &
   Company
645 Madison Avenue
New York, New York 10022
     (212) 750–8300

Lawrence, WPG Partners L.P.
One New York Plaza, 30th Floor
New York, New York 10004
     (212) 908–9500

Lubar & Company, Inc.
777 East Wisconsin Avenue
Milwaukee, Wisconsin 53202
     (414) 291–9000

Lubrizol Enterprises, Inc.
29400 Lakeland Boulevard
Wickliffe, Ohio 44092
     (216) 943–4200

Mayfield III
2200 Sand Hill Road, Suite 101
Menlo Park, California 94025
     (415) 854–5560

Memorial Drive Trust
20 Acorn Park
Cambridge, Massachusetts
   02140
     (617) 864–5770

Menlo Ventures
3000 Sand Hill Road
Menlo Park, California 94025
     (415) 854–8540
       also
230 Park Avenue
New York, New York 10169
     (212) 697–7667

Merrill, Pickard Capital
   Company
650 California Street
San Francisco, California 94108
     (415) 397–8800

Morgenthaler Management
   Corporation
810 National City Bank Building

Cleveland, Ohio 44114
  (216) 621–3070

Narragansett Capital
  Corporation
40 Westminster Street
Providence, Rhode Island 02903
  (401) 751–1000

NBR II
P.O. Box 796
Addison, Texas 75001
  (214) 233–6631

New Court Securities
  Corporation
One Rockefeller Plaza
New York, New York 10020
  (212) 757–6000

New England Enterprise Capital
  Corporation
28 State Street
Boston, Massachusetts 02109
  (617) 742–0285

New Enterprise Associates, L.P.
300 Cathedral Place, Suite 100
Baltimore, Maryland 21201
  (301) 244–0115

North American Company
P.O. Box 14758
111 East Las Olas Boulevard
Fort Lauderdale, Florida 33302
  (305) 463–0681

Northwest Growth Fund, Inc.
1730 Midwest Plaza Building
810 Nicollet Mall
Minneapolis, Minnesota 55402
  (612) 372–8770

Oak Management Corporation
2 Railroad Place

Westport, Connecticut 06880
  (203) 226–8346

Oceanic Capital Corporation
545 Middlefield Road, Suite 160
Menlo Park, California 94025
  (415) 398–7677

Orange Nassau Capital
  Corporation
Three Center Plaza, Suite 506
Boston, Massachusetts 02108
  (617) 367–1160

Pan American Investment
  Company
545 Middlefield Road, Suite 160
Menlo Park, California 94025
  (415) 398–7677

Pathfinder Venture Capital Fund
7300 Metro Boulevard, Suite 585
Minneapolis, Minnesota 55435
  (612) 835–1121

Alan Patricof Associates
545 Madison Avenue
New York, New York 10022
  (212) 753–6300

Pioneer Ventures Company
113 E. 55th Street
New York, New York 10022
  (212) 980–9090

F.H. Prince & Company, Inc.
One First National Plaza,
  Suite 4950
Chicago, Illinois 60603
  (312) 726–2232

Rain Hill Group, Inc.
80 Wall Street
New York, New York 10005
  (212) 483–9162

Regional Financial Enterprises,
  Inc.
1111 Summer Street
Stamford, Connecticut 06905
  (203) 356–1730

Research & Science Investors,
  Inc.
230 Park Avenue, Suite 1260
New York, New York 10169
  (212) 867–9535

Robertson, Colman, Stephens &
  Woodman
100 California Street, Suite 450
San Francisco, California 94111
  (415) 781–9700

SAS Associates
445 South Figueroa Street
Los Angeles, California 90071
  (213) 624–4232

Scientific Advances, Inc.
1375 Perry Street
Columbus, Ohio 43201
  (614) 424–6161

Security Pacific Capital
  Corporation
333 South Hope Street
H25-4
Los Angeles, California 90071
  (213) 613–5215

Spectrum Capital, Ltd.
208 South LaSalle Street, Suite
  1230
Chicago, Illinois 60604
  (312) 236–5231

Sprout Capital Groups
140 Broadway
New York, New York 10005
  (212) 943–0300

Stephenson Merchant Banking
899 Logan Street
Denver, Colorado 80203
  (303) 837–1700

Sutter Hill Ventures
Two Palo Alto Square, Suite 700
Palo Alto, California 94304
  (415) 493–5600

Swedish Industrial Development
  Corporation
600 Steamboat Road
Greenwich, Connecticut 06830
  (203) 661–2500

T.A. Associates
111 Devonshire Street
Boston, Massachusetts 02109
  (617) 725–2300

Technology Venture Investors
3000 Sand Hill Road, Building 4,
  Suite 220
Menlo Park, California 94025
  (415) 854–7472

Union Venture Corporation
445 South Figueroa Street
Los Angeles, California 90071
  (213) 687–6959

United Venture Capital, Inc.
120 W. State Street
Rockford, Illinois 61101
  (815) 987–2178
              also
P.O. Box 5998
Incline Village, Nevada 89450
  (702) 831–4036

Vanguard Capital Corporation
101 Lions Drive
Barrington, Illinois 60010
  (312) 381–7755

Venrock Associates
30 Rockefeller Plaza, Suite 5508
New York, New York 10112
   (212) 246–4040

The Venture Capital Fund of
  New England
100 Franklin Street
Boston, Massachusetts 02110
   (617) 451–2575

Vista Ventures Corporation
1600 Summer Street
Stamford, Connecticut 06905
   (203) 359–3500

The Wallner Company
1205 Prospect Street, Suite 542
La Jolla, California 92037
   (714) 454–1166

Warburg, Pincus Capital
  Corporation
277 Park Avenue
New York, New York 10172
   (212) 593–0300

Welsh, Carson, Anderson &
  Stowe

45 Wall Street
New York, New York 10005
   (212) 422–3232

Whitehead Associates, Inc.
15 Valley Drive
Greenwich, Connecticut
  06830
   (203) 629–4633

J.H. Whitney & Company
630 Fifth Avenue
New York, New York 10111
   (212) 757–0500

Woodland Capital Company
1401 North Western Avenue
Lake Forest, Illinois 60045
   (312) 295–6300

Wood River Capital Corporation
645 Madison Avenue
New York, New York 10022
   (212) 750–9420

Xerox Corporation
9200 Sunset Boulevard, Suite 700
Los Angeles, California 90069
   (213) 278–7940

17

Rich uncle harrys

Not all venture capitalists are professional financiers. Some are simply affluent individuals with an abundance of cash and an interest in making profitable investments. Even when the economy is sagging at the seams, when millions are unemployed and millions more are hoarding every buck, the managerial and professional elite among us seem to make more money than ever before. Doctors, lawyers, dentists, McDonald's franchisees, garment manufacturers, Exxon senior vice-presidents, and Broadway actresses are out buying Rolex watches, jetting off to Acapulco weekends, and pouring cash into CDs. Prospective borrowers with such moneyed relatives in their family trees may view them as "rich Uncle Harrys"—as easy marks for loans or cash investments.

Although many may dismiss this as wishful thinking, there is evidence to prove that "rich Uncle Harrys" can be lucrative sources of cash whether they are relatives or not. Thousands of upper-middle-class individuals are actively seeking investment opportunities in the $10,000-to-$250,000 range. As such, they fill the financing gap right below venture capitalists.

Affluent individuals, much like their counterparts throughout the organized financial community, invest not

for humane reasons but simply because they must find productive uses for their capital. Consequently, the same techniques that are appropriate for established lenders and
investors work equally well here. But now you are dealing
only with individuals. There is no corporate structure, no
approval process or other bureaucratic checks and balances
common to banks, finance companies, and investment firms
that you must consider. This means:

Emotional appeals are more likely to have an impact on sole
investors. Hot projections for a new invention may capture
their fancy, and this will not be dampened by the machina-
tions of a corporate committee.

Reliance on formal business plans will give way to greater
emphasis on personality factors. The lone investor makes
decisions more on gut feelings than on balance sheets.

Terms, conditions, interest, and the like are completely
open to negotiation. Few sole investors approach the market
according to formal standards.

William E. Wetzel, Jr., of the University of New Hampshire's Whittemore School of Business and Economics, and
Craig R. Seymour, of the university's Center for Industrial
and Institutional Development, have conducted an interesting study, sponsored by the Office of the Chief Counsel for
Advocacy of the Small Business Administration, on how to
find and work with rich Uncle Harrys, whom they call informal investors.[*]

To ferret out these special individuals, Wetzel and Seymour turned their attention to the following target groups:

High-income individuals who invest in stocks and other financial instruments

[*] William E. Wetzel, Jr., Craig R. Seymour, *Informal Risk Capital in New England*
(1981).

Presidents of major corporations

The membership of entrepreneurial organizations, such as the Smaller Business Association of New England (SBANE)

Alumni of leading colleges and universities

Registered Mercedes-Benz owners

CPAs and lawyers

Subscribers to select business magazines

Although the study focused on the New England market, the findings are valid for money seekers in all geographic regions. The selection of target groups, for example, shows the importance of imagination and creativity. Mercedes-Benz owners: What a perfect way to zero in on certified successes! It's a safe bet that many of those spending between $25,000 and $50,000 on automobiles have cash available for speculative investments.

The strategy for finding informal investors parallels the modern marketing technique of segmentation. Here the population is divided into segments, with distinct characteristics, including the predisposition to make speculative investments. Key indicators, such as luxury-car ownership, tend to identify these groups. Other groups worthy of solicitation are subscribers to *Architectural Digest* magazine, patrons of the local museums or symphony orchestras, and passengers on the *QE 2*.

Some lists are available free of charge from business organizations; others must be purchased from mailing houses at roughly $50 per thousand names.

The Wetzel/Seymour study revealed the following additional characteristics about informal investors:

The median age is forty-seven, the largest segment falling between forty and fifty years of age; only 5 percent are between twenty and thirty.

They are well-educated. Ninety-five percent have a bachelor's degree, and more than half hold advanced degrees in business, economics, and technical disciplines.

They make an average of one informal capital investment every twenty months. Cash is committed to a wide range of business interests, including start-ups (companies still in the idea or early planning stages); infant firms (those about a year old, in the red, but approaching the break-even point and with substantial profit in sight); young outfits (companies with less than five years of operation but with a proven track record and poised for rapid growth); and established companies (companies growing too fast to finance themselves internally but not fast enough to satisfy venture capitalists).

On the all-important matter of investment volume, Wetzel and Seymour found that

> compared to venture capital firms and SBICs, informal investors tend to commit relatively small amounts of capital to any individual investment. Sixty-two percent of the past investments were under $25,000, and 85 percent were under $100,000. Based on investments of $100,000 or less and using the mid-point of each range as representative of the typical investment within the range, the average investment size was $21,000. Including all size categories and using $250,000 as representative of the largest category, the average individual investment size was $51,000. . . . Clearly, informal investors have been a source of risk capital in amounts in all size categories below the typical interest threshold of professional venture capital firms, i.e., below $500,000.

In addition to the range of investment sizes available from informal investors, their tendency to participate with other individuals enhances the flexibility of the total risk capital financing available to an individual firm.*

Because our objective as million-dollar money raisers is to piece together blocks of borrowed or invested cash, informal investors can prove to be pivotal sources, as they may be willing to extend capital when more organized sources are not.

Rich Uncle Harrys show the greatest enthusiasm for ground-floor opportunities in high-technology fields such as electronics, computers, energy, and health care. The Wetzel/Seymour study found that

the principal criteria cited by these investors was that technology be in a field that they understand and can evaluate. The following representative comments illustrate this point:

"An area that I can understand or relate to."

"Fields with which I am sufficiently experienced to permit evaluation."

"It is limited to what I know and understand myself—especially about the marketplace or can get trustworthy opinions on."

The factors that most commonly lead to the rejection of investment proposals are inadequate risk/return ratios, lack of confidence in the company's management, the belief that the new venture is based too much on wishful thinking, and the fear that the proposed product's services would attract too small a market.

* Wetzel, Seymour, *Informal Risk Capital in New England*, p. 14.

The more that money seekers learn about how to turn on rich Uncle Harrys, the greater their chances of hitting pay dirt. These additional factors should be considered in designing the investment proposal:

The vast majority of informal investors expect to play an active role in the ventures they fund. Typically, they seek a consulting role or appointment to the board of directors. It is wise to make it clear that you are open to this.

Common stock is the most popular investment vehicle, followed by notes with warrants, convertible preferred stock, and convertible debentures.

Most investors seek long-term capital gains income; others seek a combination of current income and long-term gains. Deals structured to return a bit of both will likely prove highly attractive.

Informal investors are encouraged by the participation of other investors of similar means and circumstances. The important point here is that once you enlist the support of a single informal investor, he/she can tell the world of your success. The involvement of a few investors may act as a magnet to attract others.

Deals projecting the return of the initial investment within five to seven years are most attractive. Surprisingly, however, a significant minority of informal investors (24 percent) either consider the waiting period for return of the investment to be unimportant or are willing to wait more than ten years. This "patience level" is rare at established venture-capital firms.

Finally, the Wetzel/Seymour study makes this observation:

Informal investors generally learn of investment opportunities through friends and business associates. During the course of this research, it was not uncommon to discover that finding one informal investor led to contacts with several others. A network of friends and associates appears to link informal investors.

Tap the network. Put it to work for you.

18

Going public

Perhaps the most glamorous financing strategy is widely known as going public.* Glamorous, yes, because it can make unknown entrepreneurs—people with little more than a good idea and a germ of a company—overnight millionaires. Thousands have done it in the past, and thousands more are dreaming of following in their footsteps. Some will succeed.

Going public is a form of raising equity capital. The process involves selling the company's stock to outside investors. If successful, offerings of this kind can quickly generate large amounts of capital and can provide a financial base for accelerated growth. Many of the great success stories in American industry—like the fast-growing Apple Computer Company—can be traced, in part, to management's decision to take the venture to the public.

Although going public is commonly associated with giant corporations, small companies can get in on the act, too. So-called Regulation A filings, which provide for a simpler and less expensive process than standard public offerings, can be used to raise up to $1.5 million. "We are inundated with Regulation A applications from small com-

---

* For further information on going public, consult *Venture* magazine and *Going Public*, two excellent sources.

panies," says a spokesperson for the Securities and Exchange Commission (SEC), the federal agency that regulates stock offerings. "The entire process takes only about two months, the tiniest companies can qualify, and a lot of money can be raised. A wide range of companies—from theatrical producers to manufacturers to retailers—are taking advantage of Regulation A offers."

Entrepreneurs interested in taking their companies public are advised to explore the idea with an underwriter specializing in small issues. These experts help determine if there is a market for the company's stock, how many shares can be sold, and the price to be asked per share. Even more important, the underwriter forms a selling group to market the stock to investors. This is what makes the underwriter crucial to the success of most offerings: the company going public rarely has the means to sell the stock on its own.

Fees for underwriting services include a standard commission of between 10 and 15 percent of the amount of the offering plus an additional sum for expenses. The total tab, then, for a $1.5 million offering is likely to exceed $200,000, including legal fees. Most underwriters also demand warrants for 10 percent of the stock at a price that is about 10 percent above the offering price of the shares. Lawyers, accountants, and bankers can recommend the names of reputable underwriters.

Some entrepreneurs try to save money by going public without the aid of an underwriter. Although this can be done, it is advisable only for those firms that plan to sell stock to an identifiable group of friends, business associates, and relatives. Without this built-in market, the issue may never be sold.

Regardless of how the company approaches investors—with or without an underwriter—a competent attorney must be hired to handle the transaction. He or she should be a specialist in securities law and thus well versed in the latest SEC rules and regulations.

Going public does carry its share of obligations. First, the company must reveal a good deal of formerly confidential information, including comprehensive financial reports and market data. The "offering circular" used to describe the company and its stock must provide full and fair representation of the firm. This SEC requirement is designed to protect investors from unscrupulous offers. Another important consideration in going public is that management must now share ownership with outsiders. For highly individualistic entrepreneurs used to answering to no one, this may be intolerable.

"Companies that use the Regulation A filings usually believe that this simplified approach to raising a lot of money justifies putting up with the drawbacks," the SEC spokesperson adds. "For those who feel this way, the consensus is that the best time to go public is when the stock market is bullish. That's when investor confidence is strongest—and that has a lot to do with producing a successful offering."

The following is a typical scenario for a company going public.

The owner determines that the firm will benefit by raising capital in the public market. He/she has learned that there is currently an active new issues market, and he/she is willing to dilute his/her equity in the company in exchange for outside capital.

The company contacts one or more investment bankers to determine their interest in underwriting the offering and to see if both parties can work together well. The bankers visit the company's facilities, interview management and key employees, and then submit proposals on handling the offering, fees, and terms.

The company selects an investment banker and, together with the firm's accountants and attorneys, prepares the registration statement (including a prospectus) required by the SEC. This takes from one to three months, depending on the company's size and complexity.

The registration statement is filed with the SEC, and the underwriter puts together a syndicate of other investment bankers to prepare for selling the issue. The lead investment bank may approach major institutions, such as insurance companies and pension funds, with details of the offering. These cash-rich sources can be pivotal to the success of a public offering in today's market.

The SEC responds to the registration statement approximately one month after it has been filed. Examiners may seek additional information, clarification, or revision of certain items in the prospectus. The prospectus is then changed as required and returned to the SEC. Once the SEC is satisfied with the statement, it allows it to become effective.

The company and its bankers set a final price for the offering, and this is printed in the prospectus. The underwriter's salespeople begin selling the issue.

Public offerings have come to life after a period of inactivity. Investors are now pouring millions of dollars into emerging companies blessed with good management and bright growth prospects. Money is available to start and expand small ventures and to provide owners with instant liquidity.

"Throughout most of the 1970s, the public markets were just about dead as a source of financing," says Jay Cooke, managing director of Laidlaw Adams & Peck, Inc., investment bankers. "Small companies were in a terrible bind. Investors wouldn't give them the time of day. As a result, owners who did not want to sell out had to rely on short-term bank financing. Their debt-to-equity ratio went out of line, and they could not manage from a long-term perspective. The capital wasn't there.

"This began to change a few years ago and has picked up steam ever since. We are now seeing broad investor interest in small companies. The number of public offerings has increased as has the amount of money being raised. Part of this is attributable to a speculative flurry and part to the reduction in capital gains taxes, but it is based mostly on the fact that many small businesses make for good investments."

American and foreign investors alike are currently gobbling up small-company stock issues in a wide range of fields and industries. On the "most-favored list" are those firms with interests in energy, communications, electronics, computer software, and health care. "But the list is not limited to this," Cooke adds. "Any small business that has developed an interesting concept or that has carved out a special niche in the marketplace can also be highly attractive to investors. These firms can raise substantial sums of money."

It has worked that way for Systems Engineering and Manufacturing Corporation, a small maker of industrial products. When the firm held its second public offering, managers of the corporation sought to raise expansion capital and to provide some liquidity for the existing shareholders. Cash was needed to gear up production for a growing backlog of orders and to purchase part of the founders' equity.

To accomplish these goals, investment bankers offered 350,000 shares of the company's stock, priced at $8.50 a share. The value of the transaction totaled $3 million, with $1.7 million going to the selling shareholders, $1 million to the corporation, and the balance to cover the cost of the issue. Two years after the offering, the company's revenues had quadrupled, and the price of the stock had increased by 100 percent.

And this firm is one among many that have raised substantial sums in recent years. During the first quarter of
1981 alone, more than a dozen companies raised more than
$20 million each in their first public offerings. Cetus Cor-
poration, a genetic engineering company, raised a whopping
$120 million by going public despite the fact that the com-
pany registered losses in three of the four years preceding
the offering and earned only a slight profit in the other.
Investors perceived earnings potential—that the firm could
make it big in an exciting new industry with unlimited potential—and this confidence overshadowed everything else.
The offering sold out the very day it opened. This kind of
enthusiasm is helping entrepreneurs raise as much as $3.8
billion (1981) annually in initial public offerings.

In the twelve months between July 1980 and July 1981,

more than 700 entrepreneurs, investors, employees, and
individuals with a little piece of the action fulfilled an
American dream. On paper, at least, each one achieved a
net worth of a million dollars or more. And more than
100 individuals saw the paper value of their shares jump
to at least $10 million. Although many worked long and
hard, their status changed overnight—when they took
their companies public. . . .

Five millionaires were born from "penny" stocks
which sold for only 10 cents a share, including James P.
MacPherson, president and chief executive officer of Zoe
Products, who made $2.1 million on paper; and Edgar J.
Huff, president of Black Dome Energy, who made $2
million.

At the other end of the spectrum, Genetech stock
sold for the highest share price, $35, and made $32.38
million each for Robert A. Swanson, president, and Herbert W. Boyer, vice-president. . . .

Many companies put multiple millionaires on our
charts. Four firms (NIKE, Inc., Micom Systems, Inc., In-

fotron Systems, and Delta Drilling Co., Inc.) boasted at least 10 millionaires apiece. Philip H. Knight, chairman and president of NIKE, heads his company's list of 15 millionaires. He holds $178.2 million worth of stocks (and cashed in for $3.1 million). At Micom Systems, John M. Thornton, chairman, is one of 10 millionaires. He cashed in for $3.1 million and held $38.7 million worth of stock at the time of the offering. *

Clearly, for those who know how to raise money, prevailing economic conditions are of minor importance. This is obvious given today's equity markets. These are, after all, the best of times and the worst of times. While the recession is forcing thousands into bankruptcy, others are striking it rich through public offerings.

"We believe that 1981's total of 3.2 billion dollars raised through initial public offerings set the all-time record, and we expect the trend to continue," says Meredith Young, editor of *Going Public*, a newsletter that monitors the market for new corporate issues. "This is an excellent time for small businesses to use public financing to raise capital. The reduction of capital gains taxes plus the widespread disillusionment with blue chip stocks have combined to make small-business issues more attractive to investors."

Adds Ronald Koenig, managing director of Ladenburg, Thalmann & Company, an investment banking house that underwrites dozens of small-company offerings, "Wall Street's enthusiasm for initial public offerings has its peaks and valleys, and we are now at the zenith. Many ventures that might have been unable to raise any money just a few years ago can now get more than they need. Investors are clamoring for the stock of emerging companies. For entrepreneurs, selling shares to them is still the best way to get rich in America."

* *Venture*, September 1981, p. 30.

One strategy for going public is first to launch a business with venture capital, giving it time to prove itself in the marketplace before selling stock to the public. A good track record encourages investors to accept the risks that go hand in hand with new offerings. But in today's hot market, many firms are skipping the venture-capital phase and are turning to public offerings for start-up funds.

"We have handled successful public offerings for companies with virtually no sales, no customers, and nothing but a promising product or service," Koenig says. "One of our recent clients had revenues of about two hundred thousand dollars per year and was losing money when we took it public. We sold six hundred thousand shares at seven dollars each, raising 3.8 million dollars for the firm after expenses and commissions. The company designs and markets disk drives for small computers. Investors are betting that its future growth will be outstanding."

Consider the advantages of going public as described by Peter Wallace, a general partner with Hambrecht & Quest, a San Francisco investment banking partnership serving emerging companies with growth potential.

1. If a company is acceptable to the public market, its securities will generally command a higher price than in a private equity placement. This means that equity capital can be raised with minimal dilution.

2. Once a company's securities have become seasoned in the public market, the mechanism is in place for further public financings to bring in additional equity capital as needed to support a continuing growth program.

3. A viable public market creates liquidity, which can be important for shareholders in general and particularly for founders and managers, who may have substantial holdings in the company's stock.

4. The public marketplace provides an objective and credible measure of the value of the company's stock, which is of importance in attracting new management talent through equity participation, in motivating employee shareholders, and in providing for acquisition a medium of exchange with a readily acceptable valuation.

5. Being publicly held can increase a company's stature or image to its customers, suppliers, bankers, and others.*

Once the company has completed its public offering, it need not stop its ascent to the loftier heights of the business world. It can, in fact, do more than ever to capture the attention of big-league lenders and investors. By going on the stock exchange, listing with the National Association of Securities Dealers Automated Quotation System (Nasdaq), small ventures can gain the attention and visibility generally accorded only to the corporate giants. "The Nasdaq system, a computerized market for trading over-the-counter stocks, was formed to bring liquidity and credibility to these transactions," says Gordon S. Macklin, president of the National Association of Securities Dealers. "It links a network of brokers across the nation. Every trade of a Nasdaq-listed stock is reported into the system the moment it occurs. By checking computer terminals, brokers can give investors up-to-the-minute price information."

A Nasdaq listing can aid small public companies seeking to build a greater following for their stock in these ways:

Liquidity: Dealers of Nasdaq-listed stocks are required to continuously post bid and asked prices, thus assuring liquidity for the shares. This can help business owners and investors sell their interests at market value.

* Peter Wallace in Pratt, *Guide to Venture Capital Sources*, p. 96.

Exposure: Nasdaq trading activities are published daily in many newspapers and financial publications. This focuses investor attention on a select group of over-the-counter companies.

Broker supports: Market makers in Nasdaq issues are likely to promote the shares by committing research and sales efforts to them. Investors learn that even the small companies can make for good investments.

To be eligible for a Nasdaq listing, companies must be registered with the SEC as 12-G public corporations, and must have assets of at least $2 million, capital and surplus of $1 million, a hundred thousand shares outstanding, three hundred stockholders of record, and at least two brokers willing to make a market in the stock.

Nasdaq entry fees, based on the number of shares outstanding, range from $1,000 to $5,000; annual fees go from $250 to $2,500. Companies interested in exploring Nasdaq participation may contact the National Association of Securities Dealers, 1735 K Street, Washington, D.C. 20006.

"We were one of the original companies in the Nasdaq system," says J. M. Hill, president of Rangaire Corporation, a small manufacturer of kitchen appliances, "and we've been very pleased with the market. Our shares have performed well over the years and they have won a respectable following.

"Rangaire is far from being a household name, but with Nasdaq that doesn't really matter. The system is designed for firms like ours. It gives us considerable exposure in a special way. We can compete for attention with the larger corporations."

Many major companies are, in fact, listed on Nasdaq. Names like Coors, U.S. Trust, and Hoover share billing with the small businesses that make up the bulk of Nasdaq's roughly three thousand companies.

"There is a great prestige being in the same market with

some of America's leading companies," Macklin adds. "That can propel a once-obscure firm into the business spotlight." Still, a Nasdaq listing is not recommended for every company. Many entrepreneurs are uncomfortable with the higher levels of public exposure, the volatility of stock prices, and the scrutiny of security analysts. They may prefer to be either privately owned or traded over-the-counter without a central market listing. It is best to review the alternatives with local brokers, investment bankers, and accountants.

Those companies opting for a market listing can make the most of this by combining Nasdaq exposure with a public relations program designed to draw media attention to the company and its activities. As we have noted, those entrepreneurs who generate excitement for their ventures encourage lenders and investors to risk substantial sums on the businesses. Public relations agencies can help public companies move from being one of a million unknown corporations in the financial community to being center stage.

Although oil giants and merger makers seem to capture the spotlight, the media are open to small firms and entrepreneurs as well. Many of the most successful ventures have used publicity to soar from start-up to established positions. They know that making news builds a favorable image with investors, bankers, and customers.

"Small companies can get plenty of press coverage if they have innovative products or services, a new way of doing business, or a colorful owner-manager," says Leslie Schupak of Kanan, Corbin, Schupak & Aronow, Inc., a public relations agency serving small and midsize businesses. "Many entrepreneurs think there's nothing newsworthy about their firms, but that's often because they're too close to the operations to see how interesting they really are. Publicity specialists can walk in and spot hidden assets that may be of great interest to the press.

"One of our clients, for example, built a hardware store

19

Factoring

Imagine this: You start a business, it finds a niche in the market and becomes successful, and still you need money. How can that be? Here's a typical case:

Super-Duper Sweaters is a successful, profitable, well-managed garment manufacturer that turns out some of the most dazzling fashions in America. Super-Duper's sweaters make the cover of *Vogue*, are snatched off the shelves in the poshest of stores, and are sported by a Who's Who of loyal customers. Just one problem: Several times a year, Super-Duper Sweaters, Inc., finds itself without a dime to its name.

Impossible, you say! How could that be? Simple! The garment business, like scores of other industries, requires such substantial capital investments that even the most successful companies can run dry from time to time. The millions of dollars that go into producing a new spring line, for example, may not be returned for six months or more. In the meantime, Super-Duper and the thousands of firms like it must put up cash for designs, fabric, labor, warehousing, transportation, and promotion. Only then can they bill customers, and only after a time lag do they receive their payments.

But there is no time to wait: a fall line must be produced. More fabric, more labor, more designs. That's where factor-

will handle any client that sells his/her goods on terms, has a net worth of $100,000 or more, and has a base of credit-worthy customers. A factor's clientele usually falls into one of three groupings:

Small and medium-sized companies that use the services of a factor primarily for credit and collection services.

Businesses that use factors both for credit services and financial support.

Businesses primarily interested in financial support that rely heavily on the factor for funds. Clients in this category generally have limited financial resources.

One major factor, Heller Financial, provides its clients with the following services:

Reduces overhead and operating expenses by taking over the functions of credit checking, maintaining accounts receivable records, and handling collections

Provides "instant" credit approval, often on accounts that the client's own credit department might limit or reject. This enables the company to sell more merchandise to more customers.

Exerts a tighter cost control on credits and collections

Assumes the risk of bad debts.

Helps ensure sound growth and profits by turning receivables into cash when needed by the business, giving the client more elbow room for smooth and efficient operation, and improving the client's balance sheet

Becomes a stable resource, matching the client's needs with increasing credit and cash when growth is possible.

One drawback to factoring is that it can damage a small venture's reputation with its customers. Because the factor takes possession of the client's invoices, customers make their payments directly to this third party. In some industries, this can have a negative connotation, signaling that the firm is in financial difficulty; in others, such as the garment trade, factoring is considered a routine and acceptable part of a company's financing package. Just how your current or potential customers will react is a matter worthy of consideration.

20

Selling your system: becoming a franchiser

Here's another type of success-breeds-the-need-for-more-money case:

You're a small-business owner with a little shop or service outfit that makes money year after year. Not a tremendous amount, but the potential is there. You're sure of that, and you yearn to expand but don't have the capital or the know-how. If that's your dilemma, one financing strategy can help you say "today local markets, tomorrow the world."

This approach to raising money—and building a substantial business enterprise in the process—is the familiar concept of franchising, but with a twist. Rather than going the standard small-business route of buying into an established franchise, you can reverse the traditional pattern by packaging your own concept and selling it to others. Your small firm becomes the franchiser, marketing its success formula, brand name, trade secrets, and the like. In this way, the company can raise cash for an international chain of franchised units.

"Virtually any type of product or service can be franchised," says Donald Boroian, president of Franchise Concepts, Inc.,* a consulting and development outfit that has turned more than two hundred small businesses into national franchises. "We are the largest cloner of small businesses in the franchise industry. Name a type of venture, and chances are good that we have turned it into a franchise operation. The list includes sandwich shops, natural food restaurants, drive-through record stores, pizzerias, muffler shops, vision centers, a co-op buying club, and a computer store."

Businesses that are well organized and that bring a systematic approach to the market are the most successful franchisers. In the case of two similar shops on the same street, only one may be suitable for franchising. Assuming both are pizzerias, the one with written recipes, portion-control measures, and planned menus may perform well; the other, run by a disorganized owner who cooks with a "dash of this and a pinch of that," is probably better off as a single-unit operation. The formula cannot be transferred to others. Of course, those who run informal businesses but who want to become franchisers can always shift gears, changing their management style to make it more amenable to this approach. It is never too late to change.

Other major criteria for turning a small business into a successful franchise include:

A product or service that is attractive to national markets

A clear advantage over competitive offerings currently established in the market

Good credit ratings and financial stability

Reasonable cash requirements

* Franchise Concepts is located at 20200 Governor's Drive, Olympia Fields, Illinois 60461.

A prototype of the franchise concept already in operation or established, to show how the venture fares in the real world

Franchise consultants will visit small companies, analyze their franchise potential, and make a recommendation to the owner. Expect a fee of about $500 for this service.

If all signs are go, consultants can work with management throughout the development process: planning the franchise, establishing franchise fees and royalties, seeking legal registrations, preparing promotional materials, and even selling the units on the open market. Fees for this package service range from $20,000 to $100,000. The former small-business owner—now a franchiser—can anticipate collecting a minimum franchise fee of $15,000 per unit plus a 5 percent royalty based on annual sales.

The power of franchising is awesome. With good management, experienced counsel, and a healthy dose of luck, a local business can emerge from franchise development as the next McDonald's. But there are risks and drawbacks to consider. Thousands of franchises fall by the wayside, unable to survive in highly competitive markets. The best advice is to know your market and to carefully weigh all factors with an experienced attorney and CPA. Contact trade associations or accountants for the names of qualified franchise consultants.

21

Harnessing professional power

The myriad money-raising vehicles differ dramatically in rates, maturity, and ownership participation. Certainly, farmers' home loans and rich Uncle Harrys are worlds apart. Still, all capital-raising techniques are alike in one respect: they are complex legal and financial transactions. Just how a deal is structured makes an impact on the borrower's business and personal liability, tax obligations, debt service, and ultimately his profits. Consequently, wise borrowers should work with a professional team of skilled accountants and attorneys, making all major decisions in conjunction with them. These experts can clear a path through the maze of capital markets and—together with investment bankers—can help ferret out prospective lenders and investors.

The problem is that few people know how to make full use of professionals. All too often, lawyers are seen as handling wills and divorces; accountants are associated only with tax returns. In fact, members of both professions offer clients a full range of services related to raising and protecting cash. Let's take a closer look.

ATTORNEYS

Today more than ever the language of business is legal. From contracts to consumerism, from taxes to trademarks, law and commerce go hand in hand. But how can individuals obtain competent legal assistance? How can borrowers find lawyers experienced in business affairs? How can a layperson rate attorneys? How are fees established?

Although there is no single, comprehensive source of information on attorneys, a little research can go a long way in tracking down first-rate lawyers experienced in any number of specialties. The following guidelines are designed to help capital seekers select and hire qualified legal counsel:

Martindale-Hubbel law directories list virtually every attorney admitted to state bar associations. Personal descriptions for each lawyer include education, type of practice, major clients, and date admitted to the bar. The directories are available at libraries and legal offices.

Lawyer referral services sponsored by state and local bar associations provide the names of member attorneys. However, this does not imply a rating of confidence and should therefore be viewed only as a starting point for exploration of the professional's talent and experience.

A Supreme Court ruling has made it possible for lawyers to advertise their services in daily newspapers. Attorneys can now list their qualifications, education, specialties, initial consulting fees, and routine legal fees.

Clients concerned with a lawyer's professional standing may check with the state Supreme Court. Names of attorneys suspended or disbarred are generally kept on record.

Consult with friends, associates, business owners and trade associations for their recommendations on qualified legal counsel.

Narrow your search to three or four candidates, conducting exploratory sessions with each. Be sure to obtain in-depth information on educational background, previous legal experience, types of clients, number of cases handled, percentage of cases won, and fees. Seek references from existing clients.

"All too often, business people are afraid of attorneys," says a spokesperson for the American Bar Association. "They are afraid to ask them the tough questions that need answering. My advice is to overcome this timidity and to put all your concerns on the table. Only if all matters are ironed out in advance can the attorney and the client determine if they are right for each other. The process benefits both parties."

In shopping around for legal services, clients should make certain that the lawyers they interview are experienced in performing the work their businesses require. Consider the following:

Finance counseling: Attorneys can reveal the pros and cons of debt and equity sources, negotiate loan agreements, establish limited partnerships, and register public offerings. Knowing the legal implications surrounding these financial options may influence management to take one course of action or another.

"Lawyers know that most banks have stock loan forms that are completely unacceptable because of their extremely restrictive provisions," says Harold Goldberg, a lawyer active in small-business affairs. "Business owners facing bankers without legal representation may sign the form as is.

Attorneys, on the other hand, will routinely cross out the most prohibitive terms. They know what is negotiable and what is not."

Franchise reviews: Franchising remains one of the most popular yet risky routes to small-business ownership. For every promising opportunity there is a quick-buck scheme that is destined to failure. Prospective investors should have an attorney review the franchise disclosure statement, checking for total fees, royalty payments, territorial guarantees, and promotional supports. This can help weed out the shams and improve the chances for success in landing legitimate deals.

Licensing strategies: Some businesses require licenses that are issued by government agencies. Lawyers experienced in this work can often cut through the bureaucratic red tape, securing the necessary documents without the long delays a layperson may encounter.

Money seekers should be concerned not only with the types of legal services they employ but also how they employ them. A sound strategy is to move away from the traditional emphasis on defensive legal services to an offensive strategy that utilizes the law to capitalize on promising opportunities. The common practice of using attorneys solely to defend business interests is shortsighted, since it fails to take advantage of the full scope of small-business legal services.

Experts offer the following guidelines for the savvy use of legal services:

Have attorneys review major business transactions in advance and structure financing deals from the bottom up. This is the best way to utilize the law creatively and to satisfy compliance provisions.

"Because many legal issues are not apparent to a lay-
man, he must let a lawyer explore all the angles," adds Goldberg. "One client, for example, changed his clothing shop to
a wine and cheese emporium. That seemingly simple action
had a host of legal ramifications. A new corporation had to
be formed, the store lease amended, financing obtained, and
applications made to the liquor authority. Without any one
of these steps, the transaction could not have been completed."

Determine if the attorney will be handling the case indepen-
dently or calling in colleagues for highly specialized work in
patents, foreign trade, or commercial bankruptcies. Some
lawyers simply refer difficult cases to specialists and take no
share in the fee; others work along with outside counsel and
split the compensation. Clients have a right to know the
details of fee arrangements as well as the names and qualifications of attorneys involved in the case.

Seek contingent fee arrangements for complex negligence
cases. Under these terms, the attorney is paid one-third or
more of the final settlement. Clients with cash-flow problems can benefit by delaying payment until the case has been
resolved successfully.

Decide whether to hire a law firm or a sole practitioner.
Although the firms claim to have the widest range of expertise, independents insist that clients are better served
through referrals.

"General practitioners can call in the very best specialists in all business law disciplines," Goldberg observes.
"They are not limited to recommending the people within
the firm. This gives clients access to top attorneys."

Ask the attorney to integrate business activities with personal financial planning. For the self-employed, common
threads can be woven through both areas of interest.

Active money raisers may prefer a legal retainer, establishing a set monthly payment to cover all routine services, including meetings, consultations, and telephone conversations. This may foster a closer client/attorney relationship.

Clients should keep in mind that a lawyer's advice is not a dictate. It should be pooled with other business considerations in the making of any key decision. The ultimate authority and responsibility rest with the owner. These can never be delegated to an outsider. Clients should also remember that it is good policy for client and lawyer to determine, periodically, whether or not to continue the relationship.

ACCOUNTANTS

Accountants are another professional group that have moved beyond their traditional turf—of ledger books and 1040 forms. The old image of CPAs as Dickensian characters peering through green eye shades has given way to a new breed of CPAs who are full-fledged management consultants.

"Accountants are uniquely suited to handle the fiscal affairs of self-employed men and women because we gain intimate knowledge of their business and personal finances," says George Mandel, a partner with Seidman & Seidman, a national accounting firm that specializes in serving small companies and affluent individuals. "We are generalists, tieing together the threads of their financial affairs. It is all interrelated: business income, family assets, estates and the like."

Even the largest CPA firms—the so-called Big Eight—which are traditionally linked with huge, multinational corporations, are now actively soliciting and servicing small-business clients. Merchants, realtors, distributorships, and professional practices are finding that they can afford to hire some of the most prestigious names in the accounting field. Although skeptics question the Big Eight's commitment to small business, partners at the firms insist that the quality of service is the same for all clients.

Many small, local CPA firms are also capable of handling a wide scope of assignments. Clients who prefer to work with local CPAs cite the benefits of close professional relationships and of having access to the managing partners.

Fees for CPA services differ markedly according to the size and reputation of the firm, the type of assignment, and the individual performing the work. Hourly charges range from $40 to $250, with the highest rates going to senior partners at the major firms.

One clever approach to keeping costs under control is to specify that routine work be performed by junior staffers, thus saving substantially in cases where high-powered, high-priced talent is not necessary. It is also advisable, especially when dealing with large CPA firms, to demand that a partner supervise the account and be responsible for it even if subordinates put in most of the billable hours. This can be an excellent way to keep a lid on fees while still assuring that an experienced hand is at the helm.

The following are among the major services offered by CPAs:

Financial planning: The emphasis here is on anticipating long- and short-term cash needs and preparing for them in advance. For example, CPAs can help determine the amount of capital required to finance a proposed expansion or a new facility. Armed with this knowledge, the owner knows, before committing a dollar, if the project is feasible and, if so, where to turn for financing.

Raising money: If the green light is flashed, the CPA can tap personal contacts among bankers and investors, thus improving the odds of the client's obtaining the required funds. CPAs also help business owners prepare loan applications and may accompany clients to loan conferences.

"CPAs in service to small business have to think like entrepreneurs," says a principal with the accounting firm of Kenneth Leventhol. "We cannot apply standard systems or procedures to small companies. We have to be imaginative, and we must follow a project through from beginning to end. It's not enough to simply tell clients how much money they need. We have to tell them where to get it, how to get it, and we have to go out and help them fight for it."

Computer services: CPA firms provide computerized financial analyses, reports, and operating statements that can be used as management aids or as support materials for loan applications.

"Whatever their specialty, accountants catering to small business no longer simply sign off on financial statements and walk away," says Bernard Z. Lee, managing partner of Seidman & Seidman. "Our goal is to help small firms graduate from meager beginnings to substantial growth. One of our clients, for example, has expanded from its birth as a grain terminal with one employee to a major corporation listed on the American Stock Exchange. This kind of success is possible when a business gets the right financial services at each stage of its development."

In this era of "mergermania," thousands of entrepreneurs are learning that mergers and acquisitions offer some of the best opportunities for raising money. But there are no guarantees. What on paper looks like a hot prospect for a merger partner or a profitable acquisition may, in fact, be a ticket to heavy losses. Hundreds of business owners have traded highly successful ventures for what turned out to be shares of worthless stock. A layperson sees only the tip of the iceberg; it takes a professional to delve beneath the surface, to X-ray the books. CPA firms evaluate prospective deals, providing clients with informed and objective opinions on whether to accept or decline.

Learn to break the April 15th syndrome. Use accountants as year-round business consultants and confidants, relying on their wisdom and good offices throughout the money-raising process.

22

Tying up loose ends

Okay, this book has probably covered more loan plans, credit plans, investment opportunities, and professional services than you imagined existed. That should be motivation enough for you to get started on the quest for a million dollars. But first, let's tie up some loose ends.

You may be confused by the number and scope of government loan programs. CDC, SBIC, SBA, MESBIC, FHA: it's enough to leave any mortal wondering where to start and, perhaps more important, how to wade through the federal bureaucracy to get at the money. Anyone who's dealt with Uncle Sam knows that obtaining a simple form can take months. That doesn't bode well for receiving a check of $100,000 or more. But not to fear. Deep in the heart of the federal bureaucracy lies a little-known network of experts trained to help money seekers with everything from handicap assistance loans to land grants.

The shortest route to this valuable assistance is through the General Services Administration's (GSA) Federal Information Center. This agency untangles red tape surrounding government agencies, bringing outsiders directly to the source of government power and expertise.

"Our service is designed to help anyone who has a question about the government but doesn't know where to turn for the answers," says Donald Knenlein, coordinator of GSA's Federal Information Center Program. "We're here to help them find the answers or to find the right person who has the answers.

"Government is so big and complex that outsiders are often confused as to which department has responsibility for what. Take the small firm seeking to bid on government contracts. The owner may not know if he should contact the Small Business Administration, the GSA, or any of the scores of individual agencies.

"We guide management on this, putting them in touch with the right governmental units as well as with the officials best suited to serve them. This saves owners from the wild goose chase of phone calls and referrals through dozens of offices."

Working through forty-one offices across the nation, the Federal Information Center Program fields seven million queries annually. Information specialists use personal experience, government directories, and an enormous data base to match requests with the right sources to service them. Be it a question on SBIC equity investments or FHA interest rates, there is likely to be a well-versed government expert available to provide informed guidance free-of-charge.

The program operates along the following guidelines:

Queries may be directed by mail, telephone, or in person. For the address and phone number of the nearest office, write the Federal Information Center, Washington, D.C. 20405.

Sources outside government are used when they are deemed to be the most-informed experts on particular subjects.

The information service may be used as often as necessary for business and personal pursuits.

Charges for books, pamphlets, and other publications are specified in advance of shipment.

Information specialists will not service requests for legal or policy advice, will not recommend private business interests, and will not interpret laws. Firms failing to win government business loans will not be helped to change the laws but may get recommendations for revising their loan applications.

All calls and correspondence are treated as strictly confidential. Individual and business names are never released without permission.

"Our business-related activities are extremely wide in scope," says a Federal Information Center specialist, "On any given day we'll help companies gain access to experts at the SBA, the Patent Office, the Defense Department's procurement office, the Government Printing Office, the Agriculture Department, professional organizations, and state licensing authorities.

"One woman who wanted to open a liquor store called on our offices for advice on all aspects of starting the business. We put her in touch with financing sources, zoning boards, and even helped her get market research from the chamber of commerce. This way she knew, in advance, whether or not there was enough potential in the area to invest in a new business of this kind."

The best approach is to check with the FIC before contacting a government loan source. Make sure you are dealing with the right individual from the start.

On to loose end number two: the problems of women entrepreneurs. Because women have in the past remained outside business and financial circles, they now face even higher hurdles on the route to personal success. When the debits don't equal the credits, when sales suddenly slow to a crawl, or when advertising seems to have lost its zip, there is no need to panic. Women business owners can turn to a hot line for management consulting. Because many women believe they cannot get serious attention from traditional sources, the American Women's Economic Development Corporation, a non-profit organization, has stepped in to bridge the gap.

"Our national telephone counseling service is designed to assist the many entrepreneurial women out there who need help and have no place to turn," says an AWED spokesperson. "The service is offered to all women already in business or planning a business. They may have firms with serious difficulties or companies just needing a bit of direction. We try to help them all.

"AWED serves a broad cross section of women entrepreneurs. The diversity of their businesses is matched only by the diversity of the women themselves. They come from all socioeconomic and ethnic backgrounds; range in age from their twenties to their sixties; are single, married, divorced, or widowed."

All have a common interest: the need for business-financing and related assistance. Telephone counseling, one of AWED's numerous services, is simple to use. Interested parties located in the U.S. first request a hot-line application by writing directly to AWED, 1270 Avenue of the Americas, New York, New York 10020. Applications are used to provide information on the woman's business, her specific needs and problems, and where she can be reached for assistance.

Once the information is received at AWED, staffers review the application and seek an expert to consult with the business owner. Specialists are engaged to field questions in a diverse range of disciplines. All consultants are volunteers with extensive experience in the business world. If the entrepreneur's problem appears to border on several specialties, AWED makes an effort to have more than one counselor on hand for the conference.

"Sometimes you can't put a business problem into a neat category," the spokesperson adds. "A single activity can have financial, distribution, and merchandising implications. We want the women to benefit from the advice of experts in all relevant fields. It is an integrated approach to problem solving."

Business owners are notified in advance of the scheduled date and time of the telephone conference so that they can prepare thoroughly for it. The best strategy is to ready a list of questions, be armed with facts and figures, cite specific cases, and have a note pad on hand to jot down information. Those viewing the sessions as serious learning experiences benefit the most from them. There is a $25 fee per telephone conference.

Here is one final recommendation that may put all that has come before into perspective. It is wise to approach the money-seeking process with the knowledge that raising cash may not be the ultimate objective. For many it is simply a means to an end: a way to finance a product, service, invention, idea, or concept; a way to breathe life into an emerging venture and bring it to market. The big score may come not when the loan is approved but years down the road when the business proves itself and is sold on the open market. That's where the megabucks are made.

"The time you sell a business is when someone submits a bid that substantially exceeds your estimate of the firm's value," says Henry Kloss, president of Kloss Video Corporation, a small consumer electronics firm that competes successfully with multinational greats. Kloss is an entrepreneur who has raised and made millions. "In other words, it has to be an offer that you can't refuse."

The national accounting firm Deloitte, Haskins & Sells suggests that owners consider the following "sell signs":

The best time to sell is when your business is at its peak. This gives the seller the bargaining power to get full market value or more. The business may be at its peak when the operations become too large to manage personally, the owner is unable to provide more capital, or the company has achieved optimum market share.

If legitimate buyers do surface, look at your business from their perspective, determining why each is interested in your company. Recognize that a "synergistic" relationship may result in a higher asking price. Synergy, in this context, means that the seller's business will contribute far more to the buyer than its asking price would indicate. This element makes the selling equation two plus two equals five.

Other experts suggest timing business sales to coincide with major trends in the marketplace. From time to time, certain categories of businesses become hot properties with investors. If big money sources or giant corporations are gobbling up fast-food restaurants, solar-energy ventures, or real-estate brokers, owners of these sought-after firms may want to sell. When your interests are the subject of this bidding, you'll know you've arrived, that borrowing a million dollars has helped you earn many millions. Keep pointed toward that goal.

Index